Complexifying Curriculum Studies

The essays in this volume bring together leading-edge scholars to illuminate the work of William E. Doll, Jr., as a key curriculum thinker of global impact, and introduce his work and influence to new generations of scholars, teachers, and students of education. Drawing on their individual contexts, contributors cover a range of topics and themes, including engagement with pragmatism, the work of John Dewey, and the inclusion of post-modern, chaos, and complexity theories to education and curriculum. Advancing our understanding and conversation of existing problems and possibilities in education, this collection serves as both an homage to Doll and a call for action and consideration of what matters in education.

Molly Quinn is Professor in the College of Education at Augusta University, USA.

Studies in Curriculum Theory Series
Series Editor: William F. Pinar
University of British Columbia, Canada

In this age of multimedia information overload, scholars and students may not be able to keep up with the proliferation of different topical, trendy book series in the field of curriculum theory. It will be a relief to know that one publisher offers a balanced, solid, forward-looking series devoted to significant and enduring scholarship, as opposed to a narrow range of topics or a single approach or point of view. This series is conceived as the series busy scholars and students can trust and depend on to deliver important scholarship in the various "discourses" that comprise the increasingly complex field of curriculum theory.

The range of the series is both broad (all of curriculum theory) and limited (only important, lasting scholarship)—including but not confined to historical, philosophical, critical, multicultural, feminist, comparative, international, aesthetic, and spiritual topics and approaches. Books in this series are intended for scholars and for students at the doctoral and, in some cases, master's levels.

Engaging Curriculum
Bridging the Curriculum Theory and English Education Divide
Bill Green

Curriculum Studies as an International Conversation
Educational Traditions and Cosmopolitanism in Latin America
Daniel F. Johnson-Mardones

Complexifying Curriculum Studies
Reflections on the Generative and Generous Gifts of William E. Doll, Jr.
Edited by Molly Quinn

For more information about this series, please visit: www.routledge.com/Studies-in-Curriculum-Theory-Series/book-series/LEASCTS

Complexifying Curriculum Studies
Reflections on the Generative and Generous Gifts of William E. Doll, Jr.

Edited by Molly Quinn

First published 2019 by Routledge

2 Park Square, Milton Park, Abingdon, Oxon OX14 4RN
605 Third Avenue, New York, NY 10017

Routledge is an imprint of the Taylor & Francis Group, an informa business

First issued in paperback 2021

Copyright © 2019 Taylor & Francis

The right of Molly Quinn to be identified as the author of the editorial material, and of the authors for their individual chapters, has been asserted in accordance with sections 77 and 78 of the Copyright, Designs and Patents Act 1988.

All rights reserved. No part of this book may be reprinted or reproduced or utilised in any form or by any electronic, mechanical, or other means, now known or hereafter invented, including photocopying and recording, or in any information storage or retrieval system, without permission in writing from the publishers.

Notice:
Product or corporate names may be trademarks or registered trademarks, and are used only for identification and explanation without intent to infringe.

Publisher's Note
The publisher has gone to great lengths to ensure the quality of this reprint but points out that some imperfections in the original copies may be apparent.

Library of Congress Cataloging-in-Publication Data
Names: Quinn, Molly, 1964– editor.
Title: Complexifying curriculum studies : reflections on the
   generative and generous gifts of William E. Doll, Jr. / edited by
   Molly Quinn.
Description: New York, NY : Routledge, 2019. | Includes
   bibliographical references and index.
Identifiers: LCCN 2018019912 | ISBN 9781138558076
   (hbk : alk. paper) | ISBN 9781315151212 (ebk)
Subjects: LCSH: Education—Curricula—Philosophy. | Education—
   Curricula—Research. | Doll, William E.—Influence.
Classification: LCC LB1570 .C744 2019 | DDC 375—dc23
LC record available at https://lccn.loc.gov/2018019912

ISBN: 978-1-138-55807-6 (hbk)
ISBN: 978-0-367-54792-9 (pbk)

Typeset in Sabon
by Apex CoVantage, LLC

 Printed in the United Kingdom
by Henry Ling Limited

In loving memory of William E. Doll, Jr., whose life and labor has made this work possible, whose generous and generative gifts to us continue to live on gratefully through us, and those we teach and reach

Contents

Acknowledgments   x

1 Introduction—From "The Echo of God's Laughter": The Generative and Generous Gifts of William E. Doll, Jr., to Curriculum Studies   1
MOLLY QUINN

Part I
Of Influence, Inspiration, and Intellectual Adventure   17

2 Dynamics of a Scholarly Life: Conversational Complexity in Pursuit of the *Mysterium Tremendum*   21
M. JAYNE FLEENER

3 Toward the Reenchantment of Curriculum: A Study on William Doll's Post-modern Curriculum Theory   29
HUA ZHANG

4 Education as Liberating Experience: Bill Doll's Scholarship and Contested Legacies of Euro-American Curriculum Theories From Descartes Onwards   38
TERO AUTIO

5 Thoroughly (Post-Modern) Billy   48
PETER APPELBAUM

6 Travels With Bill in Search of America (and Beyond)   58
NOEL GOUGH

Part II
Of Engagement, Immersion, and Transformative Experience   69

  7 The . . . Readiness . . . To Be "All Ears"   73
      DAVID W. JARDINE

  8 Engaging Engaging: Topological Reflections Prompted by Bill Doll   80
      BERNARD P. RICCA

  9 Playful Engagement With Difference   87
      HONGYU WANG

10 A Recursive Path to Infinity   94
      LIXIN LUO

Part III
Of Play, Praxis, and Pedagogical Grace   103

11 Learning the Play of Language: Hermeneutic Acts of Interpretation While Watching Bill Doll Dance   107
      DOUGLAS McKNIGHT

12 A Life With Bill Doll: A Journey in Praxis, Patience, and Play   114
      STEPHEN S. TRICHE

13 An Extraordinary Pedagogical Figure: Bill Doll as a *Susung*   121
      JUNG-HOON JUNG

14 The Pedagogical Complexity of Story   128
      SARAH SMITHERMAN PRATT

Part IV
Of Method, Mystery, and Visionary Magic   135

15 Circling the Known   139
      KATHLEEN R. KESSON

16 An Ethics of Free Responsible Action: Examining
    Doll's Struggling With Spirituality   147
    UGENA WHITLOCK

17 Addressing "Curriculum" as an Inspirited Letter   153
    NICHOLAS NG-A-FOOK

18 The Pedagogy of the King of Chaos in a
    Post-modern Era   163
    JIE YU

Part V
Of School, Society, and the Sacred in Scholarly Tradition   171

19 Post-modern Curriculum: Reviving the Vision   176
    NEL NODDINGS

20 Complex Conversations on Curriculum: Ghosts
    and the Five C's Revisited   182
    EERO ROPO AND VELI-MATTI VÄRRI

21 "Wrestling" With Complexity: Bill Doll's
    "Dancing Curriculum"   191
    DENISE EGÉA

22 Living Poetically: The Pedagogy of William E. Doll, Jr.   201
    CARL LEGGO

23 Confronting Life and Death: Reflections on Living
    the Spirit of Education   210
    PETRA MUNRO HENDRY

24 Afterword   218
    WILLIAM F. PINAR

    List of Contributors   238
    Index   246

Acknowledgments

In 2009, at the passing of his mentor John Steven Mann, William E. Doll, Jr.—Bill—wrote of him:

> With his passing went part of my soul. Steve was my doctoral mentor; but more, he was a teacher who helped me shape my views not only on education, but also on life. The values I hold today were brought forth and refined in those years we spent as I worked on my Ph.D.
>
> (2009/2012, p. 43)

He noted, too, how Steve recognized and honored his penchant for musing; taught him that learning was an emerging, reflective process, of which failure was an important part; expanded his awareness and helped him embrace a posture of listening to the other—"entering into conversation" and "immersing oneself in what one was studying" (p. 44). Bill concluded this tribute by expressing:

> My life is richer for his presence. I pray his spirit will guide me when I cross over from life to death. Thank you, Steve.
>
> (p. 44)

    I wish likewise to acknowledge Bill—Thank you, Bill!—my doctoral mentor, here, also upon his recent passing, that what he has said of his mentor, I too would say most gratefully of him. I pray also that his spirit has guided this work. I think he would approve of the entering in and immersion it reflects, and the oh-so-rich conversation.

    There is another Bill, and mentor, whose presence has also made this collection possible: William F. Pinar. It was his generous and generative idea, that he graciously invited me to take up. He has also been a perpetual source of guidance and encouragement in its realization. The guiding influence of Donna Trueit, Bill Doll's partner, is ever felt and appreciated herein too. Of course, every contributor brings something unique, irreplaceable, and beautiful—in the intellectual sense, yes, but much more besides—to this work; it would neither be, nor be the labor of love and light that it is, without these bright authors, colleagues, and friends. I cannot thank them, with all my heart, enough.

I want to express appreciation also to those colleagues and friends, as well as family, who have been such a source of strength and solace to me, who have kept my heart in the work, also through the loss of not a few loved ones in recent years: Ugena Whitlock, Celeste Snowber, Karen Ferneding, Brett Blake, Shirley Steinberg, Kathryn Henderson, Darla Linville, Kristen Gilbert, Niki Christodoulou, Misato Yamaguchi, Petter Braathen, Jim Rhorer, Lee Lormand, Lyn Horst, Jo Mango, Maria Ricapito, Pamela Warren, Jennifer Dixon, Justine McGovern, Marti Thomas, Susie Lemieux, and Ellie Heinichen.

Finally, Mary Ann Cooke and Ozee Onwumere at Augusta University have supported me much in my work, administratively, technologically, and beyond. I wish to thank, as well, Naomi Silverman, Emmalee Ortega, Karen Adler, and the staff at Routledge for bringing this book to publication—and with much patience and flexibility, and for promoting it. Their work too ensures Doll's rich legacy endures and inspires new generations of scholars and teachers. As he himself has said, "The academic genealogy here is a joy to behold. There is comfort in knowing that one's ideas will spout elsewhere" (2012, p. xviii). I trust the reader here finds gardens of delight, fragrant bouquets, winged dandelion cypsela seeding new dreams and infinite transformative possibilities. I know Bill would have it so.

Molly Quinn
March 25, 2018

References

Doll, W. (2012). Acknowledgments. In D. Trueit (Ed.), *Pragmatism, post-modernism and complexity theory: The "fascinating imaginative realm" of William E. Doll, Jr.* (pp. xv–xviii). New York, NY: Routledge.

Doll, W. (2012). Memory of a mentor: John Steven Mann. In D. Trueit (Ed.), *Pragmatism, post-modernism and complexity theory: The "fascinating imaginative realm" of William E. Doll, Jr.* (pp. 43–44). New York, NY: Routledge. (Original work published in 2009)

1 Introduction—From "The Echo of God's Laughter"
The Generative and Generous Gifts of William E. Doll, Jr., to Curriculum Studies

Molly Quinn

Donna Trueit (2012a) in the title of a collection of his essays draws our attention to "'the fascinating imaginative realm' of William E. Doll, Jr.," also inciting this favorite quote of his from Milan Kundera:

> It is indeed a strange and marvelous world we have yet to bring into existence.... "There exists a fascinating imaginative realm, born of the echo of God's laughter where no one owns the truth and everyone has the right to be understood" (Milan Kundera, 1988).
> (Doll, 2006/2012h, p. 231)

I could not take up the same, thus, for this collection, but I could at least appeal to such, and invoke "the echo of God's laughter" via its framing in this introduction. For anyone who knows Bill—as he is familiarly called—well, intellectually at least, has probably heard him utter this *Kunderan* sentiment, the substance of which communicated herein he seems also to embody in his very person, and manner of engagement as a scholar, teacher, mentor, and colleague. "Fascinating" and "imaginative" certainly aptly describe him, as also his work; and even those who have but met him, without any particular pedagogical or scholarly inclination, would be hard pressed to forget his inexorable laugh.[1]

In fact, in a 2001 tribute to Bill I made on the occasion of his 70th birthday at the "In Praise of the Post-modern Conference," I actually began with God, and with laughter:[2]

> *In the Kabbalah, it is said that human beings are Divine Sparks, the glowing emanations of God's creative light, each one unique and*

---

1. Trueit (2012b) also makes note of this laugh, of which she says: "I would never be able to describe the sound of Bill's laughter. He laughs often and loudly" (p. xiv). A number of authors in this collection highlight such as well.
2. This tribute is printed in full in an afterword (Quinn, 2016) to Wang's (2016) compelling work on the pedagogy of William E. Doll, Jr.

> *irreplaceable. However, some sparks burn brighter than others. Bill Doll is one of those rare individuals. . . . This towering yet remarkably inviting man stood before me, a veritable post-modern pastiche; a combination of Bostonian gentleman, North Eastern Intellectual, Mystic Philosopher-Sage, Boehemian Artist-Poet, Dr. Seuss, and Santa Clause: exuberant, big-hearted (albeit thin), playful, poetic—dare I say, eccentric; yet elegant, distinguished and wise. Gorgeous snowy white hair, the classical bow tie, and a laugh that could change the world.*

It is more, though perhaps, than that Bill's laugh is so unique, robust, jovial, infectious, and surely unforgettable. It is more, though perhaps too, than that his enlivening presence, pedagogy and thought are so unforgettably influential and surely inspiring. This collection of essays is framed in this way—a kind of polyphonic harmony or symphony of voices that are themselves each echoes of a sort of Doll's divine laughter—as it also seeks to express something of/at the heart of his thought, teaching, work, influence, legacy, life, and person: certainly, an art born of spirit, and its expression of playfulness and delight in being in the world and creatively participating in its becoming. Such an art, too, embraces, embodies, dwells in, affirms, generates and calls us to that "fascinating imaginative realm . . . where no one owns the truth and everyone has the right to be understood" (Kundera, 1988, p. 164), indeed.

In his first landmark book, *A Post-modern Perspective on Curriculum*, Doll (1993) incites these ideas from Kundera as a way to frame his curricular conversations with the "fascinating imaginative realm" of postmodernism (and those emerging from complexity theory), and forward curriculum as a proliferative process—and "an art born as 'the echo of God's laughter'" (p. 151). He muses:

> Meaning and understanding . . . emerge from the process of making connections, from interpreting our being-in-the-world. . . . Negotiating . . . passages—instead of laying out the truth of a proposition, term, or viewpoint—seems to be what curriculum is or should be. In "negotiating passages" each party *listens actively*—sympathetically and critically—to what the *other* is saying. The intention is . . . to find ways to connect varying viewpoints, to expand one's horizon through active engagement with another. The engagement is a process activity that transforms.
>
> (p. 151)

He identifies this vision, too, with his own "curriculum utopia."

With utopian aspirations perhaps, I imagine this collection, too, as a kind of curriculum art born of such echoes, generative and *complexifying* reflections and conversations:[3] via active, sympathetic, critical listening to Doll, in dialogue with him; illuminating varying viewpoints on his work; expanding our own horizons of being and becoming herein, and of curriculum studies; actively engaging in a transformative process of negotiating passages, making connections, interpreting being-in-the-world—celebrating, conversing, coming together through these encounters with Doll in the divine fascinating, imaginative otherness of his thought, pedagogy and person. And my hope is that this text might similarly—and transformatively—resonate likewise with its readers.

I intentionally use the word *resonate* here too—as it summons us pointedly back as well to the notion of *echo*. For in proceeding, I would like here first to play[4] with, ruminate a bit further on, the terms by which I am framing this text—echo and laughter, and as drawn from Kundera, "the echo of God's laughter," whom Doll himself echoes oft in his work; before turning to preview something of the generative and generous gifts of William E. Doll, Jr. to curriculum studies—complexifying it so richly and beautifully—presented and reflected upon in this volume. And it is these offerings, having so aptly emerged[5] from the authors' engagements with Doll, which constitute and create the curriculum choruses that ring out and sing forth from this collection; they are hallelujahs, in the least, if not heavenly—resounding, in the parlance of Nietzsche (1883/1982), a sacred Amen, or "Yes to life"—treasures: (1) Of Influence, Inspiration, and Intellectual Adventure; (2) Of Engagement, Immersion, and

---

3. Dubbed the "King Of Chaos" (see, for example, Wang, 2016—and Gough, and Yu, in this collection), Doll has brought the insights of chaos and complexity theories to bear upon the theoretical and practical study of curriculum in rich and manifold ways. Here, building on Pinar's work (2004/2012) in positing and exploring curriculum as complicated conversation, with others, Doll (Doll, Fleener, St. Julien, & Trueit, 2005; Smitherman & Trueit, 2006; Pratt, 2008) elaborates upon such—conceptually complexifying both conversation and curriculum, and curriculum itself as complex conversation(s). Inquiry and indeterminancy play key roles herein, as do relations, reflection and emergence—the ways in which the introduction of a single idea, a small change, can effect something grand; articulating what Pratt here in her essay describes as an embodiment of our thinking the world together.
4. The use of the term *play* here is most intentional, meant to echo the spirit of Doll and his serious commitment to play (e.g., 1990/2012k, 1993, 1998/2012m, 1999/2012n, 2003/2012i, 2008/2012g, and 2009/2012j)—highlighted and taken up in myriad and compelling ways by many of the authors throughout this collection (e.g., Appelbaum, McKnight, Ng-A-Fook, Triche, and Wang, among others).
5. I say "aptly emerged" here because much of Doll's work has not only been critical of conceptions and approaches to curriculum that strive for certain, pre-set, pre-fixed and predictable outcomes pertaining to (also oft preordained and predetermined) knowledge or understanding in education (e.g., 1993); but also has been rooted in the notion of keeping knowledge alive (2005/2012f, from Whitehead, 1929/1967) via curriculum that is oriented around the unfolding, dynamic, and self-organizing purposes, processes and performances pertaining to understanding that emerge from authentic and thoughtful inquiry into, engagement with, and conversation concerning self, others, and the world.

4 *Molly Quinn*

Transformative Experience; (3) Of Play, Praxis, and Pedagogical Grace; (4) Of Method, Mystery, and Visionary Magic; and (5) Of School, Society, and the Sacred in Scholarly Tradition. To such I return—reverberate back to—in the section previews in this collection.

Of Echo in Doll's Endowment

Of echo, there might be little further of which to speak, than to reiterate its sense as that which continues to reverberate after the original word has been uttered, as that which is reflected back to its listener. An echo can also signify something possessing shared characteristics with, or which is reminiscent of, the original—expressing a close parallel of an idea or feeling or moment (*Oxford English Dictionary (OED)*, 1989).[6] Original as Doll is, the authors of each essay here certainly—as gathered around and reflectively listening to his magnanimous (laughing) vibration—emit their own unique echoes of resonance with and reverberations from it; they also do so amid harmonious ideas, feelings, moments, that are shared; and generate thus novel utterances, iterations,[7] rippling out, beyond, with growing complexity and creativity for us as well. Further, though, this very idea of the echo itself might be set forth as emblematic of something of Doll's work and influence. This can be seen in his early interest in and echoing of Dewey's thought and in his opposition to the linear, predetermined, pre-set curriculum issuing from the predominant Tyler Rationale.[8]

---

6. I intentionally here also begin to appeal to etymological examination of the language we use and the revelations issuing from such, as well as somewhat extensive footnoting, as a way to echo Doll's attention to both here in his own work, which serve also to illuminate the ways that meanings ripple out, echoing forth not only into the present but also forward and backward in time—as historical and imaginative traces, throughlines, trajectories—generating multiple interpretations, complex connections, and webs of possible meanings. Doll's (2002) introductory essay in *Curriculum Visions* on "Ghosts and the Curriculum," for example, contains thirty-six rather lengthy endnotes and draws upon etymological exploration therein. A review of the totality of his work, moreover, bears out his affirmation of the import of attention to such vestiges, shadows and echoes contained within our language and concepts which profoundly influence meaning, speech, and action. Eero Ropo and Veli-Matti Värri take up in this volume most directly Doll's work on curriculum ghosts, McKnight demonstrates his etymological influence, and Pratt also references another essay of Doll's comprising eighty-five endnotes in which he narrates something of the story of method's historical development. Doll also can be seen playing with ideas and gleaning insight through such via such notes.
7. I point here to affiliation with notions foundational to complexity theory, upon which Doll draws, involving problem-solving via repeated cycles of analysis; akin to recursion in his four R's, this self-referencing reflective process contributes to the generation and maintenance of a complex system, its path of development, its very becoming constitutive of its being.
8. See Tyler (1949) and Doll (1993) for more on this dominant curriculum approach and its critique.

He asserts with Dewey that ends that are educational arise from within authentic action, emerge from present engagement with life; that:

> Every experience is a moving force. . . . [,] the business of the educator to see in what direction an experience is heading . . . and direct it on the ground of what it is moving into.
> (1938, p. 38)

> Partial conclusions emerge . . . temporary stopping places, landings of past thought that are also stations of departure for subsequent thought.
> (Dewey, 1933/1971, p. 75, as cited in Doll, 1993, p. 138)

And for Doll, happily, one can neither fully predict nor control these landings or departures, the echoes—meeting varying surfaces, refracting, ricocheting—generated in the interactions among such moving forces; yet can delight in the patterns of meaning made, paths of inquiry generated, and evolving transformations of experience, reconstructed educationally—as well as wonderful and wondrous conversations and people generously engaged therein. Says Doll (2012a) of his own unfolding path: "The academic genealogy is a joy to behold. There is comfort in knowing that one's ideas will sprout elsewhere" (p. xviii).

From post-modern, post-structural, and complexity theories, too, Doll has poignantly illuminated the traces (Derrida, 1976, 1978), vestiges, shadows, and ghosts (e.g., of Dewey in Doll, 2002) of the past of curriculum echoing into and influencing its present and future, "the pattern that connects" (Bateson, 1972) and in profoundly nonlinear, complex, and iterative ways (with excesses and multiplicities of meaning). From the classic three R's of readin' 'ritin and 'rithmetic and modern rationale of Tyler emerges his four R's for curriculum in a post-modern world: "*rich* in problematics, *recursive* in its (nonlinear) organization, *relational* in its structure, and *rigorous* in its application" (Doll, 2008/2012g, p. 171).[9] He further develops this alternative—as he says, following Dewey who attempted to break from the paradigm of authoritarian control in which curriculum had been long mired and whose "ghost encourages us to keep on with this project" (2002, p. 53), with intellectual inroads as yet unavailable to him—via his five C's[10] of *currere*, complexity, cosmology,

---

9. Doll's four R's are indeed rich, far too much so, and too complex, to explicate here. Happily, though, a number of colleagues here in their essays illuminate such further (e.g., Appelbaum, Luo, Noddings, Wang, and Yu).
10. For more on the five C's in this collection, see particularly Hua and Wang. For inquiry specifically into *currere*, see Pinar (e.g., 2012) whose work concerning such Doll draws upon.

conversation, and community; emphasizing the whole of curriculum as a matrix, and system of relationships:

> its continuity over time depend[ing] on its relational transformations and on the emergence of present structures from structures that *were* and into structures that *will be*. . . . Interrelating and dynamically changing.
>
> (p. 43)

One cannot help but sense that Doll plays too with the traditional ABCs in his alliterative iterations,[11] also of sound—his three S's[12] (2003/2012i), another holo-sonogram through which he elatedly sings curriculum divinations into possibility. Here, he seeks to honor science, story, and spirit in relation to education's modes of thought—and the space(s) beyond and in-between; Bruner, Whitehead, Huebner, among a host of others, with Dewey, resounding here as well. Doll's work, in this way, reverberates, a fascinating imaginative symphony of manifold voices, of generous and generative encounters with otherness and dialogues across/through difference and time; creative and complex conversations, opening up to the elevation and mystery of spirit.

In Greek mythology, in the least too, Echo, a mountain nymph, is the consort of Zeus, king of the Olympian gods. While the purpose of Echo's dialogues with Hera, queen of the gods and wife to Zeus, were meant to distract, even to deceive, she did also indeed engage her extensively in complex conversation as well. Echo's is a playful spirit, born of and inhabiting and cavorting about in the high and exalted places, in conversational art and companionship with the divine. Drawn in his own work to the hermeneutic tradition, and Hermes[13]—the trickster, Doll is apt to appreciate Echo's mischievous adventures, as well, overturning the established order of things and reveling in that which it would define as diverting or excessive. As Wang (2016) of Doll's pedagogy explains: "In the context of teaching, perturbations, errors and confusions that are traditionally dismissed as negative elements become key elements for initiating students' intellectual reorganization to a higher level" (p. 46). From such emerging echoes wherein waste[14] is actually essential—whether white waves

---

11. Wang (2016) honors Doll's spirit in this way, too, in exploring his pedagogy via seven P's: play, perturbation, presence, patterns, passion, peace, and participation.
12. For more here on Doll's three S's, see Hua, Pratt, and Wang.
13. McKnight, in this collection, relates Doll's kinship with Hermes and the hermeneutic tradition; and a host of others entertain this tradition via Doll as well (e.g., Autio, Luo, and Noddings). Jardine's contribution here also embodies and enacts hermeneutics; and Yu highlights the trickster work of Doll in his identification with the Chinese myth of the monkey king, or King of Chaos, who challenges rigidity of structure and order.
14. For more here, see Doll (2008/2012g, p. 27) on waste as integral to the process of emergence, involving a requisite openness and richness for systems to sustain themselves

of delight or turbulent tensions without sense or satisfaction—might be heard, understood, and engaged "the spirit of creativity hidden in every situation, yet to be born" (Doll, 2003/2012i, p. 104).

With the excess, discarded, unusable, engaged—the inert and dead enlivened, the tension taken up—convention is challenged, knowledge is kept alive, conversation continues and creativity thrives. A story Doll relates about the guidance and insight of one of his advisors, who was departing Johns Hopkins for Teachers College (TC), comes to mind here:

> Bill, he said "TC is too professional for you; you are too much a muser to be confined. . . . Stay here at Hopkins where they will honor and develop your musings."
>
> (2009/2012j, p. 14)

The muser engages in a dynamic interplay with amusement, too, in the generation of new insights and expanding understandings. And, in such too, there is also often much requisite playfulness, delight, and laughter.

Of Laughter and Doll's Legacy

Oddly enough (although perhaps not—laugher, infectious, and catching), Iambe, the Greek goddess affiliated with laughter, is actually the daughter of Echo, and also of Pan, known too for his comradeship with the spirited nymphs. She is attributed with laughter as a healing gift—at the place of the Eleusinian mysteries compelling Demeter to smile and laugh, even in mourning the loss of her daughter Persephone. Another Spartan god, and trickster of sorts, known for his pranks—and most welcomed of the divines, too, is Gelos, who personifies laughter; companion of Dionysus (Olympian god of wine, festivity, and pleasure), he assists in reaping the harvest with utmost delight and celebration; his presence makes for more joyous and pleasant days. Comfortable with paradox and irony,[15] this god of mirth is also known for boosting morale; with honesty, he bravely confronts the darker aspects of human existence. "A sunny elegance" is attributed to him, as through laughter too, he also alleviates grief and pain and cultivates joy (Atsma, 2000–2017). Of "sunny elegance" is an apt description for Bill as well, and his playful laughter and thought have been a healing balm time again, bringing me happiness and hope amid melancholy, as I am sure it has been for many others also (to which some here attest)—and

---

dynamically and developmentally. Hendry, in this collection, takes such up similarly in relation to the cyclical mutuality of life/death, light/darkness—the spirit of education Doll embraces embedded within such.

15. Doll draws upon the ironic, as well, particularly via Rorty (1989), and paradox too, for example, through Derrida (1992/1995) and Serres (1991/1997). If not Eleusinian, he too is compelled by the mysteries of complexity. For more on mystery, in this collection, for example, see Fleener, Whitlock, and Hendry.

8 *Molly Quinn*

the curriculum field itself amid dark times. Occasions with him, too, are ever festive, and often toasted with spirits as well—of which colleagues in this collection also speak (see, e.g., Fleener, Gough).

Science itself now tells us that laughter is indeed good medicine, benefitting health.[16] Nancy Dominique (2013, March 27) in "The Origins of Laughter" reports further on not only the changes in muscle tone that occur in laughter, but also those in brain activation. Studies illuminate the act of laughing as a state of stimulation followed by that of relaxation—a dynamic interplay akin to that which Doll educationally advocates in his work,[17] and demonstrated also to be descriptive of how creative advances occur generally (e.g., Csikszentmihalyi, 1990/2008; May, 1975/1994; Robinson, 2011). As psychologically Légaré (2010) defines laughter relatedly as a subjective experience of well-being, Doll's endorsements also promote such socially, in conversation, well-being-in-the-world with others, emphasizing relations.[18] Marijuán and Navarro (2010), in "The Bonds of Laugher," speak of intellectual momentum that builds up during conversation needing, at times, relief or release. Laughter, a complex interplay between sender and receiver, shares its part, then, in creating and deepening social bonds, strengthening the quality of our relationships. "John Cleese once said: 'Laughter connects you with people. It's almost impossible to maintain any kind of distance or any sense of social hierarchy when you're just howling with laughter'" (cited in Raine, 2016, April 13). How Bill enjoys such howling and connection—relationality! We let down our defenses, we open up to the game, expressing support and admiration, in full bodied response with another via laughter (Graziano, 2014, August 14).

It's not surprising, either, that laughter is physically tied to play—a notable characteristic of Doll's theoretical and pedagogical gifts (signature elements in his approach to theory and pedagogy) to us.[19] The vocalizations of apes responding to tickling reveal that laughter served principally to communicate the intention to play, or desire to continue play. Evolutionary views of laughter, and humor, articulate three distinct adaptations involving the acquisition of a theory of mind, the development of language, and the appreciation of incongruities in symbolic

---

16. For example, see: Siegel, 1986, 2005; the popular 1998 film depicted such well also, based on the experience of physician *Patch Adams* (Farrell, M., Kemp, B., Minoff, M., and Newirth, C., producers, and Shadyac, T., director).
17. Ricca in this collection illuminates such via Doll's guidance to "engage, pull back."
18. Wang in this volume, as well as in her work on his pedagogy (2016), elucidates further the focus on relationality at the heart of Doll's life, teaching and scholarship. Hua Zhang, in this collection, speaks of responsible, "relational creativity" in such. Hendry also emphasizes his teachings of relationality. The centrality of play within Doll's relations—and teaching, scholarship, and work—is also further illumined by many authors in this collection.
19. See Wang (2016).

representations (Dominique, 2013, March 27). Doll reminds us how very much we underestimate the power and potential of laughter, pleasure, and play in our work. Here, in moving with our metaphor, we might further inquire, might laughter itself not be indelibly tied to spirit somehow? Even if not, what, then, of laughter that is divine? The echo of God's laughter? And in Doll's work?

In Conversation With Kundera on the "Echo of God's Laughter"

Bill himself also echoes such ideas—and engages them forward as he seeks to reimagine curriculum and stir us to such—from Milan Kundera (1988), who inspired him here. *Man thinks, God laughs*, says an old Jewish proverb. In Kundera's 1985 address (later published in *The Art of the Novel*, 1988) for receipt of the *Jerusalem Prize*—a biennial literary honor awarded writers whose works meaningfully explore themes of human freedom in society—he takes up this proverb, imagines Rabelais heard God laughing one day, and that thus was born the idea and art of the novel (as the echo of God's laughter). He delights in the novel as an "imaginative paradise" where no one possesses the truth; rather, each and everyone, the right to be understood. From his dissertation on Dewey's theory of change (Doll, 1972) to his reflection upon curriculum and pedagogy through such traditions as developmental biology/psychology, pragmatism, post-modernism, poststructuralism, hermeneutics, process philosophy and chaos and complexity theories, Doll, too, has reveled in the idea of such a fascinating transformative realm in/as education, by which the new, the novel, is ever artfully born within and among us. And this also ever experienced with a sense of wonder and joy amid multivocal truths, manifold meanings, and expanding understandings, dialogically and dynamically emerging in the unfolding stories of a community of human solidarity, creativity, freedom, and flourishing.

Kundera's discussion of this art's arrival, located as it is in modernity, highlights well, too, a number of ideas and issues with which Doll has wrestled in his thought and practice regarding education—in many ways stuck still within a modernist, or neo-modernist, frame—and with which he compels us to engage. Kundera (1988) explains:

> But why does God laugh at the sight of man [sic] thinking? Because man thinks and the truth escapes him. Because the more men think, the more one man's thought diverges from another's. And finally, because man is never what he thinks he is. The dawn of the Modern Era revealed this fundamental situation. . . . The first European novelists saw, and grasped . . . and on it they built the new art.
>
> (p. 157)

He speaks here also of Rabelais' despised agélaste—coined from the Greek, a humorless man, a man who does not laugh. The agélastes, having never heard God's laughter, are persuaded that truth is apparent, that all men think alike, and that they are precisely as they think themselves to be. Embracing the rationalist *Nihil est sine rationale*—There is nothing without its reason—assertion of Leibniz, they stupidly march along with the humorless, "nonthought of received ideas" (p. 163) promulgated in the name of progress, technology, and science; a science which,

> stimulated by that [same] conviction . . . energetically explores the why of everything, such that whatever exists seems explainable, thus predictable, calculable. The man who wants his life to have a meaning forgoes any action that hasn't its cause and its purpose.
>
> (p. 161)

Doll—who we might suggest would choose to forego rather than foreclose—explores this fundamental situation regarding education, curriculum, and pedagogy, raising questions about the limits of thought, the pursuits for certain truth, the reliance upon a science bent on causality, prediction, and calculation—the problem in/of our own thinking and action (e.g., 2002/2012b, 2003/2012i, 2005, 2005/2012f, 2010/2012p, 2015, 2016). Akin perhaps to the agélastes, he too takes issue with the (neo)modernists, (neo)positivists, neoliberals, once-upon-a-time Tylerians—those who all too seriously and carelessly would incarnate what he calls the ghost in the curriculum machine that is control (2002)—no laughter, no play, no interplay, no mystery, musing or surprise.[20]

Kundera (1988) continues:

> The art inspired by God's laughter does not by nature serve ideological certitudes, it contradicts them. Like Penelope, it undoes each night the tapestry that the theologians, philosophers, and learned men have woven the day before.
>
> (p. 160)

Thus, Doll's art too embraces complexity, paradox, tensionality, and temporality—complexifying curriculum studies, it challenges much of accepted, endorsed educational and curricular ideology and certitude. For example, he abandons the syllabus for evolving study issuing from dialogic engagement with and among students, wherein educational aims emerge and change in the process of living, learning, and inquiring together. He champions confusion, chaos, disequilibrium, and perturbation in education as spurs to growth and transformation. He challenges the letter of

---

20. Leggo, in this collection, beautifully explicates how Bill teaches us in his work, life and person this, a more delightful, delighting and most dearly human way, as does Hendry in her focus as well.

science in the curricular script via its spirit, and takes up the insights of the new sciences alongside, juxtaposing, those embracing narrative, myth, art, ethics, and spirituality.[21]

> But in art, the form is always more than a form. Every novel, like it or not, offers some answer to the question: What is human existence, and wherein does its poetry lie?. . . . The answer we sense in Sterne's novel[22] . . ., the poetry lies not in the action but in the interruption of the action. . . . Against that reduction of the world to the causal succession of events, Sterne's novel, by its very form, affirms that poetry lies not in action but there where action stops; there where the bridge between a cause and an effect has collapsed and thought wanders off in sweet lazy liberty. The poetry of existence, says Sterne's novel, is in digression. It is in the incalculable.
>
> (pp. 161–162)

And Doll in his penchant for historicizing and interrogating method, the form and formula so dominating educational thought and practice, calls our attention to the form that is always more than a form (e.g., 2002, 2002/2012b, 2005). Against such reduction of curriculum and pedagogy, he toys with "seeking a method-beyond-method" (2015);[23] asking the fundamental questions. Some answer his art might offer, as he loves to cite from Heidegger (1954/1977), is that "questioning [itself] is the piety of thought" (p. 31); and that we seek "an education which questions the being of all we hold sacred while at the same time manifests a faith that such questioning will lead us to the sacredness of being" (2002/2012o, p. 42). Indeed, too, in some good measure, he affirms the poetry of existence in education as in human life to be found in the

---

21. One has but merely to peruse Doll's essays in Trueit's 2012a edited collection to see the diversity and vast array of traditions/genres Doll draws upon so richly and complexly, the breadth and depth of his work here. Attention to each work singularly, as well, demonstrates well this elegant and sophisticated weaving of science, art, history, literature, ethics, etc., in his efforts to understand and reimagine curriculum.
22. Kundera here is speaking of Laurence Sterne's (1759-67/1983) *Tristram Shandy*, in which the author free-associates his tale as he follows each new attracting idea that arises.
23. Doll has illuminated in much of his work our methodological challenges in curriculum in analyzing the history and culture of method (e.g., 2005); he also takes up its linguistic heritage etymologically, which Triche addresses in this collection. From Middle English, it is interesting to note that method was tied not only to the pursuit of knowledge, systematic inquiry, but also to prescribed medical treatment of a disease. Its influence in curriculum has reflected as well this attention to pursuit, prescription, and pathology. Through Greek and Latin tracings of *methodos*, we have *meta*—expressing development, about or beyond, in pursuit of, following after; and *hodos*, meaning: way, manner, system (of doing, saying), traveling journey, path, track, or road (OED, 1989). The connections to the etymology of curriculum in a "course for running" via these meanings are intriguing here as well.

interruptions, wanderings, digressions, incalculables. Where the causal-consequential bridge collapses, where honey-dripping drowsy thought meanders off in musing, the place of poetry, new meanings, illuminations, and adventures are born.[24]

Come, then, let us attend what strange, marvelous, fascinating, and sweet delights/insights await us, and in/for curriculum studies, as we venture forward thus with Bill Doll in these echoes of/on his divine laughter.

References

Atsma, A. (2000–2017). *Theoi project: Gelos*. Retrieved from www.theoi.com/Daimon/Gelos.html

Bateson, G. (1972). *Steps to an ecology of mind: Collected essays in anthropology, psychiatry, evolution, and epistemology*. Chicago, IL: University of Chicago Press.

Csikszentmihalyi, M. (2008). *Flow: The psychology of optimal experience*. New York, NY: First Harper Perennial Modern Classics. (Original work published in 1990)

Derrida, J. (1976). *Of grammatology* (G. Spivak, Trans.). Baltimore, MD & London: Johns Hopkins University Press.

Derrida, J. (1978). *Writing and difference* (A. Bass, Trans.). London & New York, NY: Routledge.

Derrida, J. (1995). *The gift of death* (D. Willis, Trans.). Chicago, IL: University of Chicago Press. (Original work published in 1992)

Dewey, J. (1938). *Experience and education*. New York, NY: Macmillan.

Dewey, J. (1971). *How we think*. Chicago, IL: Henry Regnery. (Original work published in 1933)

Doll, W. (1972). *An analysis of John Dewey's educational writings interpreted with reference to his concept of change*. Doctoral dissertation. Retrieved from ERIC (ED065332).

Doll, W. (1993). *A post-modern perspective on curriculum*. New York, NY: Teachers College Press.

Doll, W. (2002). Ghosts and the curriculum. In W. Doll & N. Gough (Eds.), *Curriculum visions* (pp. 23–70). New York, NY: Peter Lang.

Doll, W. (2005). The culture of method. In W. Doll, J. Fleener, J. St. Julien, & D. Trueit (Eds.), *Chaos, complexity, curriculum and culture: A conversation* (pp. 21–76). New York, NY: Peter Lang.

Doll, W. (2012a). Acknowledgments. In D. Trueit (Ed.), *Pragmatism, post-modernism and complexity theory: The "fascinating imaginative realm" of William E. Doll, Jr.* (pp. xv–xviii). New York, NY: Routledge.

Doll, W. (2012b). Beyond methods. In D. Trueit (Ed.), *Pragmatism, post-modernism and complexity theory: The "fascinating imaginative realm" of William E. Doll, Jr.* (pp. 81–97). New York, NY: Routledge. (Original work in published 2002)

---

24. For more on the poetry of existence Doll's art teaches us, see particularly in this collection Gough, Jardine, and Leggo. Hendry, too, addresses such in his affirmative way of "being-toward-death" (Heidegger, 1927/1962).

Doll, W. (2012c). Complexity. In D. Trueit (Ed.), *Pragmatism, post-modernism and complexity theory: The "fascinating imaginative realm" of William E. Doll, Jr.* (pp. 169–171). New York, NY: Routledge. (Original work published in 2008)

Doll, W. (2012d). Complexity in the classroom. In D. Trueit (Ed.), *Pragmatism, post-modernism and complexity theory: The "fascinating imaginative realm" of William E. Doll, Jr.* (pp. 198–206). New York, NY: Routledge. (Original work published in 1989)

Doll, W. (2012e). The educational need to re-invent the wheel. In D. Trueit (Ed.), *Pragmatism, post-modernism and complexity theory: The "fascinating imaginative realm" of William E. Doll, Jr.* (pp. 193–197). New York, NY: Routledge. (Original work in published 1981)

Doll, W. (2012f). Keeping knowledge alive. In D. Trueit (Ed.), *Pragmatism, post-modernism and complexity theory: The "fascinating imaginative realm" of William E. Doll, Jr.* (pp. 111–119). New York, NY: Routledge. (Original work published in 2005)

Doll, W. (2012g). Looking back to the future: A recursive retrospective. In D. Trueit (Ed.), *Pragmatism, post-modernism and complexity theory: The "fascinating imaginative realm" of William E. Doll, Jr.* (pp. 23–32). New York, NY: Routledge. (Original work published in 2008)

Doll, W. (2012h). Looking forward. In D. Trueit (Ed.), *Pragmatism, post-modernism and complexity theory: The "fascinating imaginative realm" of William E. Doll, Jr.* (pp. 228–231). New York, NY: Routledge. (Original work published in 2006)

Doll, W. (2012i). Modes of thought. In D. Trueit (Ed.), *Pragmatism, post-modernism and complexity theory: The "fascinating imaginative realm" of William E. Doll, Jr.* (pp. 103–110). New York, NY: Routledge. (Original work published in 2003)

Doll, W. (2012j). A path stumbled upon. In D. Trueit (Ed.), *Pragmatism, post-modernism and complexity theory: The "fascinating imaginative realm" of William E. Doll, Jr.* (pp. 13–22). New York, NY: Routledge. (Original work published in 2009)

Doll, W. (2012k). Post-modernism's utopian vision. In D. Trueit (Ed.), *Pragmatism, post-modernism and complexity theory: The "fascinating imaginative realm" of William E. Doll, Jr.* (pp. 144–152). New York, NY: Routledge. (Original work published in 1990)

Doll, W. (2012l). Prigogine: A new sense of order. In D. Trueit (Ed.), *Pragmatism, post-modernism and complexity theory: The "fascinating imaginative realm" of William E. Doll, Jr.* (pp. 134–143). New York, NY: Routledge. (Original work published in 1986)

Doll, W. (2012m). Recursions on complexity. In D. Trueit (Ed.), *Pragmatism, post-modernism and complexity theory: The "fascinating imaginative realm" of William E. Doll, Jr.* (pp. 163–168). New York, NY: Routledge. (Original work published in 1998)

Doll, W. (2012n). Reflections on teaching: Developing the non-linear. In D. Trueit (Ed.), *Pragmatism, post-modernism and complexity theory: The "fascinating imaginative realm" of William E. Doll, Jr.* (pp. 207–221). New York, NY: Routledge. (Original work published in 1999)

Doll, W. (2012o). Struggles with spirituality. In D. Trueit (Ed.), *Pragmatism, post-modernism and complexity theory: The "fascinating imaginative realm" of

William E. Doll, Jr. (pp. 33–42). New York, NY: Routledge. (Original work published in 2002)
Doll, W. (2012p). Thinking complexly. In D. Trueit (Ed.), *Pragmatism, postmodernism, and complexity theory: The "fascinating imaginative realm" of William E. Doll, Jr.* (pp. 172–188). New York, NY: Routledge. (Original work published in 2010)
Doll, W. (2015, May). *Seeking a method beyond method*. Unpublished Manuscript, IAACS Keynote, University of Ottawa, Canada.
Doll, W. (2016). Our problem lies in our thinking. In N. Ng-A-Fook, A. Ibrahim, & G. Reis (Eds.), *Provoking curriculum studies: Strong poetry and arts of the possible in education* (pp. 205–212). New York, NY: Routledge.
Doll, W., Fleener, J., St. Julien, J., & Trueit, D. (Eds.). (2005). *Chaos, complexity, curriculum and culture: A conversation*. New York, NY: Peter Lang.
Dominique, N. (2013, March 27). *The origins of laughter*. Retrieved from https://phys.org/news/2013-03-laughter.html.
Farrell, M., Kemp, B., Minoff, M., & Newirth, C. (Producers), & Shadyac, T. (Director). (1998). *Patch Adams*. [Motion Picture]. United States: Universal Records.
Graziano, M. (2014, August 14). *Smile*. (E. Lake, Ed.). Retrieved from https://aeon.co/essays/the-original-meaning-of-laughter-smiles-and-tears.
Heidegger, M. (1962). *Being and time* (J. Macquarrie & E. Robinson, Trans.). San Francisco, CA: Harper & Row. (Original work published in 1927)
Heidegger, M. (1977). The question concerning technology. In W. Lovitt (Ed. & Trans.), *The question concerning technology and other essays*. New York, NY: Harper Collins. (Original work published in 1954)
Kundera, M. (1985). *Acceptance speech by Milan Kundera for the Jerusalem Prize for Literature at the 12th Jerusalem International Book Fair*. Jerusalem: Jerusalem International Book Fair.
Kundera, M. (1988). *The art of the novel* (L. Asher, Trans.). New York, NY: Grove Press.
Légaré, S. (2010). *Les origines évolutionnistes du rire et de l'humour*. Unpublished Master's Thesis, Université de Montréal, Montréal, Canada.
Marijuán, P., & Navarro, J. (2010). *The bonds of laughter: A multidisciplinary inquiry into the information processes of human laughter*. Bioinformation and Systems Biology Group Instituto Aragonés de Ciencias de la Salud. 50009 Zaragoza, Spain. arXiv preprint arXiv:1010.5602.
May, R. (1994). *The courage to create*. New York, NY: W. W. Norton & Co. (Original work published in 1975)
Nietzsche, F. (1982). Thus spoke Zarathustra. In W. Kaufman (Ed. & Trans.), *The portable Nietzche* (pp. 103–440). New York, NY: Penguin Books. (Original work published in 1883)
Oxford English dictionary (OED) (2nd ed.). (1989). (J. Simpson & E. Weiner, Eds.). Oxford, UK: Clarendon Press.
Pinar, W. (2012). *What is curriculum theory?* (2nd ed.). New York, NY: Routledge. (Original work published in 2004)
Pratt, S. (2008). Complex constructivism: Rethinking the power dynamics of "understanding." *Journal of Canadian Association for Curriculum Studies*, 6(1), 113–132.

Quinn, M. (2016). Afterword: Of experiencing pedagogy by rainbow light. In H. Wang (Ed.), *From the parade child to the king of chaos: The complex journey of William Doll, teacher educator* (pp. 167–178). New York, NY: Peter Lang.

Raine, J. (2016, April 13). The evolutionary origins of laughter are rooted more in survival than enjoyment. *The Conversation*. Retrieved from http://theconversation.com/the-evolutionary-origins-of-laughter-are-rooted-more-in-survival-than-enjoyment-57750.

Robinson, K., Sir. (2011). *Out of our minds: Learning to be creative*. West Sussex, UK: Capstone Publishing. (Original work published in 2001)

Rorty, R. (1989). *Contingency, irony, and solidarity*. Cambridge, UK: Cambridge University Press.

Serres, M. (1997). *The troubadour of knowledge* (S. Glaser, Trans.). Ann Arbor, MI: University of Michigan Press. (Original work published in 1991)

Siegel, B. (1986). *Love, medicine and miracles*. New York, NY: Harper & Row.

Siegel, B. (2005). *Humor and healing*. Louisville, CO: Sounds True.

Smitherman, S., & Trueit, D. (2006, May). *Complex conversations in education: Our need to move away from teaching as telling*. Paper presented at the triannual meeting of the International Association for the Advancement of Curriculum Studies. Tampere, Finland.

Sterne, L. (1983). *The life and opinions of Tristram Shandy, gentleman*. Oxford, UK: Oxford University Press. (Original work published in 1759–1767).

Trueit, D. (2012a). Preface. In D. Trueit (Ed.), *Pragmatism, post-modernism and complexity theory: The "fascinating imaginative realm" of William E. Doll, Jr.* (pp. xii–xiv). New York, NY: Routledge.

Trueit, D. (2012b). Part I: Personal reflections—Introduction: Donna Trueit. In D. Trueit (Ed.), *Pragmatism, post-modernism and complexity theory: The "fascinating imaginative realm" of William E. Doll, Jr.* (pp. 11–12). New York, NY: Routledge.

Tyler, R. (1949). *Basic principles of curriculum and instruction*. Chicago, IL: University of Chicago Press.

Wang, H. (2016). *From the parade child to the king of chaos: The complex journey of William Doll, teacher educator*. New York, NY: Peter Lang.

Whitehead, A. (1967). *The aims of education and other essays*. New York, NY: The Free Press. (Original work published in 1929)

Part I
Of Influence, Inspiration, and Intellectual Adventure

The adventure Doll engages and generates, and to which he ever invites us, is indeed illuminating, enticing the intellect, provoking the powers of the mind, advancing insight and understanding. It is also born of and by spirit, inspiring love and laughter as well as light, influential in its abiding openness to the other, to being and becoming with others, with enduring hospitality and hope in the journey. The word "adventure" invokes these ideas of wandering and of travel, and of games of chance, involving also uncertainty and risk. The adventurer is one who plays such games and seeks such experiences, wherein the outcome is unknown and destination undetermined—one who would be present to and participate in the mystery of life and living in the course, or curriculum, of its unfolding.

From *advenire*, in Old French, there is this idea of *to go—to come, to reach and to arrive at* . . . the *adventura* (from the Latin), which is the event, the happening, as much a "novel or exciting incident, remarkable occurrence" as could be "perilous undertaking" (*OED*, 1989). To adventure, takes heart, then, too (*coeur*, French): courage. From the 13th century, its meaning, tied to spirit, also embraces the wondrous, the miraculous, marvelous things. These are those to which Doll magnanimously beckons us, and as inspirational (Latin, *inspirare*, to breathe)—living, breathing, animating, arousing, affecting, divinely influential. Interestingly enough too, the word influence (Latin, *influentia, influentum, influere*) alludes in a way as well to these echoes of God's laughter—"a flow of water, a flowing in"; "to flow into, stream in, pour in . . . into, in, on upon . . . to flow" (*OED*). In the astrological sense, from early times it referred to "streaming ethereal power from the stars"; "emanation from the stars" . . . acting upon human character or destiny. From Middle English, it references more broadly an outpouring of energy producing some effect; oft this power is invisible, unseen, and immaterial, yet bears this efficacious capacity nonetheless.

Doll's influence as an internationally renowned scholar in curriculum studies who has worked in the field of American education for more than half a century is certainly acknowledged, and marked . . . it emanates (e.g., Trueit, 2012; Wang, 2016). Of such, William Pinar (2012) explains:

> Doll's genius has been to reconstruct the main moments in the 20th century intellectual history of American educational thought—pragmatism, developmentalism, complexity theory—and in so doing lay bare the through lines that link them, creating a complex interaction among the three that transforms our understanding of curriculum . . . how we understand—indeed, live in—the world.
>
> (p. 9)

The scholars in this collection clearly attest to and articulate such influence, and the ways such reaches beyond the field, indeed into their own understandings and lives in curriculum and in the world. Those in this section particularly speak to this, and the intellectual adventures and inspirations pertaining to such, and ensuing.

M. Jayne Fleener seeks to reflect upon the "largeness" and "largess" of Doll and of his work, drawing upon Heidegger on approaching the life and learnedness of a master, attentive to "the mysterious energies that drive an intellect." Here, she highlights the evolving story—propelled by passion for teaching and commitment to transforming the curriculum field—and travels therein: visits to China mirroring Dewey's, shared engagements and intellectual pursuits (e.g., process philosophy and complexity theory), sojourning together with his "scholarly entourage" and conversing over gimlets too. She describes and demonstrates well the influence of his expansive approach marked by playfulness, openness, exploration, and enthusiasm for new ideas: "The process of knowing is expanded when one understands logical inquiry as embracing intuition, inspiration, and spirit. . . . embracing essence as relationship, 'drops of experience' (Whitehead, 1929, pp. 27–28) that define emergent being. . . . emergence as vital to the dynamics of teaching and learning."

Hua Zhang also locates Doll's contributions within an intentional Deweyan legacy, and his compelling criticism of modernity in the disenchantment of the curriculum, which has rationalized and reified mind via the mechanism of methodization. Identifying him as a world curriculum scholar, Hua Zhang speaks to Doll's systematic attention to the question of method, inspiring the conceptualization of a "spiritual methodology" and new educational paradigm: "William Doll's strategy is to reenchant curriculum, animate curriculum by spirit, which is a great historical turn to post-modern curriculum." The import of such work in China and in Hua Zhang's own life and work is related, as by Doll's "deep and expansive vision" we are called to responsible, "relational creativity" through which we may rescue mind and recreate ourselves and culture via curriculum. Such reenchantment enlists us in adventure, and opens us to inspiration, indeed: "Doll's happiness is an intellectual post-modern attitude, rooted in playfulness, which is an embodiment of freedom and hope."

Working from the Finnish context, Tero Autio articulates both its and his intellectual indebtedness to and kinship with William Doll, presenting a curricular history of Finland in relation to such. Finland is not only notable in its PISA ranking, but also in its eschewal of the accountability language and high stakes testing dominating so much of education elsewhere. It shares with Doll, rather, a focus on care, trust, and responsibility. He speaks here of Doll's capacity to see curriculum matters from a larger perspective, of his enduring efforts aimed at education worthy of its name, beyond instrumental rationality and its deforming "de-complexification," and also of the dynamizing effect of his theorizing on philosophy—"Doll . . . with his perception of education based on post-modern conceptions of science that it is more complex, re-enchanted and qualitatively different from, not reducible to, and not explainable by scientism à la Descartes and Newton." Autio locates Doll's "ghosts of control"—profoundly resilient despite evidence and opposition—within the present global educational reform movement, neoliberalism, and the decay of democracy; and asserts: "For me, Bill Doll's scholarly oeuvre is convincingly demonstrating there are alternatives for that global, anti-intellectual and antidemocratic waste of human talent, imagination, and creativity in the name of education."

Creatively enacting a Doll-inspired art exploring his influence through the curricular script of *Thoroughly Modern Milly*—now Billy, Peter Appelbaum performatively plays with Doll's four R's for a post-modern curriculum (see footnote 9, Quinn, introduction) and presents the inspirations, adventures, and appreciations emerging from his own experiments with such. He critically reflects upon this journey—a dance between and bridging modern and post-modern—and the post-modern patterns and transformational processes emerging therein, located as such within various nomadic epistemological frames—to shed light on its rigorous, recursive, relational, and very rich vistas and views.

The last essay in this section, Noel Gough frames his thinking through the very notion of the journey, a search and an adventure, beyond one's capacity to control, of serendipity, sustenance, and "widening circles of affiliation." He emphasizes, too, its richness and generativity, both intellectually and personally—wherein art and science poetically and provocatively come together, as do continents and cultures intermingling, in the birth of treasured lifelong friendships, travels, experiences, and memories—inspiring creative and complex curricular conversations and collaborations too. Stumbling upon each other, a joint adventure between Gough and Doll was born—involving long drives across the American South, wine-tasting excursions, international speaking and teaching engagements and more—from which also emerged, in affiliation with others, their co-edited book *Curricular Visions*, the AERA Complexity SIG, the journal *Complicity*, and IAACS. And Gough makes particular note, too, of the laughter, and inspiration, so constitutive of their course of life, curriculum journey, together. "Bill's great gift to all who know him is his seemingly limitless capacity to find wonder and joy in almost every experience." He hopes that long may we cherish the echo of Bill's laughter.

References

Oxford English dictionary (OED) (2nd ed.). (1989). (J. Simpson & E. Weiner, Eds.). Oxford, UK: Clarendon Press.

Pinar, W. (2012). Introduction. In D. Trueit (Ed.), *Pragmatism, post-modernism and complexity theory: The "fascinating imaginative realm" of William E. Doll, Jr.* (pp. 1–10). New York, NY: Routledge.

Trueit, D. (Ed.). (2012). *Pragmatism, post-modernism and complexity theory: The "fascinating imaginative realm" of William E. Doll, Jr.* New York, NY: Routledge.

Wang, H. (2016). *From the parade child to the king of chaos: The complex journey of William Doll, teacher educator.* New York, NY: Peter Lang.

Whitehead, A. (1929). *Process and reality.* New York, NY: Macmillan.

2 Dynamics of a Scholarly Life
Conversational Complexity in Pursuit of the *Mysterium Tremendum*

M. Jayne Fleener

Introduction

In his speech to honor the composer Conradin Kreutzer in 1955, Martin Heidegger (Heidegger, 1959/1966) pronounced: "the greater the master, the more completely his person vanishes behind his work" (p. 44). To honor a great master, Heidegger explained, requires we "think," that is, we consider both the person and the work. In "thinking" we wrestle, we meditate, we engage the spirit of who we are and who they were, we get beyond the "calculative" or sterile thinking or products of an academic or public career to understand beginnings, the roots that connect and sustain. Mediation by spirit, by a being-in-relation way of thinking, is necessary "in order to bloom . . . and to bear fruit" (p. 47). Meditative thinking, Heidegger explains, "demands of us that we engage ourselves with what at first sight does not go together at all. . . . That which shows itself and at the same time withdraws is the essential trait of what we call the mystery" (pp. 53–55). The complexity of the life of the man and his work cannot be captured without engaging the spirit and the story, the *mysterium tremendum* (Doll, 2002/2012), a meditative approach to the works of Bill Doll.[1]

Complexity theory provides the lens through which Doll's work is examined. Even as Doll's work has ebbed and flowed through the chaos and complexity literature, the unfolding of his scholarship can be traced as a complex adaptive system with recursion, emergence, and increasing

---

1. To my knowledge, the early 20th-century German religious writer Rudolf Otto was the first to describe the *Mysterium Tremendum* in his 1917 publication *Das Heilige* (Trans., John W. Harvey. Oxford: Oxford University Press, 1923, *The Idea of the Holy*). As used by Doll, the *Mysterium Tremendum* describes the mystery of religious experience from a non-rational perspective, as part of a way of knowing (spirit) that is in interaction with the narratives of science and story. Doll thus extends the complex ways of knowing across scientific, spiritual, and storied experiences as the *Mysterium Tremendum*, an interplay or dynamic that creates a holistic hermeneutic. I extend this perspective of the dynamic of knowing as the *Mysterium Tremendum* to include complexity perspectives of process, perturbation, emergence, transformation, and recursive dynamics in an ongoing and unfolding hermeneutic.

layers of complexity defining the evolving story and pathways of understanding. As such, the system has particular drivers that include a passion for teaching and commitment to transform the curriculum field. Underlying dynamics of his work include sensitivity to initial conditions, recursive dynamics, and transformational processes. Exploring the work, thoughtfully, cannot separate the man from the products and must capture the products as well as the story and spirit of scholarship unfolded.

Personal Interlude

In thinking of the man and connecting his work, you cannot escape the "largeness" of Bill Doll. I think of him walking down the halls of Peabody Hall at LSU declaring his love for Donna, arms flailing, voice booming—"I'm in love, I'm in love, I'm in love." Or being with him in China where he is treated like a rock star. He stands out because of his 6-foot 5-inch frame, shock of white hair, and enormous laugh that fills the room. The Chinese are attracted to him during his visits as much to embrace the largess as to understand the thinking of this "King of Chaos"—with its double meaning bringing chaos dynamics to curriculum conversations and his self-declared affinity for the great Chinese Monkey King of myth who was known for his irreverence and bringing to humanity complexity and chaos.

The first time I met Bill was actually a non-meeting as my department chair at the University of Oklahoma, recently transplanted from LSU, declared I *had* to meet Bill Doll. Our common interests in chaos, complexity and process philosophies foretold a match made in heaven. Many gimlets[2] later, I became his colleague and dean at LSU where the adventure continued. As is common among deans, my predecessor left a letter for me describing the challenges and opportunities facing the college. What stands out about the letter, and captures the complexity of Bill Doll (and his twin giant, Bill Pinar) was the sentence "And what to do about the Bills?" Indeed!

Bill Doll and I co-taught several classes together, "played with" with many doctoral students, and continued to explore the worlds of chaos, complexity and process philosophies even as we traveled together, along with his scholarly entourage that now included Donna. And, of course, there were the parties at my house when he would announce, "It's time for a gathering . . . and we'll have it at your house. . . . I'll take care of all of the arrangements." And Hurricane Katrina, where he was "escorted" out of Destrehan as the last car out of New Orleans before the roads were closed, arriving at our house in Baton Rouge just a few hours ahead of Katrina. The conversations and opportunities I had because of Bill are too numerous and too special to delineate. To do them justice and to truly

---

2. A gimlet is a cocktail made with gin.

Dynamics of a Scholarly Life 23

honor the man, the "thinking" of Bill Doll cannot be separated from the person that he is.

Inquiry Web of Doll's Work

An inquiry web (Fleener, 2016) provides the scaffolding for exploring the complexity of Doll's scholarship (see Figure 2.1) as the scholarly connects with the personal and engages through the spirit of Bill Doll. As a mode of philosophical inquiry grounded in complexity theory, the inquiry web traces Doll's work through beginnings in history and process philosophy, to an exploration of post-modernism and complexity theories, to ultimately evolve an approach to curriculum that reveals the *Mysterium Tremendum* of the teaching and learning relationship. The

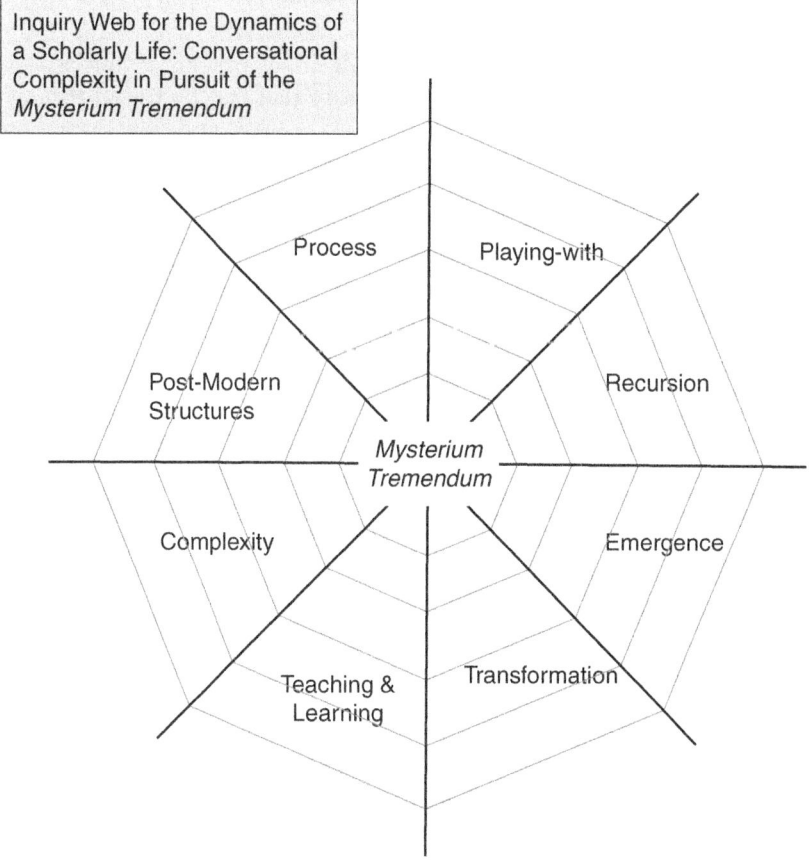

Figure 2.1 Inquiry Web for Exploring the Dynamics of William E. Doll's Scholarly Life

web offers connections and dynamic interplay while maintaining a focus on the man, beyond the works, to engage us all in continued thinking and connecting with the ideas represented by the body of his scholarly productivity. For a more comprehensive summary of Bill Doll's work, the published text edited by his wife, Donna Trueit (2012) provides in-depth descriptions and personal connections he and others have made across the body of written works that are Bill's gifts to all of us.

The inquiry web is also a fitting image to use. Bill and I explored the work out of the Santa Fe Institute that included models of emergent systems in nature. From bee hives to flocking birds, nature abounds with examples of complex dynamics that result in patterned, connected, and unfolding relationships. The inquiry web is both a tool and a metaphor for exploring the work of Bill Doll as patterned, connected, unfolding/enfolding, dynamic, and emergent.

Using the inquiry web to examine his work begins by tracing Bill's explorations of Dewey (especially Dewey, 1896, 1899, 1902, 1916, 1925, 1929, 1933, 1934, 1938) and Whitehead (especially Whitehead, 1925, 1929a, 1929b, 1938). Dewey and Whitehead, as pragmatic and process philosophers, plant the seeds of complexity that can be traced through Doll's work to key notions of relationship, process, and transformation. Over and over again, as seen in the Web, Bill's explorations engage the transformative through an understanding of being and knowing that expanded beyond sterile learning. We explored, with our friend John St. Julien while presenting to his classes and over many meals, Dewey's *Logic* (1938) to understand a logic of relationship, a logic open to ways of thinking that went beyond what is typically constrained by cognitive understandings. The process of knowing is expanded when one understands logical inquiry as embracing intuition, inspiration, and spirit. This expanded approach to inquiry, described by Dewey in his *Logic* and implicit in many of his writings that served to dispel the dualisms of modernism (*Child AND Curriculum*, 1902; *School AND Society*, 1899; *Democracy AND Education*, 1916; and *Experience AND Nature*, 1925), conveys the Both-And thinking of Dewey and the post-modern perspective of Bill Doll.

I especially remember exploring these ideas with Stephen S. Triche's students at McNeese State where Bill (occasionally accompanied by me) would typically travel at least once a semester to guest lecture. Guest lectures were a huge part of Bill's classes (where sometimes the visiting scholars equaled in numbers the students in the class) and many of his former students to this day include this strategy to "complexify" their classroom conversations. Two sessions that I recall, in particular, explored "the ghost of John Dewey" (referring to our respective chapters in Doll & Gough, 2002), and the history of curriculum related to chaos theory (as described in our chapters in Doll, Fleener, Trueit, & St. Julien, 2005). Bill first explored the influence of Ramus with Steve when Steve was completing his dissertation under Bill's tutelage. Bill always learned from and with his students. His openness to and passion for new ideas along with his ability to make connections were part of what made Bill such a great teacher. In these classes, and in other venues where we co-presented, we engaged the students in a conversation, seldom following any formal presentation plan and always including/expecting lots of time for conversation. Steve and his students were prepared for these visits and engaged in respectful and spirited intellectual playfulness of ideas by and from which Bill was always enthused and energized!

Bill and I came to Whitehead in the same way, in some respects each, independently mirroring Whitehead's own path as a mathematician, historian of the intellectual history of mathematics and science, and process philosophy challenging things as "fundamental entities in space and time," a concept I disrupted in many of my own graduate classes and writings (e.g., Fleener, 2002) while embracing essence as relationship, "drops of experience" (Whitehead, 1929b, pp. 27–28) that define emergent being. The process philosophy of Whitehead focuses on an ontology of being-in-relationship, one that pre-disposes both quantum theories and the critical phenomenology of Heidegger (1959/1966), another intellectual pursuit shared between us.

Post-modernism is an important organizing structure for understanding Doll's scholarly work and is represented in the inquiry web, even as it connects and extends his thinking in pragmatism and process perspectives. Through his explorations of and writings about Piaget, early in his career, and later his explorations of chaos and complexity theories, postmodernism provides a perspective of curriculum that, through a complexity lens, supports emergence as vital to the dynamics of teaching and learning. His seminal work, *A Post-modern Perspective on Curriculum* (Doll, 1993) connects post-modernism with process philosophy while introducing educators to complexity thinkers such as Prigogine. Through these chaos and complexity perspectives, recursive dynamics re-define the curriculum through Bill's four R's as relational, rich, recursive, and rigorous.

While the U.S. wrestled with increasing test scores and demonstrating achievement during the reign of No Child Left Behind, China was exploring how to encourage its students to think and creatively solve problems. Bill's post-modern perspective and the four R's especially resonated with audiences in China as "The Monkey King" explained how to disrupt the curriculum to support the openness (and openings) they sought. As we visited five cities in two weeks, I enjoyed watching how the four R's came alive for each audience and how chaos and complexity emerged with connections to Chinese history and traditions. Doll's travels to China during the early part of the 21st century can be compared to Dewey's own travels to China in the 1920s. Both man and country were impacted.

Although I never co-taught teacher education courses with Bill, it was through pre-service teacher preparation and the Holmes Elementary

Program that many of his teaching and learning ideas were tested and disseminated. All students in the Holmes Program left with a sense of purpose and mission after they received a healthy dose of chaos theory to propel the importance of seeding learning to support emergence of ideas. Complex learning relationships among teacher, student, and curriculum are supported when environments are created that are open to and encourage playing with ideas.

In graduate classes at LSU, Bill, and I explored the playing-with relationship and language games of Wittgenstein (1953), along with the dynamics of complexity to understand complex conversations in the classroom with a different audience. We wrestled with creating syllabi for those classes that provided just enough "seeding" for playing with ideas and emergence of pathways to learning. Opening up the curriculum to create spaces for emergent learning reveals the importance of the *Mysterium Tremendum*, the mysterious energies that drive an intellect. These mysterious energies emerge when one focuses less on the science and embraces personal story and spirit.

Driving Forces

To honor the man, one must engage thinking about the products of a life in ways that include and celebrate the person, bringing forth the spirit of the intellect. The inquiry web is an attempt to stay focused on the complex story of a life and spirit that lives through and with Bill's body of intellectual products, but comes alive when the person is part of the story. Each octant of the web can be interpreted as connected to its opposite through the *Mysterium Tremendum* of Bill Doll while the body itself, like a complex web, reveals hidden connections and relationships across, between, and among inquiry spaces. Exploring the corpus of Bill's work, thoughtfully, in a Heideggerian sense, one cannot separate the man from the products and must capture the products as well as the story and spirit of scholarship unfolded and connected, offering an

> openness to the mystery . . . [that grants] us the possibility of dwelling in the world in a totally different way . . . [for] openness to the mystery awaken(s) within us . . . a path that will lead to a new ground.
> (Heidegger, 1959/1966, pp. 55–57)

The complexity of the life of the man and his work cannot be captured by a mere listing of publications but must include the spirit and the story of Bill Doll, the *mysterium tremendum* (Doll, 2002/2012, 2010/2012), a meditative approach to the man and his thinking, a meditative approach to our own thinking, learning, and existence.

Seldom is the evolution of one's work so compatible with the driving forces of one's scholarly pursuits. There is a "double-bind" relationship between the evolution of Doll's scholarship and the purpose of his efforts to create a dynamic curriculum that engages the *Mysterium Tremendum*. There is much to learn about the man and this process by exploring the dynamics of Bill Doll's scholarly life.

References

Dewey, J. (1896, July). The reflex arc concept in psychology. *Psychological Review, 3*, 357–370.
Dewey, J. (1899). *The school and society* (Rev. ed.). Chicago, IL: University of Chicago Press.
Dewey, J. (1902). *The child and the curriculum*. Chicago, IL: University of Chicago Press.
Dewey, J. (1916). *Democracy and education: An introduction to the philosophy of education*. New York, NY: Macmillan.
Dewey, J. (1925). *Experience and nature*. Chicago, IL: University of Chicago Press.
Dewey, J. (1929). *The quest for certainty*. New York, NY: Minton, Balch & Company.
Dewey, J. (1933). *How we think* (Rev. ed.). Washington, DC: DC Heath & Company.
Dewey, J. (1934). *Art as experience* (W. James Lecture at Harvard). New York, NY: The Berkley Publishing Group.
Dewey, J. (1938). *Logic: The theory of inquiry*. New York, NY: Henry Holt and Company.
Doll, W. (1993). *A post-modern perspective on curriculum*. New York, NY: Teachers College Press.
Doll, W. (2012). Struggles with spirituality. In D. Trueit (Ed.), *Pragmatism, postmodernism, and complexity theory: The "fascinating imaginative realm" of William E. Doll, Jr.* (pp. 33–42). New York, NY: Routledge. (Original work published in 2002)
Doll, W. (2012). Thinking complexly. In D. Trueit (Ed.), *Pragmatism, postmodernism, and complexity theory: The "fascinating imaginative realm" of William E. Doll, Jr.* (pp. 172–188). New York, NY: Routledge. (Original work published in 2010)
Doll, W., Fleener, M., Trueit, D., & St. Julien, J. (Eds.) (2005). *Chaos, complexity, curriculum and culture: A conversation*. New York, NY: Peter Lang.
Doll, W., & Gough, N. (Eds.). (2002). *Curriculum visions*. New York, NY: Peter Lang.
Fleener, M. J. (2002). *Curriculum dynamics: Recreating heart*. New York, NY: Peter Lang.Fleener, M. J. (2016, December 31). Addressing educations' most intractable problems: A case of failing schools. *Emergence Complexity & Organization: An International Transdisciplinary Journal of Complex Social Systems*. Edition 1. https://doi.org/10.emerg/10.17357.e0b582abc618906c0d995c-2557c77bc3 [last modified: 2017 February 5]
Heidegger, M. (1966). *Discourse on thinking* (J. M. Anderson & E. H. Freund, Trans.). New York, NY: Harper & Row. (Original work published in 1959)
Trueit, D. (2012). *Pragmatism, postmodernism, and complexity theory: The "fascinating imaginative realm" of William E. Doll, Jr.* New York, NY: Routledge.

Whitehead, A. N. (1925). *Science and the modern world*. New York, NY: Macmillan.
Whitehead, A. N. (1929a). *The aims of education and other essays*. New York, NY: Macmillan.
Whitehead, A. N. (1929b). *Process and reality*. New York, NY: Macmillan.
Whitehead, A. N. (1938). *Modes of thought*. New York, NY: Macmillan.
Wittgenstein, L. (1953). *Philosophical investigations* (G.E.M. Anscombe, Trans.). New York, NY: Macmillan.

3 Toward the Reenchantment of Curriculum
A Study on William Doll's Post-modern Curriculum Theory

Hua Zhang

Introduction: Three States of Curriculum

Educational happiness, unity of heaven and human, and life conversations form the ancient state and wisdom of curriculum. This curriculum is charming and enchanting. I would like to call it "enchanted curriculum," which is the main state of curriculum in the ancient, agriculture-civilized, pre-modern era and society. After the Renaissance, especially the Enlightenment, accompanying the birth of Puritan-Protestant ethics, the Methodization Movement, emergence of science and technology, industrialization movement, and social efficiency movement, human society has dramatically changed. In Max Weber's words, the nature of the modern society is the disenchantment of the world (Weber, 2004). In the curriculum field, accompanying the institutionalization of curriculum and the birth of the curriculum development paradigm, a new kind of curriculum was created, which has dualism of subject and object, control-based axiology, production and transmission-based methodology as its main features. I would like to call it "disenchanted curriculum," which is the main state of curriculum in the industry-civilized modern era and society.

Since the 1980s, primarily in Western developed countries, people have been continuously reflecting on the problems of modernization, industrialization, scientism, and technical rationality. A complicated, transdisciplinary thought tide was generated. Because it focuses on the critical reflection of modernity—science-technology-industry civilization and the related mentality—it is called "post-modernism," which has anti-representationalism, anti-foundationalism, and anti-essentialism as its philosophical characters. In the curriculum field, the Reconceptualization Movement of the 1970s, led by famous curriculum theorist Professor William F. Pinar, is the symbolic event to systematically criticize the disenchanted curriculum and curriculum theory. During this movement, Professor William E. Doll, Jr., created a new curriculum paradigm—post-modern curriculum theory—which is a magnificent curriculum vision for our time and world. I would like to call it "reenchanted curriculum," which is the main state of curriculum in the information-civilized post-modern era and society.

William Doll's great contributions to the curriculum field can be generalized into two parts: the first is the deep criticism on the disenchantment of curriculum, which forms Doll's diagnosis of modern curriculum; the second is the fascinating construction on the reenchantment of curriculum, which forms Doll's vision of post-modern curriculum. These two aspects have great significance to our time and world.

Methodization and the Disenchantment of Curriculum: Doll's Diagnosis

About 100 years ago, when science and technology were rapidly developing and industrialization was flourishing, great German sociologist, historian, and philosopher Max Weber predicted the problems of modernity and modern society, and wisely diagnosed it. Weber pointed out that the process of rationalization has lasted for thousands of years in the Western world and reached its peak in modern society, and scientific progress is the most important fraction in it. The main outcome of this process is "the disenchantment of the world," which means magic, ghosts, and all the mysterious forces are rooted out and everything can be controlled by scientific calculation. "We can in principle *control everything by means of calculation*" (Weber, 2004, p. 13, emphasis in original). When everything is forced to be calculated, human minds become calculating mentality, human society becomes calculating society, and human civilization becomes calculating civilization. Under this condition, the brilliance of humanity and dignity of sublime values disappear. Weber said, "Our age is characterized by rationalization and intellectualization, and above all, by the disenchantment of the world. Its resulting fate is that precisely the ultimate and most sublime values have withdrawn from public life" (p. 30). The essence of rationalization and intellectualization is the expansion of purposeful or instrumental rationality and atrophy of value rationality, which inevitably give rise to sick personalities and put the society in crisis, even danger. In this society, "specialists without spirit, hedonists without a heart, these nonentities imagine they have attained a stage of humankind [*Menschentum*] never before reached" (Weber, 2002, p. 121). Instrumental rationality, and the related rationalization of society, is a firm iron cage, which imprisons human freedom and creativity. In order to escape from the shell, we must shed instrumental rationality, recover value rationality, and reenchant the world. That is Max Weber's era diagnosis.

William E. Doll's diagnosis of the curriculum field echoes Max Weber's. Very similar to Weber, Doll also revealed the root of the disenchantment of curriculum in Protestant culture and ethic. But Doll concretely found that the mechanism of disenchantment is the Methodization Movement. Even more deeply, Doll raised the idea that Protestants, Puritans, and their followers created a "new ghost" to replace the old ones and finished the process of disenchantment. The name of this ghost is called "control" or "method." In the world curriculum field, Doll is probably the only scholar who systematically studies the method issue of curriculum and pedagogy. As early as the late 1970s or early 1980s, when Doll was chair of the Education Department and chair of the College Curriculum Committee at SUNY-Oswego, he had the idea to study the Methodization Movement (Doll, 2009/2012e, p. 17). He has published a series of high-quality and strong papers on the culture of method in the curriculum field (Doll, 2002/2012a, 2002, 2005). Studying curriculum method and the culture of method is the main academic strategy for Doll to understand the essence of "modern curriculum" and reveal its problems.

The intrinsic mechanism and essence of curriculum modernization and disenchantment is the rationalization of the educational field. Because a specific type of rationalism is peculiar to Western culture, mentality, and society, we can only find the typical rationalization of curriculum in the Western world. Just as Max Weber mentioned, even "mystical contemplation" is rationalized in Western society, although it is specifically "irrational" in other cultures. "And there can equally well be rationalizations of the economy, technology, scientific work, education, war, the administration of justice, and other forms of administration" (Weber, 2002, pp. 365–366). In a culture where everything is rationalized, the curriculum field is inevitably trapped also in this fate.

The process of curriculum rationalization is the process to rationalize human minds, including the minds of curriculum specialists, teachers, and students. Mind rationalization is mind reification and alienation. Human minds become reified, alienated, and dull. Emotions, love, caring, and a whole person disappear. Weber's judgment of "specialists without spirit" and "hedonists without a heart" is also true in the curriculum field. When curriculum is rationalized, modernized, and disenchanted, the predetermined educational purposes will actually be made by without-spirit specialists and without-a-heart hedonists. The rich values of curriculum are reduced to the only one: control. Doll said, "As we control, we accept the idea of control and become, ourselves, controlled" (Doll, 2002/2012f, p. 38). The rationalized mind is a controlling mind, which has technical rationality as the only value to pursue, and results in persons without spirit. This is the disenchantment of an individual. When technical rationality is applied to rule a society, the society will be bureaucratized, stratified, and dehumanized, which is a society without spirit. This is the disenchantment of a society. When technical rationality is used to control nature, the nature will be dominated, tamed, and destroyed. Mountains and rivers, lakes and oceans, forests and grasslands, birds and animals, and all of nature become raw materials and resources for human beings to machine in factories, and nature loses its naturalness, which is a nature without spirit. This is the disenchantment of nature.

It is urgent to rescue curriculum and pedagogy from their rationalization in today's world and the coming world of "big data." Referring to the problem of rationalism in modern society, Weber said, "The first problem is therefore once again to recognize the *distinctive characteristics* [*Eigenart*] of Western rationalism, and within this, of modern Western rationalism, and to explain how it came into being" (Weber, 2002, p. 366, emphasis in original). That's why he studied the Protestant ethic. William Doll's unique and great contribution to reveal the secret of rationalism in the Western curriculum field is his systematic study on the culture of method in curriculum and pedagogy, from Ramism to the Tyler Rationale. How to solve the problem? If William F. Pinar's strategy to go beyond the rationalized curriculum is to recover the dignity and value of individuals and cultures by autobiography (*currere*) and internationalization (Pinar, 1975/2000, 2014), William Doll's strategy is to reenchant curriculum, animate curriculum by spirit, which is a great historical turn to post-modern curriculum. Pinar and Doll influence and benefit each other. Their friendship goes beyond the personal. It is a great curricular friendship.

Post-modern Curriculum as Reenchanted Curriculum: Doll's Vision

Bill Doll embodies post-modernism in his work and life. As always, he is in a happy and passionate mind. Happiness with passion is the intrinsic value of education. A real educator is a happy person. Confucius is an optimist. John Dewey is an optimist. John Dewey's most famous student Hu Shih called himself an incurable optimist. So is Bill Doll. This optimism is a spiritual happiness. Everybody who knows and contacts Bill Doll must have opportunities to enjoy his joyful laughter, and his morning greeting phrase "happy everyday." I am so lucky and honored to know Bill Doll for nearly twenty years, from classrooms and conference auditoriums to everyday life, from LSU to UBC, from America to China, Canada, and other countries, I have been deeply plunged into his happiness and thoughts, which help me grow in academic study and personhood. Doll's happiness is an intellectual post-modern attitude, rooted in playfulness, which is an embodiment of freedom and hope.

Reenchanted Philosophy of Curriculum

Bill Doll is one of the most important curriculum theorists who can skillfully, deeply, and wisely handle the relationship between philosophy and curriculum. He consciously inherits John Dewey's legacy. Dewey said, "philosophy was defined as the generalized theory of education" (Dewey, 1916/1980, p. 341). "Education is the laboratory in which philosophic distinctions become concrete and are tested" (p. 339). We can infer that philosophy is the general theory of curriculum, and curriculum is the laboratory of philosophy. Based on this valuable legacy, Doll raises up a deep and far-sighted vision of curriculum.

As for curriculum ontology and axiology, Doll thinks that all reality is the reality of relationships, which is always in process. No relations, no world. No process, no world. Individuals, societies, cultures, social systems, nature, ecological circles, and universe are relational and formed by relations. The forming process is creations, and creations in emergence. These creations are cosmological creations. These relations are the relations of being, or relations per se. These relational acts of creation are from spirituality, which is the relational creativity per se. Relationality is creative, and creativity is relational. So creativity must be responsible, respectful, and ethical. Relational creativity is a moral creativity. Here we find the commonality between Doll's post-modernism and Chinese traditional Confucianism. Doll said, "I am responsible without sacrificing myself or my being to the other. I am freely responsible and within this 'free' responsibility there lies the possibility of new possibilities" (Doll, 2002/2012f, p. 41). Relationality gives rise to responsibility, and responsibility gives rise to possibility and creativity, and vice versa. These are the essence of spirituality. "I believe our spirituality must be . . . a relationship of being we develop, with awe and reverence toward all creation. This relationship is . . . a relationship of being" (p. 42). From this perspective, curriculum is not an entity, but a relation; not atomic and static, but dynamic, relational, and creational. Based on this point, Doll raises his "new vision of education":

> Education in the sense I am considering is education which focuses on our being-on our engagement with life as this is manifest in humanity, the world, the universe, the cosmos. Such an education does struggle with the spiritual, and is infused with the spiritual at the same time it infuses the spiritual with us.
> (Doll, 2002/2012f, p. 42)

This vision is the ontological and axiological vision of curriculum.

As for curriculum epistemology, Doll thinks that the essence of knowledge is understanding. His eternal motto is from Czech-born French writer Milan Kundera: "There does exist a 'fascinating, imaginative realm where no one owns the truth and everyone has the right to be understood'" (from Kundera, in Doll, 1993, p. 155). For Bill Doll, this "fascinating, imaginative realm" is curriculum, pedagogy, classrooms, schools, subject matters, and societies. Go beyond "objective truth," towards truth as shared or conversational. Go beyond idle, isolated, and dead facts of various subject matters, towards core ideas, alive knowledge, and lived experience. Doll writes, "a fact by itself is really nothing; it acquires its 'factness' only as it enters into relationships with other facts, only as it is contextualized" (Doll, 2005/2012c, p. 117). Knowledge is relational. In order to enter into knowledge, we should keep a relational way of thinking. Doll fully absorbs the knowledge theories of Whitehead and Dewey, integrates them into his own three S's (science, story, spirit), and forms his unique epistemology.

The central question for Whitehead's educational thought is to keep knowledge alive and free students from inert knowledge. To realize this goal, "Let the main ideas which are introduced into a child's education be few and important, and let them be thrown into every combination possible" (Whitehead, 1929, p. 2). Only when students have opportunities to apply and create with the important ideas can they keep knowledge alive and develop creative intelligence. The central question for Dewey's educational thought is to learn to think well or reflectively. He said, "The real problem of intellectual education is the *transformation* of natural powers into expert, tested powers: the transformation of . . . casual curiosity and sporadic suggestion into attitudes of alert, cautious, and thorough inquiry" (from Dewey, in Doll, 2002, p. 51). Intellectual education is to provide opportunities for students to do thorough inquiry and develop expert thinking. This is one of Dewey's main educational ideals. Based on the thoughts of Dewey, Whitehead, Jean Piaget, Jerome Bruner, and Ilya Prigogine, Doll raises his epistemology of the three S's:

> Discrete facts in and of themselves are quite useless; however, facts embedded in a matrix of relationships provide us with the "richness" . . . necessary for knowledge and knowing to transform themselves via creative development built upon creative development, upon creative development.
>
> (Doll, 2003/2012d, p. 106)

This is Doll's epistemological vision of curriculum.

As for curriculum methodology, Doll thinks that method is essentially the intellectual, creative, and spiritual habit, attitude, action, and passage to solve problems in specific situations. Method is idiosyncratic and situational, not a one-size-fits-all model to follow. The modernist method, from Ramism to the Tyler Rationale, "is formal, rigid, universal—a path or way for all to follow"; the post-modern method, is "a new livelier, spirit-filled method, is more like a habit—personal, private, varied according to circumstances and above all reflected upon" (Doll, 2005, p. 48). The modernist method is disenchanted, and the post-modern one is spiritual, which is full of relational creativity. The main problem of modernist method is rationalist and universalist, which pursues control-based values in the name of scientific principles or rationales. In Dewey's words, this method "breeds mediocrity in all" (Dewey, 1916/1980, p. 173). The nature of post-modern method is freedom, creativity, and spirituality. From this perspective, the real method of curriculum development, pedagogy, and learning is not proceduralism, transmission, and reception, but deliberation, research, and inquiry. Both *currere* (self-study) and conversation are rich and spiritual methods in the curriculum field. Doll raises his methodological vision as follows: "I believe spirit lies in personal struggle . . . with all its complexities and chaotic happenings (irrationalities); and that in bringing forth this struggle and reflecting on it, a new, more humane, method can be found" (Doll, 2005, p. 48). This spiritual methodology implies a new curriculum practice.

Conclusion: Doll's Significance to Our Time and World

Our time is the age of information civilization. For education and the development of individuals and societies, this age is a double-edged sword. On the one hand, technical rationality and control-based values are unprecedentedly expanded because of the universal use of information technology in societies. Under this background, the Tyler Rationale and its derivations might come to life in the curriculum field because of their character of technical rationality. On the other hand, the new opportunities for personal fulfillment and well-functioning society are created by information civilization. The coming society of knowledge calls for the development of critical thinking, creative thinking, and collaborative thinking, which conversely calls for the transformation of curriculum and pedagogy from transmission to innovation. The development of "key competences" or "21st century competences" for students and teachers is an urgent theme of our time. I think Doll's post-modern curriculum theory can meet the challenge of this information age. As early as 1984, Doll raised a new competence model and transcended the behavioristic one (Doll, 1984/2012b). His three S's can clear up the problems of technical rationality because of its emphasis of spirit and story. His five C's (*currere*, complexity, cosmology, conversation, community) are both a value system and pedagogical way for 21st-century curriculum. His four R's (richness, relations, recursion, and rigor) are an enlightening frame for competence-based curriculum in the age of information. Doll's post-modern curriculum theory is far-sighted, and has long-term vitality for our time.

Doll's post-modern curriculum theory is rooted in cultural differences and the world because it emphasizes relationships, spirit, story, and cosmology. Worldliness is one of the main characteristics of Doll's post-modernism. Doll's curriculum thought deeply influences Chinese educational theory and practice. After the publication of the book *A Post-modern Perspective on Curriculum* in Taiwan in 1999 and in Mainland China in 2000, post-modernism has been a persisting hot theme in the Chinese curriculum field. For example, from 2000 to 2012, there are 1,940 papers published on post-modernism in Mainland China. All of Doll's works were published in China and warmly welcomed. Both educational researchers and schoolteachers have been heartily reading Doll's works. His book *A Post-modern Perspective on Curriculum* (Doll, 1993) has been continuously reprinted and universally recognized as a true classic. It is ranked 7th among the highly cited foreign academic books about pedagogy, while Dewey's *Democracy and Education* is ranked 5th (Su, 2011). In a practical field, Doll's post-modernism becomes one of the theoretical foundations for the ongoing national curriculum reform in China.

I am always moved when I read Doll's following words:

> curriculum is not just a vehicle for transmitting knowledge, but is a vehicle for creating and re-creating ourselves and our culture. . . mind is a verb, an active verb; an active, seeking verb; an active, seeking, self-organizing verb. It should not be wasted.
> (Doll, 1993, p. 131)

I understand why Bill Doll is so heartily welcome in China. Our education today, at least in China, is still wasting mind. Rescuing mind, creating and re-creating ourselves and our culture through curriculum studies and curriculum reform are our mission. Doll's words are eternally sounding in our curriculum world.

References

Dewey, J. (1980). Democracy and education. In J. A. Boydston (Ed.), *John Dewey's middle works* (Vol. 9). Carbondale, IL: The Southern Illinois University Press. (Original work published in 1916)

Doll, W. (1993). *A post-modern perspective on curriculum*. New York, NY: Teachers College Press.

Doll, W. (2002). Ghosts and the curriculum. In W. Doll & N. Gough (Eds.), *Curriculum visions* (pp. 23–70). New York, NY: Peter Lang.

Doll, W. (2005). The culture of method. In W. Doll, J. Fleener, J. St. Julien, & D. Trueit (Eds.), *Chaos, complexity, curriculum and culture: A conversation* (pp. 21–76). New York, NY: Peter Lang.

Doll, W. (2012a). Beyond methods. In D. Trueit (Ed.), *Pragmatism, postmodernism, and complexity theory: The "fascinating imaginative realm" of William E. Doll, Jr.* (pp. 81–97). New York, NY: Routledge. (Original work published in 2002)

Doll, W. (2012b). Developing competence. In D. Trueit (Ed.), *Pragmatism, postmodernism, and complexity theory: The "fascinating imaginative realm" of William E. Doll, Jr.* (pp. 66–80). New York, NY: Routledge. (Original work published in 1984)

Doll, W. (2012c). Keeping knowledge alive. In D. Trueit (Ed.), *Pragmatism, postmodernism, and complexity theory: The "fascinating imaginative realm" of William E. Doll, Jr.* (pp. 111–119). New York, NY: Routledge. (Original work published in 2005)

Doll, W. (2012d). Modes of thought. In D. Trueit (Ed.), *Pragmatism, postmodernism, and complexity theory: The "fascinating imaginative realm" of William E. Doll, Jr.* (pp. 103–110). New York, NY: Routledge. (Original work published in 2003)

Doll, W. (2012e). A path stumbled upon. In D. Trueit (Ed.), *Pragmatism, postmodernism, and complexity theory: The "fascinating imaginative realm" of William E. Doll, Jr.* (pp. 13–22). New York, NY: Routledge. (Original work published in 2009)

Doll, W. (2012f). Struggles with spirituality. In D. Trueit (Ed.), *Pragmatism, postmodernism, and complexity theory: The "fascinating imaginative realm" of William E. Doll, Jr.* (pp. 33–42). New York, NY: Routledge. (Original work published in 2002)

Pinar, W. (2000). *Curriculum studies: The reconceptualization.* Troy, NY: Educator's International Press. (Original work published in 1975)

Pinar, W. (2014). *Curriculum studies in China.* New York, NY: Palgrave Macmillan.

Su, X. (2011). *A report on academic influence of humanistic and social sciences books in China.* Beijing: China's Social Sciences Press.

Weber, M. (2002). *The protestant ethic and the "spirit" of capitalism* (P. Baehr & G. Wells, Eds. & Trans.). New York, NY: Penguin Books.

Weber, M. (2004). *The vocation lectures* (D. Owen & T. Strong, Eds., R. Livingstone, Trans.). Indianapolis, IN & Cambridge: Hackett Publishing Company.

Whitehead, A. (1929). *The aims of education and other essays.* New York, NY: The Free Press.

4 Education as Liberating Experience
Bill Doll's Scholarship and Contested Legacies of Euro-American Curriculum Theories From Descartes Onwards

Tero Autio

I engage with some associations related to discourses on European and American curriculum theory and history to express my intellectual debts to my dear friend, my *Doktorvater*, and the great and creative curriculum theorist, professor William E. Doll, Jr. Since "the intellectual breakthrough" in Anglo-American curriculum theory starting from the late 1970s, Anglophone curriculum theory has experienced a profound transformation first in the U.S. and Canada, and it has also found resonance and partners in dialogue in different parts of the world: in Argentina, Brazil, Chile, and Mexico in Latin America, South Africa, India, China, South Korea and Japan—as well as my country of origin, Finland, due to relatively short but democratic tradition where the quality of education was tied from the very beginning to social equality: for promoting the overall well-being of society and single individuals.[1]

The education system was harnessed for optimal social equality and inclusiveness that is expressed not as test scores but as non-stigmatizing support for disadvantaged children, as professional and intellectual autonomy of teachers, as master's degrees for all teachers, and as cost-free access to education up to PhD studies. In this context, Bill Doll's ideas find a strong and genuine resonance both in education policy and teacher education. In 2014 my alma mater, Tampere University, awarded Professor Doll an honorary doctorate in education for his contributions and personal visits in Finland. Bill Doll's scholarship has decisively affected the rise of popularity of curriculum studies in Finland among the students and a new generation of curriculum scholars and their intellectual interests (Saari, Salmela, & Vilkkila, 2014).

I would prefer disclosing to some extent the special Finnish receptivity to the style of curriculum research Bill Doll's insightful and imaginative scholarship embodies. Finnish education policy analyst Pasi Sahlberg's dissertation (Sahlberg, 1996) was the first Finnish research to employ Bill Doll's doctoral supervising and his post-modern perspective on

---

1. Finland celebrates her 100 years' independence this year 2017.

curriculum and teaching. Later Sahlberg (2011) wrote an education best-seller, *Finnish Lessons: What Can the World Learn From Educational Change in Finland?* Sahlberg's book, whose first printing was sold out in a couple of weeks, awoke a discussion of the "Finnish exceptionalism" that was initially based on the surprising and quite unexpected success in the first PISA results in 2001.

Peruskoulu, the Finnish Comprehensive School that covers grades 1 to 9, from age seven to sixteen, was fiercely criticized since its first blueprints in the 1960s by the political right, and from 1980s onwards the harsh critique was extended by the representatives of the economy and industry, the Education Committee of the Confederation of Finnish Industries and Employers (CIE). For this "noisy minority" the Finnish *Peruskoulu*—that was considered among parents, the elite, and the media in a typical modest Finnish style "good enough, but far from excellent"—was seen as a catastrophe. The timing of the irony of history couldn't be more perfect:

> Just two weeks before the publication of the first report, PISA 2000, on 24 November 2001, the influential and powerful Confederation of Finnish Industries and Employers (CIE), which has been fiercely criticizing *Peruskoulu* since the early 1980's, organized an autumn seminar at one of Helsinki's main conference venues, Finlandia Hall. Key players in business and industry once again criticized Finnish comprehensive schools for their mediocrity and ineffectiveness, with reference to international evaluations of their quality and efficiency. This time they argued in particular for more competition and better conditions for private schools. Following the first PISA report the CIE became completely mute about *Peruskoulu* and all traces from the seminar quickly vanished.
>
> (Simola, 2015, p. xiv)

There is another, international, source for irony in Finland's success that contrasts it with other nations: international PISA was the first national systematic test in the history in Finland. The Finnish basic education system lacks altogether externally mandated tests and exams that is a Finnish rarity in basic education on the global scene: no inspecting, no testing and no ranking. All tests are teacher driven. There is a silent and consensual antipathy among teachers, their unions, and the education administration to issues, which particularly in English-speaking countries, are "implemented" as "quality assurance and evaluation" (QAE) measures. A telling episode took place when Professor Diane Ravitch—who during the President George W. Bush administration advocated *standardization, accountability*, and *privatization* as drivers of the U.S. basic education policy—spoke at the publication event of Pasi Sahlberg's book *Lessons From Finland* in December 2011. She asked during her lecture what is the state of teacher accountability in Finnish education, and the audience instinctively replied as one choir:

we do not have that term in education; accountability belongs to book-keeping and business, not to education; the topics in Finland are about teachers' responsibility, their care for children and trust in teachers.

> Finnish hostility towards ranking, combined with bureaucratic tradition and a developmental approach to QAE strengthened by radical municipal autonomy have resulted in the construction of nationally and locally embedded policies that have been rather effective in resisting a trans-national policy of testing and ranking. It is significant, however, that those policies represent a combination of conscious, unintended and contingent factors.
>
> (Simola, 2015, p. xv)

Acknowledging complexity, chaos, and contingency as natural elements in Finnish basic education policies—in contrast with the self-sufficient and arrogant grasp of the Anglophone mainstream instrumental rationality and system closure—is greatly benefiting from the spirit, theoretical, and moral sensitivities exemplified in Bill Doll's scholarship. Still one more ironic trait in the present Finnish education success is that it can be claimed to be based on a kind of unarticulated but powerful educational tradition rather than on well-argued education theories or philosophies and their practical and political adoption and translation. In this sense, I think, Bill's historically long and theoretically insightful analyses unravel the often-unarticulated or implicit legacies not only in Finland. Particularly, in the U.S. tradition of presentist, ahistorical context and against the recent, astonishing narrowly defined U.S. education reforms (NCLB; TRTT), insufficiently informed "reforms" seem misguided; a fresh air and genuinely democratic spirit may be needed, assisted by radical theoretical reorientation where the education of children and work of teachers—seen from the Finnish perspective—would be qualitatively different from the dispirited and antidemocratic education *monologue* indeed: from the treadmill of learning, testing, and learning outcomes. In academic terms, Bill Doll's intellectual capacity to see things of teaching in larger perspective seems indispensable in the U.S. context too, where the reach of historical consciousness and "the domain of curriculum history" hardly cover more than "the development of the twentieth century public school curriculum" (Franklin, 2009, p. 297).

A Short History of a "De-complexification" in Education

I see Bill's lifetime long scholarship as an intellectual struggle for the education worthy of its name against the modes of instrumental rationality which the founders of the Frankfurt School, Theodor Adorno and Max Horkheimer, defined in the 20th century as "half-education," or *Halbbildung* (Horkheimer and Adorno, 1947/1969). *Halbbildung* is yet the core of present transnational education policy where instrumental excesses have reached the point of what Sahlberg (2011), while juxtaposing the Finnish basic school policy with the transnational policy model lead by the Anglophone example, coined the education acronym GERM (Global Education Reform Model): "a virus that is killing education."

An essential preceding trajectory in that unintellectual GERM simplification, anti-Dollian "de-complexification" indeed, is rendered by the long European-American historical and theoretical developments Bill Doll insightfully weaves when he threads his intellectual needle from Petrus Ramus (1515–1572) via René Descartes (1596–1650) to Ralph Tyler (1902–1994). Common to all of those historical figures are efforts to tame the quite normal chaos and complexity of life and consciousness by disciplining reality with pre-set, decontextualized, assumedly universal methods.

"Ramus's new methodology—a taxonomic, hierarchical ordering from the general to the particular in a linear, 'unbroken progression'—was denounced by his colleagues as a vulgar 'shortcut,' which diluted the ancient and noble profession of dialogue" (Doll, 2002, p. 31). The "dilution of dialogue" as a kernel of curriculum and teaching gained decisive momentum in the next century by the most influential contributions of René Descartes. Ignoring Descartes, I think, the intellectual-historical reception of the modern and post-modern worlds with their patterns of education and curriculum may remain incomplete. I have dealt more broadly with Descartes's contribution on the shape modern education took (Autio, 2012), but here I will briefly focus only on some remarks on Descartes that are closely related to Doll's critique of Descartes's impact on modern education still effective in today's policies and practices.

In my view, the fateful and far-reaching shift in education from dialogue to monologue was structurally instigated as an unintended but inevitable by-product of René Descartes's groundbreaking intellectual achievements, particularly in his *Principia Philosophiae* and *Discourse on Method*, where he presented his revolutionary theory of knowledge and vistas for New Sciences dissociated from the religious as well as old Greek authorities (Descartes, 1985). Descartes is more often than not misperceived in philosophy textbooks and classified under the rubric of *Rationalism*, yet, arguably, to view him as one of the most influential curriculum theorists would do more justice to him and dynamize his epistemological views beyond conceptions of standard philosophy. (In my view, curriculum theory is dynamizing all philosophy; philosophy of education is arguably stagnated and seems to be unable to reach the social, political, moral, and psychological dynamics of curriculum theory.)

For a devoted Catholic, the creation of his theory of knowledge—which Descartes felt urgent and indispensable amidst the political and theological chaos in Europe plagued by the Thirty Years' War—was a huge and formidable leap from faith to secular reason. Descartes implicitly revived the dissident insight created by some disciples already within the Ancient Church when the eschatological belief in salvation as a real historical possibility of fulfillment ceased in the early decades of the first millennium: the expected *Parousia*, the prophesied return of Christ to Earth, obviously, will not occur in human history. Hope turned to fear and the future became a focus of anxiety rather than redemption. The only hope available to humanity to walk with confidence in this life was to invest not in Divine revelations but human thought; *faith came to be substituted by human knowledge*, Gnosis (see Autio, 2012, pp. 126–135).

Thus, the seeds for secularization seem to have been sown early on within Christianity itself, not caused by the advent of modernity and secular science sixteen hundred years later. Descartes's intellectual honesty forced him to articulate his subliminal insight amidst the real threat of losing his life at the hands of Catholic and Protestant zealots alike. The modern age can be claimed as an outcome of the struggle within Christianity as particularly evidenced by Descartes's personal and intellectual biography.

In the re-emergence of Gnosticism, in the advent of the modern age and particularly through Descartes's brave and insightful mind, eschatological despair transformed into a new interest in *the qualitative condition of the world*. Up to the point of Descartes's time, the world turned out to be more persistent than expected, "attracted once again the old questions regarding its origin and dependability and demanded a decision between trust and mistrust, *an arrangement of life with the world rather than against it*" (Blumenberg, in Autio, 2012, p. 132).

Descartes synthesized Francis Bacon's (1561–1626) and Galileo Galilei's (1564–1642) ideas of *Nuova Scienzia* that advocated, respectively, the then revolutionary ideas of *inductive reasoning* and *experimental method* as a reconfiguration to combining the study of nature and providing the pragmatic Baconian "helps, beneficial to man." Descartes, "the great formulator of the new worldview" (Randall, in Autio, 2012, p. 27), through his secularized and dynamic concept of knowledge and its methodology, envisioned huge vistas for the well-being of humanity.

> His interests were not confined solely to the methodological advancement of science but were spiced by a specific political and educational flavour; one might see in them the seeds of rising Western democracy and a good measure of the educational optimism with a concern for educational equality later reflected in the French Revolution and in the education theories and systems from the Enlightenment to this day.
> (Autio, 2012, p. 27)

In Descartes's eyes, mathematics with its "clear and distinct ideas" provided the perfect answer for a long and arduous search for trust and certainty in human life. The enthusiasm Descartes attached to mathematics expanded in his mind to the fantasy of *a universal method of discovery and learning, mathesis universalis*.

> This discipline should contain the primary rudiments of human reason and extend to the discovery of truths in any field whatever. Frankly speaking, I am convinced that it is a more powerful instrument of knowledge than any other with which human beings are endowed, as it is the source of all the rest.
> (Descartes: *Discourse on the Method*, Rule Four, quoted in Autio, 2012, p. 29)

The Urgency to Save Complexity Again in Education and Curriculum

Descartes predicted the success of his Method based on the ideology of mathematical exactitude and "efficient causes" to be manifested in three major areas: *mechanics, medicine*, and *morals* (Autio, 2012, p. 51). In retrospect, we can just appreciate and admire the historical precision of his estimate of future development—with one fatal and consequential exception. The idea of progress inherently in the Cartesian triad tacitly presupposes that the *improvement of morality is dependent on the progress of scientific knowledge*. Jean Jacques Rousseau (1712–1778) was the first who strongly challenged the validity of this claim; on the contrary, Rousseau asserts in his *Emile* in 1762, moral decay and corruption rather than moral improvement has accompanied scientific progress.

Rousseau broke with his critique the unity of Descartes's vision of all-encompassing rationality and by his observation of moral decay he genuinely politicized the concept of education not any more in accordance with or reducible to scientific knowledge only. Doll reinstates Rousseau's main point with his perception of education based on post-modern conceptions of science that it is more complex, re-enchanted and qualitatively different from, not reducible to, and not explainable by scientism à la Descartes and Newton:

> The centerpiece of this vision, cause-effect determinism measured mathematically, depended on a closed, nontransformative, linearly developed universe. Stability was assumed, nature was in all ways consonant and simple, and the disciplines were organized in a reductionist hierarchy from mathematics and physics through sociology and psychology. . . . Despite its miraculous accomplishments in fields like medicine and microbiology, [modern thought] has been quite ineffective in dealing with growth, development, and personal [. . .] interactions. . . . *In short, modern thought has not provided a good model for the education of human beings.*
> (Doll, 1993, p. 26, my italics)

Modern thought which Bill refers to is to be encapsulated within the series of thinkers from Petrus Ramus to René Descartes via Isaac Newton to Ralph Tyler. Despite Tyler's iconic position in modern educational thinking, he is not the only education advocate of a "closed system" (Doll), the self-sustaining, self-enclosing curriculum model that the Rationale elegantly represents. Johann Friedrich Herbart (1776–1841) himself, one of the pivotal figures in Western education, was ambivalent with his two models of education study—hermeneutic or mechanistic ones. At last he ended up with an intellectual ambition to develop a universal model of a "mechanics of mind and to go down in history as the Newton of psychology" (Benner, quoted in Autio, 2012, p. 107).

Epilogue

The long history of modern thought with its mechanistic overtones still exists with us as the hyphen in Bill Doll's "post-modernism" implies, as an erudite marker of his sense of intellectual history. At the same time when international curriculum theorizing has been powerfully challenging obsolete Cartesian-Newtonian concepts in North and South America, South Africa, Asia, Australia, and Europe, the "closed," dispirited, mechanistic educational thinking is equally strongly present in education policies and reforms. Even the North European *Bildung* tradition, which has over hundreds of years opposed the Anglophone mainstream instrumentality in terms of behaviourist-cognitive learning discourses, is falling apart—Finland this far as a lone exception (Autio, 2017; Sahlberg, 2011; Simola, 2015). Sweden and Germany, former models for Finland, have adopted the Anglophone *standardization, accountability*, and *privatization* as the guiding beacons for their education policies with detrimental effects on the appeal of the teaching profession.

Ghosts of Control (Doll, 2002) have taken different shapes in the intellectual history of education and they seem astonishingly resilient despite their deeply unconvincing intellectual and moral appeal and the opposition of teachers. Today's ghosts in education policies are intellectually indebted to Anglo-American educational psychology and learning theories that draw on Herbart's fantasies of a "mechanics of mind" in the late 19th century and developed later in the 20th century to behaviorist and cognitivist learning theories. As a result, education in all its political, social, and psychological complexity is reduced to instrumental, context-free "learning" and since the Coleman Report (Coleman et al.,1966), where education (e)quality was reinterpreted, context-free again, in terms of test scores, learning theories have been replaced in practice by "learning outcomes."

Neoliberalism—"economic thought is coterminous with rationality" (Couldry, 2013)—redefines the basic curriculum question: *What Knowledge Is of Most Worth?* to *What Skills and Competencies Are of Most Worth?* General education from kindergarten to university is atrophied and "vocationalized" as conveniently measurable skills and competencies. The primitive simplification of education is an outcome of education policies purposefully informed by obsolete methodologies of learning theories in tandem with political intentions of neoliberalism. The existential original *Quest for Certainty* (Dewey, 1930) has been vulgarized into standardization, accountability, and control, the political consequence of which we may be witnessing in the decay of democracy. Pinar (2011) emphasizes the historical succession of the U.S. mainstream educational policy logic by a comment that critically underlines the current political connection between behaviorist-cognitive psychology and neoliberal education policy:

> Since *No Child Left Behind*, "behavior" itself has been reduced to test-taking. It is in this sense that I have asserted that accountability in the United States is a form of neo-fascism.
>
> (p. 185)

The increasing evidence of the social and political failure of economic globalization, neoliberalism, implies political consequences, one of the most obvious being what the German columnist Jochen Bittner (2016) for *The New York Times* terms *Orderism*:

> it is ideological without being an ideology. It is mercurial, pragmatic and cynical; its meaning and values change to fit the circumstances. . . . Orderism prioritizes stability over democracy and offers an alternative to the moral abyss of laissez-faire societies. Russia stands as a model for this new social contract. . . . What is striking, though, is how compatible orderism is with the attitudes of many voters in the United States and Europe. Donald J. Trump's campaign boils down to a promise of tough order. And the decision of British voters to leave the European Union, catalyzed by the promise of the U.K. Independence Party and others of an orderly, independent England, was nothing but an attempt to stop the frightening and discomfiting effects of globalization.

The long-standing Cartesian *Culture of Method* (Doll, 2002; Autio, 2012), with its positivist belief system and isolated variables insufficiently informed by big pictures—often technically sophisticated, but based upon an ideologically and psychologically naïve belief in mechanistic, "evidence-based" accounts of systems and behaviors—make education easy prey for neoliberalism. Neoliberalism has drastically intensified the historical detrimental grip of instrumentalism—encouraging a disenchanting and alienating education policy variant of the political *Orderism* in the teaching profession in most countries. The theoretically flawed background assumption is to imagine the relation between teaching and learning as a cause-effect one that is supposed to legitimize the focus on "products" and "outcomes" of learning as an index of "effective" teaching. For me, Bill Doll's scholarly oeuvre is convincingly demonstrating there are alternatives for that global, anti-intellectual and antidemocratic waste of human talent, imagination and creativity in the name of education.

References

Autio, T. (2012). *Subjectivity, curriculum and society: Between and beyond the German didaktik and Anglo-American curriculum studies*. New York, NY: Routledge.

Autio, T. (2017). Reactivating templates for international curriculum consciousness: Reconsidering intellectual legacies and policy practices between Chinese, Anglo-American and European curriculum studies. In J. Chi-Kin Lee & K. Kennedy (Eds.), *Theorizing teaching and learning in Asia and Europe*. New York, NY: Routledge.

Bittner, J. (2016). *The new ideology of the new cold war*. Retrieved from www.nytimes.com/2016/08/02/opinion/the-new-ideology-of-the-new-cold-war.html?_r=0

Coleman, J. S., Campbell, E. Q., Hobson, C. J., McPartland, J., Mood, A. M., Weinfeld, F. D., & York, R. L. (1966). *Equality of educational opportunity*. Retrieved from http://files.eric.ed.gov/fulltext/ED012275.pdf

Couldry, N. (2013). *Why voice matters: Culture and politics after neoliberalism*. London: Sage.

Descartes, R. (1985). *The philosophical writings of Descartes* (Vol. I, J. Cottingham, R. Stoothoff, & D. Murdoch, Trans.). Cambridge, UK: Cambridge University Press.

Dewey, J. (1930). *The quest for certainty: A study of the relation of knowledge and action*. London: George Allen & Unwin.

Doll, W. (1993). *A post-modern perspective on curriculum*. New York, NY: Teachers College Press.

Doll, W. (2002). Ghosts and the curriculum. In W. Doll & N. Gough (Eds.), *Curriculum visions* (pp. 23–70). New York, NY: Peter Lang.

Franklin, B. (2009). Epilogue: Some musings on what's new in the *new curriculum history*. In B. Baker (Ed.), *New curriculum history*. Rotterdam, Netherlands: Sense Publishers.

Horkheimer, M., & Adorno, T. W. (1969). *Dialectic of enlightenment*. New York, NY: Continuum (Original work published in 1947)

Pinar, W. (2011). *The character of curriculum studies: Bildung, currere, and the recurring question of the subject*. New York, NY: Palgrave Macmillan.

Rousseau, J. (1979). *Emile or on education*. New York, NY: Basic Books. (Original work published in 1762)

Saari, A., Salmela, S., & Vilkkila, J. (2014). Governing autonomy: Subjectivity, freedom, and knowledge in Finnish curriculum discourse. In W. F. Pinar (Ed.), *The international handbook of curriculum research* (2nd ed.). New York, NY: Routledge.

Sahlberg, P. (1996). *Who would help a teacher? Post-modern perspective on change in teaching.* University of Jyvaskyla, Institute for Educational Research. Publication Series A. Research Reports 119. 263 + 14 pages.

Sahlberg, P. (2011). *Finnish lessons: What can the world learn from educational change in Finland?* New York, NY: Teachers College Press.

Simola, H. (2015). *The Finnish education mystery: Historical and sociological essays on schooling in Finland.* New York, NY: Routledge.

5 Thoroughly (Post-Modern) Billy[1]

Peter Appelbaum

Seismic epistemic shifts are only recognized retrospectively. Yet some prophets sense it coming. As they speak, they are received as portending chaos and confusion. Only later are they labeled prophets. During the one step forward, two steps backward, one leap forward, twisting moments of cultural transition, the world feels like it is going to rack and ruin. And then people propose things that simply don't make sense—at first. Then, the fashions are outrageous, only to become coopted. We label the newfangled ideas as nothing new, and perhaps do not even recognize what is or was profoundly powerful in their newness. In this essay I claim that sincere genius lies in making the new accessible while maintaining the potential for significant transition.

Just imagine, for example, if we did *not* create a curriculum by starting with objectives and working backwards to find how to meet them. Suppose as well that we did *not* design our curriculum following step-by-step instructions designed to mold learners into producers of expected outcomes, and that we did *not* evaluate our curriculum based on how efficiently those learners moved through planned tasks toward a predetermined set of criteria for matching how accurately these learners' products matched our intended outcomes.

The 1967 film, *Thoroughly Modern Millie*, set a thoroughly "modern" objective claimed to be symptomatic of the 1920s Americana, marrying for money and not love, in the context of a cultural shift evident in the new era of post-industrialization. This newfangled, modern attempt to seize control of one's life goes comically awry as wealth, power, money, and gender roles are multiply mixed up in a carnivalesque, anything-goes sort of way. In the end, the "modern" is perhaps understood as nothing new; and yet, at the same time, new gender roles and new forms of courtship and identity are inscribed as acceptable and proper even as they are dramatically new. Similarly, Bill Doll set a thoroughly post-modern set of

---

1. With apologies to Jimmy Van Heusen and Sammy Cahn, who composed the original title tune for the 1967 film, *Thoroughly Modern Millie* (Hill, 1967). Copyright issues require the reader to find lyrics to the original song external to this volume.

concepts and processes in a context of a newly changing cultural context of the 1980s and 1990s. His notions of curriculum might be taken as surprisingly unoriginal if read through a modernist lens; yet as I illustrate in this essay, his ideas and processes are only misunderstood this way, and are instead processes that lead the modernist into new ways of thinking and acting that are no longer modern, yet feel like nothing new.

Teacher-Student #1: What we think is chic
Teacher-Student #2: Unique
Teacher-Students #3 and #4: And quite adorable

... but could there ever be anything else that we would do? Are we not abdicating our moral responsibilities if we do not proceed according to truth and wisdom?

Some alternatives have been used over the past centuries as the starting points of curriculum:

- Canonical experiences (Bruner, 1960; Eisner, 1982)
- Learner questions (Block, 1999)
- Arbitrary changes of geographical location (Ellsworth, 2005; Tarc, 2013)
- And more recently, any "thing" or concept that has not yet been attempted (Morris, 1996; Jardine, Clifford, & Friesen, 2002; Appelbaum, 2007).

BILLY: **But the fact is, everything today is—*was* thoroughly modern**
ENSEMBLE: **Check your rationality**

Bosley Crowther (1967) of the New York Times *called the 1967 film,* Thoroughly Modern Millie, *"thoroughly delightful," "a kidding satire, in a rollicking song-and-dance vein," "a joyously syncopated frolic," and "a romantic-melodramatic fable that makes clichés sparkle like jewels." He concluded, however, that "the whole thing's too long. If they'll just cut out some of those needless things, all the faults will be corrected and it'll be a joy all the way."* TV Guide *rated the film three out of four stars and commented, "Although it ultimately runs out of steam, this charming spoof of the 1920s is still one of the 1960s' better musicals. . . . Andrews is a comic delight, Moore is charming, and Channing steals scene after scene in this enjoyable feature."*

The film was one of four nostalgic movies directed by George Roy Hill; he subsequently made Butch Cassidy and the Sundance Kid, The Great Waldo Pepper, *and the Oscar-winning hit,* The Sting.

The film begins in 1922 New York, with flapper Millie Dillmount (Julie Andrews) determined to find work as a stenographer to a wealthy businessman and then marry him—a "thoroughly modern" goal. Millie befriends the sweet yet naive Miss Dorothy Brown (Mary Tyler Moore) as the latter checks into the Priscilla Hotel. When house mother Mrs. Meers (Beatrice Lillie) learns Miss Dorothy is an orphan, she remarks, "Sad to be all alone in the world." Millie has no inkling this woman is selling her tenants into white slavery; those without family or close friends are her primary targets.

Millie meets a devil-may-care paper clip salesman, Jimmy Smith (James Fox), to whom she takes an instant liking; nevertheless, she carries on with her plan to work for and then marry a rich man; and when she gets a job at Sincere Trust, she sets her sights on the attractive but self-absorbed Trevor Graydon (John Gavin). Jimmy later takes her and Miss Dorothy on an outing to Long Island, where he tells them that his father was the former gardener. Millie begins to fall for Jimmy, but sees him summon Miss Dorothy from her room for a late-night rendezvous, and assumes the worst. She is determined to stick to her plan and marry Trevor. One morning, she goes to work dressed as a flapper and attempts to seduce him, but her effort fails. Eventually, Trevor sees Miss Dorothy and falls in love with her and vice versa, leaving Millie heartbroken.

BILLY: **Everything today makes yesterday slow**
ENSEMBLE: **Testing is reality**
BILLY: **It's not insanity? —It's "Wall Street Air" In fact, it's stylish, not engaging, to . . .**
BILLY AND ENSEMBLE TEACHER-STUDENTS: **Raise your scores and lose your art!**

Bringing a fresh and inspired interest in post-structural, post-modern philosophy to Bill Doll's work in the 1980s, it was tempting to dismiss the suggestion of four new R's as a reproduction of modernist discourse rather than the construction of a post-modern transformation. What my naïve initial reading missed, however, was how Bill's (1993) *Postmodern Perspective on Curriculum* carefully attended to the slow and confusing transformation underway in culture, social institutions, and knowledge/curriculum. Instead of whining arguments for a post-modern curriculum, Bill handed me a post-modern *perspective* on curriculum. Some interesting experiments followed. I designed university courses, professional development workshops, and committee meeting agendas using richness, recursion, relations, and rigor as my guiding mantra (Doll, 1993). Because these courses, seminars, workshops, and committee meetings were not experienced as well-structured, objectives-based, efficient models of "schooling" according to modernist criteria of judgment, they tended to be highly praised for engagement and personal reflection, but somehow existing outside of expectations for what they were supposed to "accomplish."

Jimmy's attempts to talk to Millie, continually thwarted by no-nonsense, head stenographer Miss Flannery, lead him to eventually climb up the side of the building; when he finally gets to talk to Millie, she tells him she is quitting her job since Mr. Graydon is no longer available. Comedic mayhem and complications ensue, making heavy use of miscues, complex deceptions, and elaborate masquerade. Wondrous though it may be, Millie finally discovers Jimmy and Miss Dorothy are millionaire siblings sent out into the world to find partners who would love them for who they were and not for their money. Millie marries Jimmy, and Miss Dorothy marries Trevor. Nice closure for a nice, modernist tale, linking modern Millie with modernist narrative.

BILLY: **Complexity, not sleeping minds . . .**
ENSEMBLE TEACHER-STUDENTS: **But that would be heretical!**
BILLY AND ENSEMBLE: **Relations replace the factual . . . Generative, not presentable**

A transformative discourse suitable to a transformative cultural moment is like a Deleuzian nomadic epistemology: existing in more than one world. The four R's are possible to misinterpret as new objectives. We start with these objectives and use the assigned topics and concept goals to meet them. It can work as a pitiable approximation of some sort of alternative. Indeed, my own experiments in this way really did make us—the ostensible teacher and students—interact and explore in ways that were characteristically *different*. At the same time, however, these concepts also exist in a transformative, process-based world of flux and becoming, a post-modern plasma of complexity and uncertainty. For example, university students planning and assessing project-based learning with groups of eight to ten elementary children countered the norms of a curriculum "selling the children into modern forms of slavery" with an exuberant simultaneous accomplishment of modernist outcomes and humanistic empowerment.

In the same way that the film uses a recreation of 1920s struggles with changing technologies, mores, gender roles, and associated power relationships to parody the same struggles continuing into the late 1960s, Bill Doll used the discourse of objectives to analogously parody the struggles with changing technologies, mores, gender roles, and associated power relationships in the 1980s and '90s. This parallel struggle decade upon decade was driven home to me as I was given the opportunity to chair the program for the American Educational Research Association (AERA) special interest group on Critical Issues in Curriculum and Cultural Studies. The online submission system and review process demanded categories of scoring that would lead to a summary result supposedly useful for determining proposals included in the program. What I needed was a set of criteria for judgment that existed in the system that assumed empirical, quantifiable criteria, yet would also be possible to co-exist in a postmodern parody of that very same system. I used Bill's four R's:

AERA Review Criteria, Critical Issues in Curriculum & Cultural Studies, Peter Appelbaum, Chair 2007–10

- *Choice of Topic/Issue*—Is the proposed presentation situated well within curriculum studies and/or cultural studies? Does it promise to add to the ongoing conversations in our field, as opposed to regurgitating previously published or presented ideas, results, conceptions, challenges, etc.?
- *Relation*—Does this presentation demonstrate a good awareness of other, related work in the areas of curriculum studies and/or cultural studies, so that we can understand the links and disruptions pursued by the proposer(s)?
- *Rigor*—Does the proposal help you believe that the scholarship presented in this proposal remains honest to its commitments, both as a source of meaning and as a tool of pushing beyond the envelope?
- *Recursion*—How well does the proposed presentation promote the kinds of dialog and reflection that causes thoughts to leap back upon themselves, to explore into oneself as a meaning-maker while also challenging the presumptions such concepts persist in reconstructing?
- *Richness*—How well does this proposal promise a conference discussion that has depth in the sense of layers of meaning, multiple possibilities or interpretations? Does the work promote and question indeterminacy, anomaly, inefficiency, disequilibrium, dissipation, lived experience, etc.?
- *Provocation*—How well does this scholarship provoke new thinking, re-thinking, alternative practice (research/teaching/scholarship/art), questions, declarations, and, especially . . . ACTION???
- *Membership Appeal*—How well does this work push the envelope of curriculum studies and/or cultural studies? Our SIG has traditionally provided a platform for presentations that would not be accepted by the usually Divisions. Does this proposal need an audience not found elsewhere on the AERA program?
- *Would you attend this session?*—Surely you should support our SIG, right?

Significant here is the way the review process was transformed. Previously, reviewers would check off numbers and write one or two sentences about why they did or did not think the proposal would lead to a worthwhile presentation, criticizing more than critiquing. In response to the four R's, reviewers composed letters of love and appreciation, entering into complex conversations about the potential of the research described to engage its audience, transform the field, and open up new lines of inquiry!

What I noticed is the ways that the four R's began their lives as modernist categories and were themselves transformed through the process of using them in modernist ways into post-modern processes of transformation. Similar four R's applications have begun as professional development for teachers, becoming new collaborations among urban and suburban schools on the creation of new community gardens; began as the introduction of writing in mathematics and becoming a new sex education program led by youth in the school; initiated as a grant funding search to support a new science lab and turning into a teacher study group on responses to community violence; and more.

BILLY: **No more goody-good curriculum, The sacred in complexity**

The four R's, and Bill's later cousins—the three S's, science, spirit, and story (Doll, 1998), and the five C's, *currere*, complexity, cosmology, conversation, and community (Doll, 2002)—work in dialogic ways for pretty much anybody who attempts to use them. My graduate students in introductory curriculum studies courses begin semester-long community projects with Tyler-esque objectives stemming from content, learners, and community; as they run into the same quandaries that most curricula have since the advent of the modern, rational, recipe approach became synonymous with curriculum design, they turn to Bill's R's, and later Bill's C's and S's for solace and comfort. These R's, C's, and S's start out as simplistic objectives, observable, measurable, and quantifiable for many of these novices. Rapidly, however, our discussions shift into self-reflection on the transformation that is occurring in our very conceptions of what a curriculum could mean, what it might not mean, what a program design can and cannot entail, the value of an indefinable encounter, and more. The nomadic epistemological frames of these terms, living in both modern and post-modern landscapes, are transformative and especially generative.

Bill called for a curriculum that would *dance!* (Doll, 1993, p. 103): the teacher's role is transformative rather than causal; metaphors might be more useful than logic in generating community dialogue; planning and evaluation focus on processes and patterns, not standardized products. A dancing curriculum's patterns and improvisations facilitate relations, recursions, rigor, and richness of experience. These words sound modern to a modernist; they are also post-modern as steps generating relations and conversations among curriculum workers themselves, functioning as perturbations, provocations of disequilibrium, self-organization, chaotic order, and lived experiences. As I did in my course planning, workshops and meetings, program chairing, and support of new curriculum projects by emerging teachers, administrators, and district officers, post-modern curriculum transformers soon recognize emerging patterns of recursion, relation, richness, and rigor. Together, we name them things like science, spirit, and story, . . . *currere*, complexity, cosmology, conversation, and community. The coalescing patterns themselves take form, dissipate, and reorganize.

ENSEMBLE: So gather 'round, 'cause here comes Complexity-modern Billy now What we think is dissipative, affordable . . . They find most deplorable! But the fact is Everything today is thoroughly modern
ENSEMBLE: Richness, Rigor, Recursion, Relations
ENSEMBLE: Everything today is starting to go
ENSEMBLE: Alter-global, no more nations
ENSEMBLE: Professors say it's criminal what Neoliberals'll do What they're forgetting is
BILLY: This is—*was* 2018!

****

(Musical Interlude, Dance Routine)

Bill's point with *A Post-modern Perspective* was that we need to match the transformative nature of culture, society, and shifting regimes of truth better than the modernist reliance on linearity and predictability tied to a mechanics of curriculum. As the world of knowing and being shifts away from Newtonianism toward a world more appropriately modeled by complexity theories, open systems, interaction, transaction, and organic change, Bill found inspiration in Prigogine (e.g., 1980, 1988), Piaget, Whitehead, and the emerging complexity sciences. My own orientation grew out of anthropology (Geertz, 1973; Sahlins, 1985) and its concerns for the coevolution of technology and culture, history and social transformation; social theory (Therborn, 1980) and its concerns for the interactions between ideology and power, agency and social structure; and popular culture studies with its opening of questions about the dualities of commodity and cultural resource, and social change and social reproduction (Fiske, 1990). Cornel West (1994) was playing with the nomadic concepts of self-esteem and matter to lead social change via discursive ambiguity. Arts-based approaches to educational research interrogated patterns of evidence, argument, method, clarification, and emotion in increasingly institutional ways (with the formation of a special interest group at AERA, new journals and conferences, and new formats sneaking into the more resistant threads of research and practice at stodgy conferences and journals). Kieran Egan (1989, 1992) established alternative curricular approaches via imagination and storytelling. I pursued this in/by interchanging curriculum, content, skills, and objectives with popular culture, cultural resources, problem-posing and relations of power, by demonstrating the efficacy of these concepts in what I perceived as the least obvious disciplinary regime for such efforts, mathematics, hoping to make the argument that it could be done at least as well in any area of the traditional school subject curriculum (Appelbaum, 1995).

By the time we entered the new millennium this practice of replacing critique with the construction of nomadic terms had become a powerful tool for reconceptual curriculum theory. A masterful example of this is Jardine et al.'s (2002) *Back to the Basics of Teaching and Learning*. William Doll himself wrote the foreword to this book, naming the characteristic of a powerful nomadic vocabulary: "This book is, by any standard, amazing. It plays, in a wonderfully hermeneutic manner, with common themes in an uncommon way." Learning, as Doll sifts out of this book, "comes from being immersed, fully in a situation, not from counting the number of correct answers on a test" (p. ix). The basics of a rich and powerful curriculum, as culled from countless hours of research and practice in classrooms, ordinarily assumed to be modular building blocks of a piecemeal instructional program, are transformed through rich storytelling and recursive reflection on these classrooms into "relation, ancestry, commitment, participation, interdependence, belonging, desire, conversation, memory, place, topography, tradition, inheritance, experience, identity, difference, renewal, generativity, intergenerationality, discipline, care, strengthening, attention, devotion, transformation, and character" (p. xi). Doll's foreword recognized this example of such "things" as "basic" to generating relation, rigor, recursion, and richness:

> to look at an issue like "the basics" differently, interpretively, affects not only how we might teach . . . but will also affect "how we live out" life itself and especially our relationship with our children. Such an effect brings with it a host of ethical issues about how we treat the planet with which we live, how we treat those who are other to us (ourselves the others, other), how we treat our children, and how we treat that which we call knowledge.
>
> (p. x)

We might summarize Jardine et al.'s longwinded list of basics with Doll's five C's: *currere*, complexity, cosmology, conversation, and community (Doll, 2002)—or, with my own contribution to this strategy of discursive and hence epistemology transformation: poaching, weirding, dark matter, the jazz, and criteria for ways of working (Appelbaum, 2007). In his 2002 "Ghosts and the Curriculum" introduction to *Curriculum Visions*, Bill suggested we are still in a transition period between paradigms, still entering that new world where systems of control formed from the webbed interactions of everyday life, and he invited us to use these four "multiple personalities of curriculum" (p. 54) to develop that new paradigm.

Bill gave us the *strategy*, not the mundane vocabulary.

Oh, Bill. You are so thoroughly modern! ☺ Might you be looking at things with the old technology? Are nomadic epistemological C's merely old-fashioned gadgets to help us find the right words? No. The key, as Bill so graciously urges us to live with, is the *process*, not the product—not the R's, the S's, the C's, not my poaching, weirding, jazzing, mattering, and criteria-ing; but the *transformative process* via any nomadic terms. Bill's "lesson" is to look at the ideological and cultural transformations with processes that themselves take on the character of transformation in a self-similar way (well described by complexity sciences). For, just as surely as nomadic epistemological terms have been at the heart of curriculum reconceptualization, so have nomadic terms such as "reform," "accountability," and "assessment" shifted policy and practice from democratic empowerment and the support of teaching and learning into a nightmare of corporatization, children as unpaid slave labor, and teachers as abused foremen. The processes of transformation are characteristic of every ideological practice and the policies that enact them. Indeed, any set of terms can be used in this transformative way, to live in and out of the dominant power/knowledge regime, to foster institutional transformation, within complex webs of self-similar transformations taking place in myriad ways and at unending levels of transformation and ideological reproduction.

BILLY: One's always becoming, and wow!
ALL: So gather 'round, 'cause here flew by Complexity-science, oh my—
Don't look now! Whoops! Never saw it coming! We're so thoroughly modern
BILLY: **Billy!**
ALL: **Does "Now" have meaning now?**

References

Appelbaum, P. (1995). *Popular culture, educational discourse, and mathematics*. Albany, NY: SUNY Press.
Appelbaum, P. (2007). *Children's books for grown-up teachers: Reading and writing curriculum theory*. New York, NY: Routledge.
Block, A. (1999). Curriculum from the back of the bookstore. *Encounter: Education for Meaning and Social Justice*, 12(4), 17–27.

Bruner, J. S. (1960). *The process of education*. Cambridge, MA: Harvard University Press.
Crowther, B. (1967, March 23). Screen: "Thoroughly Modern Millie": Pleasant spoof of 20's opens at Criterion. *The New York Times*. Retrieved August 7, 2017, from www.nytimes.com/movie/review?res=9e06e3de163ae63abc4b51dfb566838c679ede
Doll, W. E., Jr. (1993). *A post-modern perspective on curriculum*. New York, NY: Teachers College Press.
Doll, W. E., Jr. (1998). The spirit of education. *Early Childhood Education*, 31, 3–7.
Doll, W. E., Jr. (2002). Ghosts and the curriculum. In W. E. Doll & N. Gough (Eds.), *Curriculum visions* (pp. 23–70). New York, NY: Peter Lang.
Egan, K. (1989). *Teaching as storytelling: An alternative approach to teaching and curriculum in the elementary school*. Chicago, IL: University of Chicago Press.
Egan, K. (1992). *Imagination in teaching and learning: The middle school years*. Chicago, IL: University of Chicago Press.
Eisner, E. (1982). *Cognition and curriculum: A basis for deciding what to teach*. New York, NY: Longman.
Ellsworth, E. (2005). *Places of learning: Media, architecture, pedagogy*. New York, NY: Routledge.
Fiske, J. (1990). *Understanding popular culture*. New York, NY: Unwin Hyman.
Geertz, C. (1973). *The interpretation of cultures*. New York, NY: Basic Books.
Hill, G. R. (Director). (1967). *Thoroughly modern Millie*. [Motion Picture]. Hollywood, CA: Universal Pictures.
Jardine, D., Clifford, P., & Friesen, S. (2002). *Back to the basics of teaching and learning: Thinking the world together*. New York, NY: Routledge.
Morris, M. (1996). Toward a ludic pedagogy: An uncertain occasion. *JCT: The Journal of Curriculum Studies*, 12(1), 29–33.
Prigogine, I. (1980). *From being to becoming: Time and complexity in the physical sciences*. San Francisco, CA: W. H. Freeman and Company.
Prigogine, I. (1988). The rediscovery of time. In F. Kitchner (Ed.), *The world view of contemporary physics: Does it need a new metaphysics?* (pp. 125–143). Albany, NY: SUNY Press.
Sahlins, M. (1985). *Islands of history*. Chicago, IL: University of Chicago Press.
Tarc, P. (2013). *International education in global times*. New York, NY: Peter Lang.
Therborn, G. (1980). *The ideology of power and the power of ideology of power*. London: Verso Editions.
West, C. (1994). *Race matters*. Boston, MA: Beacon Press.

6 Travels With Bill in Search of America (and Beyond)

Noel Gough

Prologue (2016)

In July 2016, I revisited the National Steinbeck Center in Salinas, California, and acquired a 50th anniversary edition of his delightful non-fiction work, *Travels with Charley in Search of America*, to replace an earlier edition consumed by a house fire in 1987.

> A journey is a person in itself; no two are alike. And all plans, safeguards, policing, and coercion are fruitless. We find that after years of struggle that we do not take a trip; a trip takes us. . . . In this a journey is like marriage. The certain way to be wrong is to think you control it.
>
> (Steinbeck, 1962, pp. 1–2)

I first encountered Steinbeck's writing in 1961 as a senior high school student of American history. An enlightened teacher encouraged us to explore an episode of U.S. history by reading novels that interpreted it. I chose to explore what became known as the Great Depression (1929–1939), and began by reading Steinbeck's *In Dubious Battle* (1936), *The Grapes of Wrath* (1939), and *Of Mice and Men/Cannery Row* (1947), each of which expressed his passion for social justice and his compelling and intimate sense of the American people in their natural and human habitats. I found *Cannery Row* especially appealing (and have re-read it many times), and it also helped me to resolve a dilemma I then faced: my academic aspirations were towards the biological sciences, but I achieved academic success more easily in the humanities, especially English language and literature and history, and was receiving conflicting advice from my teachers about the subject specializations I should choose in my final year of high school (which had consequences for the university courses I could apply to enter). I am convinced that the character of "Doc" in *Cannery Row*, based on marine biologist Ed Ricketts—Steinbeck's close friend and occasional coauthor (Steinbeck & Ricketts, 1941)—helped me (albeit unconsciously at the time) to make up my mind. Somewhat later, I recognized that Steinbeck's dramatization of the interconnected lives of the marginalized inhabitants of *Cannery Row* is the fictional complement to Steinbeck and Ricketts's exploration of marine life in *Sea of Cortez*. As Richard Astro (1995, p. xxiii) writes:

> We see John Steinbeck fusing science and philosophy, art and ethics by combining the compelling if complex metaphysics of Ed Ricketts with his own commitment to social action by a species for whom he never gave up hope, and he believed could and would triumph over the tragic miracle of its own consciousness.

Subsequently I realized that "Doc" (and his encounters with *all* life within and beyond the Great Tide Pool of the Monterey Peninsula) personified the possibilities for counteracting C. P. Snow's (1959) contention that a split in the intellectual life of Western society between the sciences and humanities hindered resolution of the world's problems. Thus, I chose to undertake my first undergraduate degree in the biological sciences, majoring in zoology and botany, but my interests in the other branch of Snow's "two cultures" never waned. I eventually read almost everything Steinbeck wrote (and much else besides) and in due course completed another degree in arts, majoring in English literature and psychology, before undertaking graduate studies in education.

Re-reading *Travels with Charley* in 2015, I was reminded that 1987 was also the year that marked the beginning of my travels with Bill Doll, a journey that began in the academic landscape of American curriculum studies but took us in directions that neither of us anticipated. In the years before email and the internet made transnational collaborations commonplace, we did not foresee that an Australian and an American curriculum scholar—neither of whom had any previous knowledge of one another's work—would initiate and sustain a productive personal and professional working relationship that would grow and strengthen across three decades. In this essay—apropos of Steinbeck's assertion that a journey is "a person in itself"—I attempt to characterize the idiosyncratic "personality" of the journeys—academic and geographic—that Bill and I took together. Bearing in mind that "trip" is not only a synonym for "journey," I also recall that Bill refers to his own career trajectory as "the path stumbled upon" (Doll, 2009, p. 55), so my account will attempt to elucidate the serendipities that produced the conversations, friendships, and widening circles of association and affiliation through which our journeys materialized. And although we spent far too much time apart to think of our journey as being "like marriage," I am certain that we never thought we could control it.

In the Beginning (1987)

I attended my first AERA Annual Meeting in Washington DC in 1987. I had recently been appointed Australian Editor of the *Journal of*

Curriculum Studies (*JCS*), and Bill Reid (then *JCS* General Editor) and Ian Westbury (then *JCS* U.S. Editor) invited me to join them in a symposium on ways of studying the past, present, and future in curriculum inquiry. I recall that one of the first sessions I attended was a symposium chaired by Bill Schubert, which included a number of other presenters whose names I had encountered in my reading (e.g., Bill Pinar, Hugh Munby) and the (then) unknown to me William E. Doll, Jr.

This was my first visit to the U.S., and I had already experienced some mild episodes of "culture shock," including (1) seeing more handguns worn openly than I had previously seen outside of a television program; (2) realizing that if a sign said "ice cream $3.00," a mysterious (to us aliens) combination of state and federal taxes meant that I had to tender an amount greater than $3.00 to purchase it, which led to me rapidly accumulating an inconvenient pocketful of small coins; (3) deciphering the arts of "tipping" (which in my part of Australia refers primarily to forecasting the results of Australian Rules football matches; tipping as understood in the U.S. is much less common in Australia because hospitality workers are relatively well paid); and (4) trying (and failing) to understand why many Americans evidently tolerated—and enjoyed—insipidly weak coffee and beer.

It would be an exaggeration to say that my first experience of Bill Doll was any kind of culture shock, but he exemplified some marked differences between Australian and American cultural norms. For example, his self-identification as "William E. Doll, Jr." resembled names that I associated with an earlier (and more conservative) era—for example, William F. Buckley, Jr. To me, Bill reinforced this hint of conservatism with his distinctive manner of dress and wardrobe coordination, notably his preference for bow ties. Outside of formal wear, Australian men rarely wear bow ties, except for comic or theatrical effect. Bill reinforced my initial sense of conservatism with his distinctive manner of speech, a strong and forceful declamatory style that seemed to descend from a height greater than his own (which is not inconsiderable). If pressed, I would have described his manner as somewhat patrician (which I later learned is sometimes used to describe a Bostonian accent).

Although Bill's presentation style seemed a little strange to me (given the much less formal manner adopted by most Australian academics), what he actually said was unlike anything I had heard before. I don't recall the precise title or contents of his presentation, but I silently applauded every word. I later found much of its substance in an essay, "Prigogine: A New Sense of Order, A New Curriculum" (Doll, 1986), which he elaborated in "Foundations for a Post-modern Curriculum" (Doll, 1989) and in *A Postmodern Perspective on Curriculum* (Doll, 1993). Bill argued that, since the mid-17th century, the Newtonian paradigm governed not only science but also social science, including education, and formed the foundation of the "measured curriculum." As a biologist skeptical of psychology's claims to be "scientific," I had long shared Joseph Schwab's (1958, p. 169) view of "the corruption of education by psychology," and thus very amenable to Bill's suggestion that the dependence of American psychologists and educators on Newton's paradigm might explain their misinterpretation of Piaget's work on adaptive biological and cognitive structures, which have more in common with Prigogine's work on self-organizing chemical and biological structures.

In retrospect, I acknowledge that my attendance at Bill's 1987 AERA presentation was the moment at which I "stumbled" upon a path that he was already treading and that I would soon join. Bill was nearly halfway through his fifty-year career at the time our paths intersected—by comparison, I was a novice, and did not identify myself as a curriculum scholar until I commenced my doctorate in 1978—thus I was largely unaware of his substantial scholarship around Dewey, Piaget, Bruner, and Whitehead. But I was enthusiastic about, and encouraged by, his argument that Prigogine's work could bring a new scientific paradigm to educational issues, and ultimately provide the basis for an educational model that goes beyond and stands as an alternative to the measured curriculum. I had been attempting (with little success) to advance some "new paradigm" arguments of my own among my Australian peers in science and environmental education (Gough, 1987). Bill inspired me to persevere, and with his encouragement, my arguments found more appreciative audiences internationally (Gough, 1989).

Because this was my first AERA meeting, I did not understand many of its rituals and protocols, but I was fortunate that Ian Westbury (then vice president of Division B) guided me in matters such as for whom and for what purposes "receptions" were intended. Bill and I were unfashionably early for that year's Division B reception—we were the only people there for five to ten minutes—and so we began a complex conversation that continued for thirty years. Initially our conversation was sustained via what we now call "snail mail," but it rapidly introduced me to many new friends and colleagues, and to many new places. In what follows, I will recount just a few highlights.

Excursions Post-AERA (1989–1993)

Between 1987 and 1989 Bill and I maintained a paper-based correspondence, one result of which was a symposium at the 1989 AERA meeting in San Francisco, which involved Bill, me, Daiyo Sawada, and Francis Klein. After AERA, Bill generously used his air miles to enable my travel to New Orleans, from where we drove (courtesy of fellow *JCS* editorial board member Jean King, who was then chair of Education at Tulane University) to Baton Rouge, where Bill had arranged for me to speak to faculty and graduate students at Louisiana State University (LSU), after which Bill Pinar hosted a memorable party. This was the first of many such visits, and my first indication of just how special Bill was to his graduate students, and of the reasons that so many of them remained lifelong friends.

As a long-time aficionado of traditional jazz, I was delighted to have my first opportunity to visit New Orleans but, like Steinbeck decades earlier, some aspects of the America I found there disturbed me. In 1960, Steinbeck was horrified by the so-called Cheerleaders protesting the integration of black children in a New Orleans school:

> a group of stout middle-aged women who, by some curious definition of the word "mother," gathered every day to scream invectives at children ... a small group of them had become so expert that ... a crowd gathered every day to enjoy and to applaud their performance.
> (p. 180)

Steinbeck had looked forward to reacquainting himself with "the New Orleans of the great restaurants," but after listening to the Cheerleaders' words, "bestial and filthy and degenerate," he writes: "My body churned with weary nausea.... And I could no more have gone to Gallatoir's for an omelet and champagne than I could have danced on a grave" (pp. 188–189). The traces of racism that I encountered—my visit was shortly after David Duke (a former grand wizard of the Ku Klux Klan) was elected to the Louisiana House of Representatives—were less confronting than Steinbeck's, but my first visit to a U.S. school, Beauregard Junior High School, remains memorable for two illustrations of the thin line many Americans perceive between heroes and villains. First, the principal began her warm but obviously well-rehearsed welcoming ritual by drawing attention to a yearbook that lay open, in readiness for visitors to inspect, at a page that displayed a photograph of the young Lee Harvey Oswald. I got the distinct impression that the principal saw this not only as a matter of historical interest but also of something approaching pride—that here, so to speak, was proof that Beauregard JHS could produce graduates who were famous for more than Andy Warhol's fifteen minutes. My second memory of Beauregard JHS is that, while browsing in the school's library, I found a well-thumbed copy of a slim book titled *Vice Presidents of the USA*, which consisted of short biographies of each incumbent. The last entry was for Spiro Agnew and reported his early resignation from office without mentioning the criminal charges that precipitated it. Apart from this sanitizing of history, I was bemused that such a book existed at all. I cannot imagine a book titled *Deputy Prime Ministers of Australia* being written, published or acquired by a school library—let alone that it might be consulted by students. In retrospect, the more I learned about education in the U.S., the less these two events seemed to be particularly surprising or sinister—rather (as Hannah Arendt, 1963, might say) they are signs of the banality of evil.

One way or another, my encounters with Bill at AERA meetings led, more often than not, to further travels. For example, in 1990, at the AERA meeting in Boston, Bill invited me to join him at a dinner meeting at Harvard University, where he introduced me into a network of curriculum theorists and "process philosophers," a memorable result of which was meeting Kathleen R. Kesson. This initiated another enduring friendship (and future collaborations), and Kathleen's invitation for me to visit Oklahoma State University in Stillwater in 1991.

After another AERA meeting in San Francisco (1992), Bill and I (together with my partner, Annette Gough, and Molly Quinn, who was then one of Bill's doctoral students and research assistants), drove to a farmhouse in Mendocino, where we were joined by Bill Schubert and his family, to begin our initial planning of what would eventually become *Curriculum Visions* (Doll & Gough, 2002). En route to Mendocino we paused at Bodega Bay (an unexpected treat for us Alfred Hitchcock fans, because it was the location for many scenes in *The Birds*). We fortunately chanced on a time when there were few visitors, and the quiet fishing harbor and surrounding bleak treeless hills eerily evoked the movie's ominous silences. Our visit to Mendocino coincided with the 1992 Cape Mendocino earthquakes—a series of events that included an $M_w 7.2$ thrust mainshock at around midday on April 25, followed early the next morning by two sleep-disturbing aftershocks measuring M_w 6.5 and M_w 6.6 (these were perhaps an omen for the ups and downs that preceded the ten-year gestation of our book). Returning to San Francisco, Bill led us in taking time out to sample the local (Anderson Valley) wines—a pastime that would provide us with many more shared pleasures in various parts of the world.

Our third post-AERA excursion followed the meeting in Atlanta in 1993. Bill and I drove to New Orleans via Callaway Gardens—a two-day journey across Georgia, Alabama, and Mississippi that took us through parts of the deep rural South that I would never have visited as a tourist. I have memories of sparsely populated stretches of highway, bordered by scattered, often ramshackle dwellings (including many repurposed railroad cars) surrounded by pickup trucks in various stages of decomposition (although there was usually one new vehicle in the mix). I felt some apprehension as we approached Montgomery, Alabama, because I remembered that segregationist George Wallace was one of the longest-serving governors in post-Constitutional U.S. history, and that it was the destination of the 1965 Selma to Montgomery marches led by Martin Luther King, Jr.

Enter "the King of Chaos"

For the 1994 AERA meeting in New Orleans, Bill, Kathleen R. Kesson, and I proposed a two-hour interactive symposium and multimedia presentation on "Chaos and Curriculum Inquiry," but the organizers programmed us for a forty-minute roundtable with around ten seats. To our surprise we attracted a standing-room only crowd of at least forty people, which prompted Bob Kahn (then a PhD student), to suggest forming a new special interest group (SIG), Chaos and Complexity Theories, which rapidly flourished with Bill as program chair finding innovative ways to increase participation. I recently found some notes I prepared as chair/discussant for one of the SIG's sessions in 1998, in which I wrote: "between them Bill and Bob brought sufficient non-linearity, reflexivity, recursiveness, and irreversibility into play for this SIG to self-organize." Members of the SIG were actively involved in initiating a series of Complexity Science and Educational Research conferences and founding the journal *Complicity*. This indirectly led to travel beyond the U.S. for many of us, including a conference on Complexity, Chinese Culture, and Curriculum Reform, hosted by the Institute of Curriculum and Instruction, East China Normal University, Shanghai, in 2010. Bill's stature and leadership in these activities was readily apparent and justifies his designation as "the king of chaos," a title bestowed on him by students in the Holmes Elementary (and Middle School) Education program he directed at LSU, which also forms part of the title for Hongyu Wang's (2016) fine account of Bill's pedagogical life history.

Beyond AERA Meetings

In the (Northern Hemisphere) summers of 1989 and 1992, Antoinette Oberg invited me to teach courses in the Master's Program in Curriculum Studies at the University of Victoria (UVic), Canada. Antoinette used her networking skills to recruit selected curriculum scholars from around the world to teach in these summer sessions. In 1993, I taught a course that was audited by three of Bill's LSU graduate students, and I encouraged him to visit the class. Subsequently, Bill too became a regular (and popular) visiting professor in Antoinette's summer program.

Bill, Annette, and I taught in the 1995 UVic summer program, after which Annette and I spent three months as Royal Bank Fellows at Queen's University, Kingston, Ontario. In September I flew to New Orleans to join Bill and two of his doctoral students (Al Alcazar and Jeanne Robertson) for another long drive across Mississippi and Alabama from New Orleans to Monteagle, Tennessee, for that year's "Bergamo-that-wasn't-at-Bergamo" conference.

In a rare lapse of Bill's oenological radar, he found a winery near Monteagle, but the wines were undrinkable. Notwithstanding this dismal experience, the Monteagle conference provided other indelible memories, including a joyful outdoor gathering to witness Shirley Steinberg and the late Joe Kincheloe renew their wedding vows (they reminded us that they made their first vows in a parking lot) and an out-of-season Mardi Gras party featuring Bill Pinar as the Mardi Gras Queen.

And so we continued, despite the geographical distance that separated us most of the time, to find many opportunities to enjoy each other's company, collegiality, and shared experiences—such as the five summers between 1997 and 2003 in which we taught at UVic (and where we also tasted at first hand the rapid improvement in the quality of Vancouver Island's cool climate wines), and our collaboration on the nearly never-ending story of *Curriculum Visions*. Our shared commitment to the International Association for the Advancement of Curriculum Studies led us to productive conferences in China, Finland, and South Africa.

I am immensely grateful to Bill for directly and indirectly introducing Annette and me into an ever-widening circle of very dear US and Canadian friends and colleagues with whom we have enjoyed productive relationships and might not otherwise have become so closely acquainted.

Postscript: The Echo of Bill's Laughter

Donna Trueit's (2012, pp. xiii–xiv) preface to a recent collection of Bill's writing concludes with these words:

> Just as surely as I could never describe the echo of God's laughter (as you will note, one of Bill's favorite lines from Milan Kundera), I would never be able to describe the sound of Bill's laughter. He laughs often and loudly. He is eternally optimistic. It is the strongest recommendation I can think of for the academic work he does that he sees possibilities in any situation.

The lines Bill quotes from Kundera are in turn quoted from the frontispiece of Richard Rorty's (1989, p. xvi) *Contingency, Irony, and Solidarity*, but Kundera (1986, p. 74) precedes the words Rorty quotes with the following:

> There is a fine Jewish proverb: Man thinks, God laughs. Inspired by that adage, I like to imagine that François Rabelais heard God's laughter one day, and thus was born the idea of the first great European novel. It pleases me to think that the art of the novel came into the world as the echo of God's laughter. But why does God laugh at the sight of man thinking? Because man thinks and the truth escapes him. Because the more men think, the more one man's thought diverges from another's.

I am struck by the convergence of Kundera's thinking here with Astro's (1995, quoted above) interpretation of Steinbeck's "commitment to social action by a species for whom he never gave up hope, and he believed could and would triumph over the tragic miracle of its own consciousness." I recently stumbled upon some Chinese literary scholarship on Steinbeck and found Tao Jie's (2008, p. 126) summary of Wen Jiexia's argument that Steinbeck, in *Of Mice and Men*, carries on the tradition of Rabelais (*Gargantua*) and Cervantes (*Don Quixote*). The influence of Cervantes is obvious in *Travels with Charley*—Steinbeck paints the name Rocinante (Quixote's horse) in 16th-century Spanish script on the side of his customized three-quarter-ton pickup truck—but it pleases me to see him located within the tradition that Kundera sources to Rabelais. Elaborating on his admiration for Rabelais, Kundera (1986, p. 75) also writes:

> François Rabelais invented a number of neologisms that have since entered the French and other languages, but one of his words has been forgotten, and this is regrettable. It is the word *agelaste;* it comes from the Greek and it means a man who does not laugh, who has no sense of humor. Rabelais detested the *agelastes*.

Bill Doll is the antithesis of an *agelaste*. Bill's great gift to all who know him lies in his seemingly limitless capacity to find wonder and joy in almost every experience, no matter how trivial or insignificant it might seem to those of us who are more suspicious or cynical. I hear Bill's laughter whenever I listen to the medieval plainsong composed by Saint Hildegard von Bingen (1098–1179), a Benedictine abbess, writer, composer, philosopher, Christian mystic, visionary, and polymath considered by some to be a pioneer of scientific natural history in Germany. And as if that were not enough to remind me of Bill's faith, talents and dispositions, Hildegard described herself as "a feather on the breath of God," an image of Bill's humility, buoyancy, and lightness of being that I will long cherish.

References

Arendt, H. (1963). *Eichmann in Jerusalem: A report on the banality of evil.* New York, NY: Viking Press.

Astro, R. (1995). Introduction. In J. Steinbeck (Ed.), *The log from the Sea of Cortez* (pp. vii–xxiii). New York, NY: Penguin Books. (First published by Viking Press 1951)

Doll, W. (1986). Prigogine: A new sense of order, a new curriculum. *Theory Into Practice, 25*(1), 10–16.

Doll, W. (1989). Foundations for a post-modern curriculum. *Journal of Curriculum Studies, 21*(3), 243–253.

Doll, W. (1993). *A post-modern perspective on curriculum.* New York, NY: Teachers College Press.

Doll, W. (2009). The path stumbled upon. In E. C. Short & L. J. Waks (Eds.), *Leaders in curriculum studies: Intellectual self-portraits* (pp. 55–66). Rotterdam, Netherlands: Sense Publishers.

Doll, W., & Gough, N. (Eds.). (2002). *Curriculum visions.* New York, NY: Peter Lang.

Gough, N. (1987). Learning with environments: Towards an ecological paradigm for education. In I. Robottom (Ed.), *Environmental education: Practice and possibility* (pp. 49–67). Geelong: Deakin University.

Gough, N. (1989). From epistemology to ecopolitics: Renewing a paradigm for curriculum. *Journal of Curriculum Studies*, 21(3), 225–242.

Jie, T. (2008). Steinbeck studies in China. In K. Ariki, L. Li, & S. Pugh (Eds.), *John Steinbeck's global dimensions* (pp. 117–132). Lanham, MD: The Scarecrow Press.

Kundera, M. (1986). *The art of the novel* (L. Asher, Trans.). New York, NY: Grove Press.

Rorty, R. (1989). *Contingency, irony, and solidarity*. Cambridge, UK: Cambridge University Press.

Schwab, J. (1958, Summer). On the corruption of education by psychology. *School Review*, 66, 169–184.

Snow, C. P. (1959). *The two cultures and the scientific revolution*. London, UK: Cambridge University Press.

Steinbeck, J. (1962). *Travels with Charley in search of America*. New York, NY: Viking Press.

Steinbeck, J., & Ricketts, E. F. (1941). *Sea of Cortez: A leisurely journey of travel and research*. New York, NY: Viking Press.

Trueit, D. (2012). Preface. In D. Trueit (Ed.), *Pragmatism, post-modernism, and complexity theory: The "fascinating imaginative realm" of William E. Doll, Jr.* (pp. xii–xiv). London: Routledge.

Wang, H. (2016). *From the parade child to the king of chaos: The complex journey of William Doll, teacher educator*. New York, NY: Peter Lang.

Part II
Of Engagement, Immersion, and Transformative Experience

The Dewey scholar, Doll is never far from experience in his thinking and practice, and its import in understanding curriculum, that which has centrally organized educational activity in schools (Pinar, 2012). In articulating theoretically, and enacting pedagogically, such experience, he not only embraces its meaning as "to test, try, learn by trial or proof," and to "feel, undergo"—its lived *currere* sense (see footnote 10, Quinn, introduction) and its experimental one, involving knowledge gained by repeated trial, recursive reflexivity; but also its transformative possibilities—as that through which we change form, undergo a change in form, reach across and beyond form (*OED*, 1989)—become our "not yet" (Freire, 1970/1990), realize our "moreness" (Huebner, 1999), our "to come" (Derrida, 1990). For Doll, such attention to experience that is educational in the largest sense necessitates, as well, immersion and engagement. From the verb, *immergere*, such calls us "to plunge in, dip into, sink, submerge"; to "absorption in some interest or situation." Figuratively, the notion of immersion is incited in relation to work, study, and passion therein. Definitions thereof even reference such as a method of teaching (e.g., foreign language education) (*OED*, 1989).

Additionally, in engagement, we are summoned, "to bind, to pledge" to (that which) "attract(s) or occupy(ies) the attention of," to make a certain "appointment" or "promise" (*OED*). While Doll might not invite us to "enter into combat," he would have us enter into the work, the experience, which also oft means a readiness to wrestle with complexity, perturbation, contestation, confusion, difference. Still, we engage, we commit, to listen, to understand, to evolve, to grow and be changed.

Genuine experience, engagement, immersion, transformation, requires a posture of readiness for and toward such, a studied and cultivated openness, marked by lightness in seeking, questioning and conversation. This is the focus of David W. Jardine's essay concerning Bill Doll, "the refuge of Bill's presence"—his joy in being "all ears" that creates such in others. As we are each and all perpetually vulnerable before the petrifying reifications of articulated reality, ossifications of thought in and beyond our curricular work, and opacity and solidity of the world of education, we need ancestors like Bill who disrupt our fixed gaze, teach us to rise above that which impinges upon us, and in petitioning against closure, properly study in order to see those powers and potentialities that might be presently available to us. He shows us how to take time to work out all that is at work, by which we carry the burdens of the world a bit more lightly, in light, and with, too, the sword of insight, and such "refreshing courtesy."

Barney Ricca illuminates further the power and potential of this engagement Doll exemplifies in his person and work in examining one of his well-known tropes: "Be engaged. Pull back." Whereas this co-requisite for fullness of attention and engrossment Jardine discusses in terms of the readiness to be all ears in concert with the "deflected glance," Ricca approaches such via the lens of complexity theory, rooted in emergence, complementary processes among differing elements and levels, and flexible connections and change. Drawing upon such, Doll embodies engagement—demonstrates how in honoring and promoting emergence, belying control, one can remain radically open, stay connected and support rather than hinder the learner's growth and the birth of new understanding.

It is play, Hongyu Wang sets forth, and playful engagement with difference, relation and relationality—intellectual, social, and spiritual—to which Doll inventively calls us, enacting both theoretically and pedagogically. Such supports the openness that is a precondition for understanding. Surprised by the other, difference presents us with the opportunity for transformation: for entertaining alternative viewpoints and questions, integrating and crafting experiences anew, gleaning manifold patterns and depths of meaning and connection, generating fresh ideas and complexifying curriculum. Losing the self in play, immersed, engaged, in relational emergence, we enter into the spirit of the subject, experience or interplay, and transcend ourselves, move beyond the given, in humility and awe. Doll, Wang submits, asks "us to rethink the meanings of play, engagement, and difference in keeping knowledge alive and enabling personal growth and communal inquiry."

Examining her experience of recursively re-teaching and re-learning in a mathematics course as inspired by Doll's four R's (see footnote 9, Quinn, introduction) and in mentoring email communications with him, Lixin Luo reflects upon the hermeneutic dance between complexity and simplicity she learned from him, opening up to infinite possibilities wherein confusion, uncertainty, dissipation, and unpredictability are generatively engaged rather than eschewed. Here, the teacher, too, is transformatively involved with the subject matter and spirit of the discipline under study as much as is the student, via the experience of recursion that brings new insights into the work, both conceptually and pedagogically.

References

Derrida, J. (1990). Force of law: "The mystical foundation of authority." (On deconstruction and the possibility of justice). *Cardozo Law Review*, *11*(5–6), 919–1044.

Freire, P. (1990). *Pedagogy of the oppressed*. New York, NY: Continuum. (Original work published in 1970)

Huebner, D. (1999). *The lure of the transcendent: Collected essays by Dwayne E. Huebner*. Mahwah, NJ: Lawrence Erlbaum Associates Publishers.

Oxford English dictionary (*OED*) (2nd ed.). (1989). (J. Simpson & E. Weiner, Eds.). Oxford, UK: Clarendon Press.

Pinar, W. (2012). *What is curriculum theory?* (2nd ed.). New York, NY: Routledge. (Original work published in 2004)

7 The . . . Readiness . . . To Be "All Ears"

David W. Jardine

Preamble

What better description than this could I find for my thirty-year love affair with Bill Doll?

> Without the readiness of the person who is receiving and assimilating [*des Aufnehmenden*] the text to be "all ears" [*ganz Ohr zu sein*], no . . . text will speak.
> (Gadamer, 2007a, p. 189)

His unwavering joy in conversation, commiseration, his whiling over a question, a spark, bespeaks a lightness that produces joy while it seeks it. And this, too:

> We welcome just that guest who promises something new to our curiosity. But how do we know that the guest we admit is one who has something *new* to say to us? Is not our expectation and our readiness to hear the new also necessarily determined by the old that has already taken possession of us?
> (Gadamer, 2007b, p. 82)

There is the coupling, here, of the arrival of the new and the insistence that Bill embodies, that my readiness for that arrival is, in part, determined by what I have already come to know and how I have come to hold myself in that knowing. It is not an amassed blockage to that arrival, but is a condition of it, a condition of recognizing the new when it arrives.

A readiness to be all ears is thus not an innocent, or naïve or blank-faced openness, but a studied one, one won and re-won over time. It is an outcome of study properly done. This or that topic "compels over and over, and the better one knows it, the *more* compelling it is" (Gadamer, 2007c, p. 115), not *less*. This sort of knowledge, thus held, is a petition against hardening and closure, a summons on behalf of what can be thus hard-won: the lightness of gravity.

Readiness needs to be sought, cultivated. It needs to be taken care of properly and repeatedly and relentlessly. Readiness takes work, it takes energy, *energeia*, "aliveness" (Gadamer, 2007a, p. 211; Ross, 2006, pp. 107–108), and it not only takes it. It *produces* it. And when it works, it hits the still spot between give and take and begins to glow. As anyone who has met Bill or even heard or read him from afar knows full well, his being "all ears" extents such a glow. Such whiling stillness "is not a function of lackadaisical, meandering contemplation, least of all passive in any way, but is a function of the fullness and *intensity* of attention and engrossment" (Ross, 2006, p. 109) and watch out! It's contagious.

In around 1406, Tsong-kha-pa (2000, p. 179) noted that what pleases one's teachers most are not material gifts, but rather "offerings of practice." It is the pleasure taken in the practice of others that allows a teacher to "act as a refuge for everyone" (p. 179). Otherwise they are mere hoarders of their own expertise, weighty but sullen and full of complaint over new arrivals that always and only have nothing new to say. We've all been around enough of that.

In early September 2015, Bill invited me to speak to graduate students and Faculty at the University of British Columbia in Vancouver on a topic of my choice. That talk was given a title cited from Kevin O'Leary (2012), wherein he described clearly and distinctly how he profits, as an astute businessman, from desperate parental concerns over "literacy": "I love the terror in a mother's heart." That particular issue was written about elsewhere (Jardine, in press), about how one can profit from those who are petrified and how maintaining one's customers in a state of terror while providing purchasable relief from that very terror that one secretly maintains, has become a great contemporary art, in business, in politics, in education. What follows here is a reconstruction of some other threads of that talk offered as a wee gift of practice given to one of my teachers.

Again, we all know this much in having been around the refuge of Bill's presence. The joy he takes in being "all ears" *creates* joy.

"As in love, our satisfaction [in this joy] sets us at ease because we know that somehow its use at once assures its plenty" (Hyde, 1983, p. 22).

Thus a Fleet

A quick and fleeting scenario from a recent graduate class full of practicing teachers meeting at a local school, where someone on leave from the local school system visited his old place of work and was surprised and frustrated by the level of relentless complaint he encountered, some former colleagues even complaining about how much others complained. He mentioned how he had never quite noticed it before when working there and how now, having, shall we say, broken the fixed stare of living and breathing it day-to-day, he could see what was once hidden from view.

In our class, we all laughed at first, in recognition and commiseration. But then this: there was an at first gradual then ever-increasing falling forward into this culture of complaint. We all got drawn towards it, into it, deeper, deeper, so that our conversations became wedded to its roil, and it became more and more enormously engorged by our attention which it both fed and fed upon. It loved our attention, especially since that attention was only geared to more attention.

All of us were drawn in because of how very enlivening it *felt* to join in and how vigorous we each felt in feeling its stirring in us resentment, condescension, look-at-that-ness, this-bugs-me-too-ness. Everyone had something to say. Anecdotes scattered and shot and ricocheted around the room. Everyone was compelled to listen in that funny way, sitting on the verge of wanting a turn to tell, some urgency, some example, some frustration, some blame, this teacher, that face, those words, tut-tut, and the class of twenty-four broke up into a dozen ever-louder crisscross sideways conversations.

It *appeared* that everyone was "all ears" but no one was. Each of us already knew the anecdote we had waiting its turn to turn and spin and expend itself in this whirl. The game was already set, already fully determined and there was little readiness to hear something new. You can't be "all ears" if the only audible message offered is "Oh, yeah? Listen what happened to me!" Dramatic. Grotesque.

And, admit it, terribly temporarily enjoyable. Arousing.

The Weight, the Inertia, the Opacity

> I tried to identify myself with the ruthless energies propelling the events of our century, both collective and individual. I tried to find some harmony between the adventurous, picaresque inner rhythm that prompted me to write and the frantic spectacle of the world, sometimes dramatic and sometimes grotesque. Soon I became aware that between the facts of life that should have been my raw materials and the quick light touch I wanted for my writing, there was a gulf that cost me increasing efforts to cross. Maybe I was only then become aware of the weight, the inertia, the opacity of the world—qualities that [can] stick to writing. At certain moment I felt that the entire world was turning into stone: a slow petrification, more or less advanced depending on people and places but one that spared no aspect of life. It was as if no one could escape the inexorable stare of Medusa.
>
> (Calvino, 1988, p. 4)

Here, then a sideways glance at this lovely piece written by Italo Calvino (1988) called "Lightness." How the direct stare into these circumstances of complaint tends to harden that stare and therefore, at the same time, turn the object of that stare into its own version of "concrete" reality, thus turning our stare to stone, no longer able to turn away. The snaky roil mesmerizes—it *seems* like "aliveness"—but then it only petrifies. Like terror in a mother's heart, I suppose, stood stock-still and immobilized, susceptible to false promises of relief proffered by precisely that which caused the petrification in the first place.

As the object turns to a stony stare ("Look at that!" "Listen to them!" "You think *that's* bad, wait till you hear this!—I think," here, of Ivan Illich's [& Cayley, 1992, p. 127] hilariously apt description of this as "apocalyptic randiness"), we become attached to this monster wrought, in part, by our petrified stare, and then we blame it for our woes, turning effect into cause and making thinking impossible. This hostility in its turn once again further hardens and reifies, and this reification invokes hostility ("It's getting worse, don't you think!" "Why doesn't somebody do something!"), and that hostility, in its turn, reifies, adds gravity and weight. What happens, essentially, is that complaint is deeply and sincerely *experienced*, but it is no longer visible as *perpetrated*.

Energy just spent and temporarily exhausted.

Meeting Medusa in a Mirror

> Unskilled persons whose eye of intelligence is obscured by the darkness of delusion conceive of an essence in things [things are fixed, reified, concrete, inert] and then generate attachment and hostility with regard to them.
>
> (Tsong-kha-pa, 2000, p. 210)

This is why the "inertia and opacity of the world" is described as a wheel (Sanskrit: *Samsara*) in Buddhist thinking and imagination. It wheels and, when we become caught in its stare, we are wheeled, around and around, both adoring and complaining of this wheeling. The heavy solidity of "the real world" of schooling is met only with greasy, squirming of snakes. But then, Calvino:

> To cut off Medusa's head without being turned to stone, Perseus supports himself on the very lightest of things, the winds and the clouds, and fixes his gaze upon what can be revealed only by indirect vision, an image caught in a mirror.
>
> (Calvino, 1988, p. 4)

Medusa's roiling can be caught in a mirroring wherein we can remain not simply caught up in her stare and battered in the roil, but somehow "outside" of it: this is Gadamer's (1989, p. 444) "freedom from the environment" that makes us not simply caught in the earth's immediacies and tethers. We can "rise above what impinges on us from the world":

> This does not mean that [we] leave [our] habitat but that [w]e ha[ve] another posture towards it—a free, distanced orientation.
>
> (p. 445)

In this free distance, this "free space" (Gadamer, 1992, p. 53), I am not simply caught in the impinging of things, of actual circumstances and heat, but gain a sense of what might be possible, here, over and above the embodied reactions of mutual impingement, what potentialities and powers might be at work in this spell-binding immediacy.

But to break the spell of its immediacy and begin to glimpse its perpetration requires a deflected glance. In study, in writing, we support ourselves on the very lightest of things, thinking, but we don't then look away from our lot and up into the clouds:

> As for the severed head, Perseus does not abandon it but carries it concealed in a bag. Perseus's strength always lies in a refusal to look directly, but not in a refusal of the reality in which he is fated to live' he carries the reality with him and accepts it as his particular burden.
> (Calvino, 1988, p. 5)

Study, writing, carries our burden more lightly.

It may be that in the confines of schools our complaint has little recourse beyond its own continuance. This is why we study. Within the orbits of school and its language and accelerated time, there is not enough recourse available to work *out* what is at work, here. It cannot wing. It has no gush of coolness and musing:

> Medusa's blood gives birth to a winged horse, Pegasus—the heaviness of stone is transformed into its opposite. With one blow of his hoof on Mount Helicon, Pegasus makes a spring gush forth, where the Muses drink.
> (Calvino, 1988, p. 5)

As per this class of ours, someone had to simply say, "Stop!" in a voice loud enough to break the spell, loud enough to remind everyone that we are surrounded by ancestors who can help us, quite literally, *out*. So we read Bill Doll's work. And Maxine Greene. Bill Pinar. Thich Nhat Hanh, Wendell Berry. David G. Smith. Cynthia Chambers, on and on. Once we summoned them, they broke our fixed gaze and cultivated our readiness. We studied our circumstance instead of falling for it. They provided us with a field rich enough to work *out* what was happening, here. They helped us be all ears.

The bodhisattva Manjushri is associated in Buddhism with wisdom. He carries a sword used to cut through the spell, especially through the petrifying reifications of "the real world."

Like Perseus' sword, it cuts. It stops.

Studying and the Arts of Writing

Studying and the arts of writing don't precisely make lighter the burden of the world. They make it translucent, thus, shall we say, lightened:

> Whenever humanity seems condemned to heaviness, I think I should fly like Perseus into a different space. I don't mean escaping into

dreams or into the irrational. I mean that I have to change my approach, look at the world . . . with a different logic. The images of lightness that I seek should not fade away like dreams dissolved by the realities of present and future.

(Calvino, 1988, p. 7)

Thus the wonderful burden of writing and its wonderful reprieve, because, when it works, readers can recognize themselves in it as *already wiser* than they might have first imagined (precisely the act of a good teacher in relation to a student):

> What writers have is a license and also the freedom to sit—to sit, clench their fists, and make themselves be excruciatingly aware of the stuff that we're mostly aware of only on a certain level. And that if the writer does his job right, what he basically does is remind the reader of how smart the reader is. Is to wake the reader up to stuff that the reader's been aware of all the time.
>
> (Wallace, 2010, p. 41)

And this:

> One of the things about being a writer is you're able to give the impression—both in the lines and between the lines—that you know an *enormous* amount. That you know and have lived intimately all this stuff. Because you want it to have that kind of effect on the nerve endings. And its like—it's something that I'm fairly good at. Is I think I can seem, I think I can *seem* like I know a whole lot about stuff that in fact pretty much everything that I know is right there. It's a very tactical research-type thing.
>
> (pp. 144–145)

In writing, in studying, my own lure towards complaint becomes vivid. I myself am at stake. This sword is for me, for my sake.

> Ovid has some lines (IV. 740–752) that seem to me extraordinary in showing how much delicacy of spirit a man must have to be a Perseus, killer of monsters: "So that the rough sand should not harm the snake-haired head (*anquiferumque caput dura ne laedat harena*), he makes the ground soft with a bed of leaves, and on top of that he strews little branches of plants born under water, and on this he places Medusa's head, face down." I think that the lightness, of which Perseus is the hero, could not be better represented than by this gesture of refreshing courtesy toward a being so monstrous and terrifying yet at the same time somehow fragile and perishable.
>
> (Calvino, 1988, pp. 5–6)

Postscript

So there we have it, this gesture of refreshing courtesy that comes when I think over the past thirty years of friendship and camaraderie with Bill Doll. Study. Light air that bears a sword. Terrifying but not petrifying. Readiness. And, too, somehow, fragile and perishable.

References

Calvino, I. (1988). Lightness. In I. Calvino (Ed.), *Six memos for the next millennium* (pp. 3–30). Cambridge, MA: Harvard University Press.

Gadamer, H. G. (1989). *Truth and method*. New York, NY: Continuum.

Gadamer, H. G. (1992). The idea of the University – Yesterday, today, tomorrow. In D. Misgeld & G. Nicholson, eds. and trans. Hans-Georg Gadamer On Education, Poetry, and History: Applied Hermeneutics. Albany NY: SUNY Press, 47–62.

Gadamer, H. G. (2007a). Text and interpretation. In R. E. Palmer (Ed.), *The Gadamer reader: A bouquet of later writings* (R. E. Palmer, Trans.) (pp. 156–191). Evanston, IL: Northwestern University Press.

Gadamer, H. G. (2007b). The universality of the hermeneutical problem. In R. E. Palmer (Ed.), *The Gadamer reader: A bouquet of later writings* (R. E. Palmer, Trans.) (pp. 72–88). Evanston, IL: Northwestern University Press.

Gadamer, H. G. (2007c). From word to concept: The task of hermeneutics as philosophy. In R. E. Palmer (Ed.), *The Gadamer reader: A bouquet of the later writings* (R. E. Palmer, Trans.) (pp. 109–120). Evanston, IL: Northwestern University Press.

Hyde, L. (1983). *The gift: Imagination and the erotic life of property*. New York, NY: Vintage Books.

Illich, I., & Cayley, D. (1992). *Ivan Illich in conversation*. Toronto, ON: House of Anansi Press.

Jardine, D. (in press). I love the terror in a mother's heart. In J. Seidel & D. Jardine (Eds.), *The ecological heart of teaching: Radical tales of refuge and renewal for classrooms and communities*. New York, NY: Peter Lang.

O'Leary, K. (2012). *Dragon's den*. Produced by the Canadian Broadcasting Company. Series 6, Episode 19, first aired March 14, 2012. Retrieved from www.cbc.ca/dragonsden/pitches/ukloo.

On-line etymological dictionary. Retrieved from www.etymonline.com.

Ross, S. M. (2006). The temporality of tarrying in Gadamer. *Theory, Culture & Society, 23*(1), 101–123.

Tsong-Kha-Pa. (2000). *The great treatise on the stages of the path to enlightenment* (*Lam rim chen mo*) (Vol. 1). Ithaca, NY: Snow Lion Publications.

Wallace, D. F. (in conversation with David Lipsky). (2010). *Although of course you end up becoming yourself*. New York, NY: Broadway Books.

8 Engaging Engaging
Topological Reflections Prompted by Bill Doll

Bernard P. Ricca

As a mathematician, which in one sense is where Bill Doll started his own career in education, I want to engage a (still!) nagging email exchange that I had with Bill more than a few years ago. First, however, I invite the reader to explore one of the wonderful territories of mathematics. All you will need are scissors, pen or pencil, some paper, and tape. (Seriously, put down this text and go get those items.) Once you have come to a point where you are ready to abandon the explorations, you can return to the text. Even if you have done these explorations before, you should do them again, if for no other reason than they're fun!

The investigations involve a Möbius strip, and are quite easy to do. First, create a Möbius strip by taking a long strip of paper (say, about 2 feet by 1 inch), putting a half twist in it, and then connecting the two short ends.[1] Once that is done, try the following:

- Place a pen or pencil about halfway between the edges, and draw a line on the strip, staying about halfway between the edges. Continue drawing until you return to the original spot(!). Then, answer this question: What will happen when you cut along that line? Finally, cut along the line.
- With a second strip, draw a line all the way along the length of the strip that is about one-third of the way from one edge. Again, what do you think will happen when you cut along that line? Finally, cut along the line.

While there are many other investigations that are worth pursuing—What happens if you cut the objects resulting from the original cuts? What happens if you put more than one half twist in the strip?—these explorations will do for starters.[2]

---

1. The Wikipedia page on Möbius strips has a nice illustration that might help, if you are having problems.
2. In fact, these investigations actually touch on some very advanced mathematics; I think that this is the reason we don't often encounter them in schools. See Friesen et al. (2006).

Now that you are ready to return to this piece—and those of you who are too boring to have done the investigations should stop right here and do them—you should be able to answer some questions (e.g., "What happened?" "Were you surprised?") while (probably) being completely unable to answer other questions (e.g., "Why does the Möbius strip in three space behave this way?"). Both the Möbius strip and these questions are important anchors for the investigations that follow.

"Be Engaged. Pull Back"

This phrase, used by Bill Doll in the classroom, was the beginning of the email exchange which prompts these reflections. And while it is possible to take a rather surface-level interpretation of the seeming paradox—sometimes to engage we must pull back and regroup—both the difficulty that students had grappling with the phrase, and Bill's own character, suggest that there is a deeper meaning.

Levels

Deeper is routinely taken to imply that there are multiple levels to meaning. And therein lies the first hint of the problem we face in examining the statement. "Be engaged. Pull back." Although we are accustomed to looking at different levels of situations, the very word itself—levels—almost immediately implies a hierarchy. But as Bill is not a fan of hierarchies, this is worth some further examination.

In complex systems theory, the concept of emergence is prevalent (Bedau & Humphreys, 2008; Holland, 1999). Although it is typically considered that behavior at one level (say, the group) emerges from behavior at another level (the individual), and although it may appear to be so, levels do not provide a full explanation for emergence. Consider rush-hour traffic, for example: The overall behavior (i.e., the never-ending backup) emerges from the behavior of the individual drivers. Agent-based model simulations (see Open ABM, n.d., for a simple example) show that, usually, the congestion would be greatly relieved if everyone backed off a bit, so that there was less need for each driver to push the brake pedal. Of course, in another example of the tragedy of the commons, this only works if every driver behaves that way. Any one driver who attempts to exploit the situation by suddenly changing lanes will trigger a cascade of braking cars, which will, in turn, institute the return of the congestion. This simple example shows problems with the explanations of emergence that rely on emergence across levels.

First, the pattern of stopping and starting travels as do waves, propagating backwards from the perturbation (the driver changing lanes). In fact, the propagation of braking waves can be well modeled by considering the cars as particles in a fluid, and the offending driver as a sudden impulse applied at a particular point in the fluid. Hence, by taking an even more bird's-eye view—another level!—than just the drivers caught in rush hour, we can see that apparently emergent behavior may not actually be emergent.

Second, Andrighetto et al. (2007) note that the emergence of behavior in groups requires not only a "lower" level creating patterns at a "higher" level, but also a reciprocal process from "higher" to "lower":

> Dealing with autonomous social agents, emergence is in the loop between bottom-up and top-down processes. Emergence of properties at aggregate level cannot be effectively accomplished unless properties feedback on the lower level through a complementary process of immergence into behaviours of units at the lower level.
> (p. 11)

It is the failure of the aggregate level (society) it be immergent into the lower level (the offending driver), by not successfully imparting important behaviors in all drivers, that produces the pattern that is seen. Hence, although it may appear that behavior at one level emerges from behavior at another (lower) level, without a complementary process, emergence is but an illusion. Given the need for complementary processes, the hierarchy of levels that is often assumed by "deeper" and its ilk, collapses. Levels, yes. Hierarchy, no.

Ryan (2007) *attempted to pick up the pieces of emergence by considering emergence being coupled to scope*, and not to scale. *Scope* is, essentially, the number of different measurements that are used to fully describe something, whereas scale is the extent of each measurement. An example will help here: Consider a high-resolution digital picture, say one that is 1024 × 2048 pixels. The scope of that picture is the entire two megapixels, while the scale is one pixel. Now, let us consider a lower resolution image of the same scene, say 480 × 960 pixels. This latter image would certainly seem fuzzier than the former image, because each pixel is now much larger; the scale used for each pixel has been increased. Ryan would say that the scope used in the pictures has also changed, decreasing from the former to the latter. However, a segment of the original picture, shown with pixels the same size as the original, could have a smaller scope than the original, while retaining the same scale. Although there is some benefit to considering this approach, it suffers from the same issues as levels.

The problem with all approaches to levels, whether or not they are hierarchical, is that they are inherently geometric in nature. Geometry, with its precise metrics (ways to measure distance), and clear notions of scale, between, above, larger, and so on, does not match the essence of complex systems, and hence, is inappropriate to use in understanding such systems. Even *fractal geometry* (Mandelbrot, 1982), although it does move beyond scales, is not sufficient to discuss complex systems. Fortunately, the world of mathematics provides us with an alternative approach that does provide the necessary tools for complex systems: topology.

Topology

Topology is a branch of mathematics that can be initially understood by considering all objects to be made of infinitely flexible material. Topological objects can be distorted in myriad ways, such that the joke goes that to a topologist, a coffee cup and a donut are identical (because they both have one hole in them). And you, the reader (at least, the obedient ones of you who partook of the explorations presented at the beginning of the paper), have some experience in the strange world of topology: the Möbius strip!

Although this paper is not part of a topology course, a few words about topology will be helpful. First, the strangeness of the Möbius strip has to do with the fact that it has only one edge, and only one side; this is different than most common physical objects that have a front and a back. (Any odd number of half-twists will produce such a figure, although each such figure will have its own idiosyncracies.) Second, topological investigations do not admit any measure of closeness, or ordering, or size. Notice that these geometric ideas are at the heart of many of the analyses we make, and, more to the point here, at the heart of the paradox of "Be engaged. Pull back." How can one be close enough to engage and farther away at the same time? Third, because topology does not admit to size, it is, like fractal geometry, scale-free. Fourth, topology considers connections and holes, known as *genus* in topology-speak. (Both a coffee cup and a donut are genus 1.) And fifth, topology has different ideas about inside and outside (an extension of the Möbius strip's strange properties of front and back sides).

In many ways, topology is similar to the study of networks; in fact, we often speak of the *network topology*, and networks—with ideas about connections, betweenness, and distance that are someplace between geometry and topology—are an enticing metaphor (in the sense of Thelen, 1999) for exploring engagement. However, the limitation of networks for the current examination is that networks consider discrete entities, with hard boundaries, connected to one another; these hard boundaries seem inappropriate when talking of people in the personal context of "Be engaged. Pull back." Furthermore, networks are usually populated by nodes that do not change in character,[3] and this static approach is likewise inappropriate for the personal context. For all these reasons, and more, topology is a better branch of mathematics on which to base

3. Epidemiology is an exception to this; however, virus spreading is probably also not the metaphor to use for these explorations.

investigations into complex systems in general, and for the particular exploration here.

Engagement and Emergence

> *If you want to change something you have to understand it, and if you want to understand something you have to change it.*
> (Gravemeijer & Cobb, 2006, p. 163)

Armed with some topology, what does it mean to engage? And what does emergence have to do with engagement?

Engagement and Teaching

Much of Bill's life has been spent in classrooms, where change and understanding are key activities. Students, as individuals, are constantly changing, striving to understand and hoping to be understood. External pressures exerted on classrooms constantly change, although because of the attempt to change the classroom without understanding it, those pressures are often destructive. In the midst of all this change (or not) and understanding (or not) lives a teacher. And it is the teacher who must find ways to engage with students.

It is here that topology can open our thinking: Teachers engage students not by becoming "close" (that geometric misnomer for teacher-student relationships) but by being connected to students in particular ways; without connections between students and teachers, there is very little learning. (I dare say that all readers of this piece will agree that their best teachers were ones with whom they had a particularly good *connection*.) It is important, however, that these connections are flexible enough to change without being broken; the "genus" of the teacher-student relationship, whatever that might be, endures through the changes, but the relationship may change radically over time. Furthermore, it is unclear, at least in good teacher-student relationships, which of the two is "the learner," as both individuals take on both roles, just as it is unclear which side of the Möbius strip is which. And perhaps most importantly in this post–No Child Left Behind era, metrics of teachers do not do a good job of capturing the essence of teaching, of ordering teachers from "good" to "bad," and so on.

Emergence (Again)

Ultimately, learning, growth, and change—which are the goals teachers have for their students—are emergent processes; the transfer of knowledge from teacher to student has been widely debunked, and many other ideas (e.g., constructivism—see Doll, 2008) have also been found wanting. And because this process requires both emergence and immergence, it is impossible to state clearly whether the teacher or the student is on the "higher" level. Certainly, we can establish metrics by which to measure how much knowledge has been mastered (controlled!) by teachers and students, but the results are at least as much a reflection of the instrument as they are a reflection of the teachers and students.

If emergence is not something that is easily measured, and hence, not something that can be controlled, the implication is that emergence requires openness, which is in many ways the opposite of control. But it is not just that openness is the antithesis of control: for emergence to occur, a very radical openness must be present. Good teachers never know what students will come up with, but they are willing to travel with their students wherever the students may go. However, while always connected, the teacher stays out of the way of the student; this is the best engagement.

"Be Engaged. Pull Back" (Again)

Full engagement, then, implies a rather radical openness: We do not know what will come out, and we cannot control it; in fact, control is the opposite of engagement. And pulling back is an essential part of this engagement: we must remove ourselves from that with which we engage—while still maintaining engagement!—so that we may allow the system to become itself.

No two sentences can sum up Bill Doll (or anyone else, for that matter), but I believe that it is this ability to be engaged while pulled back that are a hallmark of Bill Doll. Anyone who has been engaged with Bill in any way knows that he has an expansive personality (and that his laugh can literally fill a room) but that neither his personality nor his engagement control outcomes. Rather, he is connected enough to allow for the other to grow. And Bill's curriculum works are perhaps best understood in this same light: It is important to engage with ideas, with topics, and so on, but the goal has never been to become the idea, the topic, or even to be controlled or directed by them. Rather, the goal is to promote emergence.

References

Andrighetto, G., Campennì, M., Conte, R., Paolucci, M., Istituto, L., & Martino, S. (2007). *On the immergence of norms: A normative agent architecture*. AAAI Fall Symposium, 11–18. Retrieved from www.aaai.org/Library/Symposia/Fall/fs07-04.php

Bedau, M., & Humphreys, P. (2008). *Emergence: Contemporary readings in philosophy and science*. Cambridge, MA: MIT Press.

Doll, W. (2008). "Maturana is not a constructivist" . . . nor is Piaget. *Complicity: An International Journal of Complexity and Education, 5*(1), 27–31.

Friesen, S., Clifford, P., & Jardine, D. (2006). Anh Linh's shapes. In D. Jardine, S. Friesen, & P. Clifford (Eds.), *Curriculum in abundance*. Mahwah, NJ: Lawrence Erlbaum Associates Publishers.

Gravemeijer, K., & Cobb, P. (2006). Design research from a learning design perspective. In J. van den Akker, K. Gravemeijer, S. McKenney, & N. Nieveen (Eds.), *Educational design research*. New York, NY: Routledge.

Holland, J. (1999). *Emergence: From chaos to order*. Cambridge, MA: Perseus Books.

Mandelbrot, B. (1982). *The fractal geometry of nature*. Gordonsville, VA: W. H. Freeman and Company.

Open ABM. (n.d.). *Traffic flows*. Retrieved from www.openabm.org/book/3138/63-traffic-flows

Ryan, A. J. (2007). Emergence is coupled to scope, not level. *Complexity, 13*(2), 67–77. https://doi.org/10.1002/cplx.20203

Thelen, E. (1999). The dynamics of motor development: Commentary on Wimmers and Vereijken. In G. Savelsbergh, H. van Der Maas, & P. Van Geert (Eds.), *Non-linear developmental processes* (pp. 151–157). Amsterdam: Edita KNAW.

9 Playful Engagement With Difference

Hongyu Wang

In the field of education, "play" is usually associated with early childhood and elementary education, in which hands-on activities are emphasized as a way of facilitating students' learning, while in the educational debates in recent decades, "difference" is often associated with social and cultural differences. There is no inherent relationship between "play" and "difference." However, in William Doll's curriculum and pedagogical theory and practice, "play" and "difference" take on quite different meanings, and his playful engagement with difference as a teacher and as a scholar has opened up a new landscape in education. Drawing upon his work and my recently completed study of his pedagogical life history (Wang, 2016), this paper highlights Doll's play—"a complex form of play" (Pinar, 2016, p. xi)—with difference in multiple dimensions: intellectual, social, and spiritual.

Playful Engagement With Intellectual Difference

For Doll (2012), difference plays an essential role in students' and teachers' intellectual growth. In Gadamer's (1960/1998) notion of experience, there is a built-in element of "surprise" that cannot be fully captured. Without surprise, an authentic experience does not occur. The key to opening students and teachers to this surprise is playful engagement with intellectual difference. The Derridian notion of "learning" requires learning something *other* and *different* that cannot be fully mastered (Egéa-Kuehne, 1995). Therefore, openness to something different is the precondition for transformative learning and teaching. Also influenced by Piaget's cognitive development theory and Prigogine's chaos and complexity theory, Doll (1993, 2012) affirms the positive role of perturbation, difference, and disequilibrium in learning, teaching, and curriculum.

If difference is necessary for reaching another level of understanding, one way to keep perturbation generative is through play, although intellect and play are often perceived as antithetical. As Ted T. Aoki (1990/2005) acknowledges, work and play do not come together. However, for Doll (1993, 2012), playing with different ideas and playing with patterns of subject matter, which bring newness and surprise, are important for "keeping knowledge alive" (Doll, 2012, p. 118). It is important to point out here that playing with ideas is different from the common understanding of play as hands-on activity. For Doll, following Dewey's notion that experience must include the element of reflection, play is not only of the body but also of the mind as both are integrated in experiencing. To reduce play to hands-on activities in the classroom neglects the importance of meaning-making in students' intellectual growth.

Playing with ideas can use various tools—hands-on, imaginative, performative—but what is essential for such play is not delivering knowledge but for students to interact with the subject structure. Doll believes that each subject has its own patterns and that educators need to have a deeper, structural understanding of the subjects they teach so that they can guide students to play with the patterns of those subjects. In his teaching at school and in teacher education, Doll (2012) demonstrates such play with patterns that goes beyond the factual, linear, accumulative mode. When students at different levels have a chance to imaginatively and intuitively play with subject structures, they not only reach a more advanced level of understanding, they also become immersed into a process of experiencing.

Such play is transactional and associated with the process of "crafting an experience" (Doll, 2012, p. 98). The transactional nature of play between and among students, texts, teachers, and situations requires participants to lose themselves in the process of engagement in a to-and-fro movement of making sense to generate new meanings. Doll (2012) refers to such immersion while finding ways to respond creatively as "crafting an experience": "It is this process of interactive doing, undergoing, and responding which turns experience into *an experience*" (p. 99; italics in the original). As students play with ideas and craft an experience, richer and deeper understandings as well as creativity can come forth.

Playing with ideas is also related to the spirit of questioning. Heidegger's notion that "questioning constitutes the piety of thought" has been influential to Doll (quoted in Doll, 2012, p. 81). He encourages his students to look at issues from multiple angles and to not stay with only one interpretation. Searching for alternatives is the reformulated quality of rigor in Doll's (1993) post-modern curriculum. For Doll, questioning generates new lines of thinking, but questioning is also connected with the joy of learning and teaching. Engaging in intellectual conversations, for Doll, is often accompanied by sharing lunch with students and colleagues, walking and talking on and off campus, driving together to attend conferences, and other activities of nourishing companionship (Wang, 2016). Questioning that happens in the midst of laughter, nourishment, and communal sharing is both enlightening and endearing. Playfulness accompanying questioning prevents critique from becoming rigid and blind to its own limits.

The blending of sharing food, walks, and talks in his intellectual relationships with students and colleagues infuses social dimensions into intellectual life, which is usually marked by independence and seriousness. Here, the intellectual dimension of play is intertwined with Doll's playfulness in social relations to create a communal space for everybody's intellectual exploration and personal growth.

Playful Engagement With Social-Relational Difference

Social and cultural differences, for which race, ethnicity, gender, class, or sexuality are the markers, and their meanings for education have been explored for decades. Refusing to see a person or/and an issue through one particular lens, Doll is known for not getting involved in politics of education that is oriented by identity. However, he emphasizes the importance of social relations and the necessity of playing with tensionality in the relational in order to negotiate more room for educative possibilities. In his curriculum visions, whether the four R's, five C's, or three S's, playful engagement with relations is an important component, as reflected in Relation in the four R's (Richness, Recursion, Relation, and Rigor), Community in the five C's (*Currere*, Complexity, Cosmology, Conversation, and Community), and the relational quality of Story in the three S's (Science, Story, and Spirit) (Doll, 2012).

There are two intertwined layers of Relation in the four R's: pedagogical relations within the curriculum and cultural relations that are "local in origin but global in interconnections" (Doll, 1993, p. 180). To enrich curriculum through such a relational matrix, Doll does not set up fixed structures but plays with relationality to keep curriculum open and generative. Here the term "interplay" is important, as it emphasizes an interactive approach that negotiates curriculum passages through play. Dewey's experiential, interactive approach to education, Piaget's theory on peer interactions, and the importance of the relational interplay in complex social systems have influenced Doll's perspective on the role of interplay in curriculum and pedagogy (Doll, 1993). Doll's teaching in the classroom is distinguished by the complicated interplay that students engage in through interacting with texts, with one another, with the instructor, and with the outside world (Wang, 2016).

Community, proposed as the last of the five C's (Doll, 2002), emphasizes the importance of the interplay between the individual and the communal. For Doll, community should have elements of both "care and critique" (p. 50) so that it can help us "both develop and be critical of our basic assumptions" (p. 51) to enable transformation of the curriculum and its participants. A community of learners develops a high degree of trust, in which playing with social relations in "a community of *dissensus*" (Ziarek, 2001) goes hand in hand with playing with different ideas. A dialogic community—many of Doll's classes demonstrate such a quality (Wang, 2016)—allows more space for the diversity of students and the instructor to come into play than does a community based upon sameness. Janet Miller (2010) argues for curriculum communities without consensus, in which a communal space is not based upon any universal notion but "re-forms daily and differently in response to difference and to the unknown" (p. 96). While intellectual difference excites Doll's imagination, he also approaches tensions and turbulence in social relations as a great opportunity for transformative change.

Story in the three S's highlights the importance of the relational in the personal and cultural context (Doll, 1998, 2003/2012). While the role of interpretation and relationships in stories goes beyond scientific logic, interestingly, Doll blends the storied quality of human life as "allied with complexity theory's mode of considering relationality itself as always being in process, of always forming a dynamic system" (Doll, 2012, p. 109). While social relations are necessarily more complicated than relationality in a biological or scientific system, a sense of emergence also applies to social systems (Fleener, 2002). The notion of playing with boundaries in complexity science to generate transformative processes is also important for dealing with tensions in social relations. Playing with tensionality and differences in social relations, rather than being stuck in the either/or mentality to find one solution, is essential to creating a "shared flourishing" community (Hershock, 2012, p. 21) in which differences make complementary contributions to sustainable relationality. For Doll (2013), ethical relationship with the other in a post-modern approach lies in respecting the alterity of the other and being willing to let go of the pursuit of certainty to welcome enriching opportunities.

Doll's approach to social difference is also based upon the acceptance, since his teenage years, of his own difference from others. Never quite fitting into the crowd in his youth and any particular intellectual camp in his academic career, he has followed a unique pathway, creating his own niche by thriving on differences and mobilizing others (Wang, 2016). Creating his own space in the midst of difference has cultivated in him the capacity to stand on his own while at the same time initiating conversations across differences. Relationship with the self and relationship with the other cannot be separated. Furthermore, Doll's capacity to playfully engage the relational has been developed through many years of organizing groups of students, teachers, and scholars for intellectual conversations and years of leading curriculum change on various occasions (Doll, 2012; Wang, 2016). Doll narrates how his experiences of interacting with others who have different viewpoints has developed his ability to listen to those who disagree while building personal relationships with them. He has used this skill in both teaching and leadership experiences.

Both relations and community are not only social and human, but also ecological and cosmological, which leads to the next dimension of play: spiritual play with difference.

Spiritual Play With Difference

Play and spirituality seldom come together as spirituality is a serious matter, but contemplative wisdom places them together because getting in touch with the vital energy of the universe requires a sense of playfulness that goes beyond attachment to one's individual ego to reach the ecological and cosmological realm of life where sacredness lies. "Playfulness is transcendent" (Wang, 2014, p. 85) as play goes beyond dualism, bridges separateness, and keeps curriculum and teaching alive. When we introduce play into our engagement with difference, the fluidity, flexibility, and fun aspects of life can open up. Religious dogmas and doctrines, when perceived as absolute and permanent, drain the vitality out of life and cannot lift people to a higher level of awareness and sacred interconnectedness. Spiritual play with difference, on the other hand, takes people out of their immediate realm to listen to the sound of the cosmos and to get in touch with something that is greater than humanity.

Doll calls himself a "heretical Catholic" (Wang, 2016). He is committed to Catholicism's sense of interconnectedness but not confined by any of the restraining doctrines that he experienced as a child in a Catholic school. For him, the spiritual requires one to be open to difference so that one can, with humility and awe, keep pursuing what is more than oneself and what is beyond the given. Spirituality is not a fixed ideal, but emergent, cosmological, and ecological. This open-ended sense of spirituality has infused creative energy into his curriculum and teaching approaches.

Doll (2012) argues that "our accepted concepts of God, religion, spirituality assume a type of permanence—a cosmology of permanence as it were—we no longer find valid" (p. 35). In a post-modern age, change rather than permanence is accepted as a fundamental feature of life. An emergent sense of spirituality is fluid, dynamic, and life-affirmative. In chaos and complexity theory, "emergence" describes a systematic change as a result of interactions between and among all components within the system. This notion calls for "thinking in a relational way" because it is through "the relations among the objects, particularly their differences, that we begin to understand the objects themselves" (p. 36). This focus on the relational asks us to shift our attention from the particular component to the interconnected pattern in order to allow new structures of a system to emerge.

The concept of relational emergence is compatible with Gregory Bateson's (1979/1988) notion of the "pattern which connects" (p. 8), a pattern both ecological and spiritual, connecting not only human beings but also all living creatures. Moreover, cosmological creation is also "emergent—the universe coming out of itself—in a mysterious but natural way" (Doll, 2012, p. 39). If the universe itself is mysteriously emergent, spirituality is related to the cosmic energy, a relationship that does not bring the conventional religious control that produces fear but brings heartfelt awe at the intricate, complex process of creation and the throbbing, underlying interconnectedness of life.

Acknowledging that spirituality has a strong element of passion, Doll emphasizes the need to balance passion with play, the Wittgensteinian sense of play *with* boundaries, so that the binding force of passion "is counterbalanced with the liberating force of play. The tension between these two, an essential and productive tension, produces that 'third space' where newness, creativity, generativeness reside" (Doll, 2012, p. 110). An emergent sense of spirituality that is based upon a relational view is playful; in such spiritual play, difference is honored, not dissolved, to allow newness to be cultivated so that passion breathes life into a situation but does not dominate.

Doll also believes that each subject matter has its own spirit and that teachers' and students' play with subject patterns enables them to get in touch with the spirit of a subject. He explains:

> Spirit has a long history, going back in Western thought to the early Christian communities and the visitations of the Holy Spirit that gave life and vitality to those communities. Analogously, spirit refers to the life and vitality of a subject. It comes to us as we look at the history and structure of a subject; through that looking, we become filled with awe at the aliveness and vitality of a subject.
> (Doll, 1998, p. 6)

Going a step further than Jerome Bruner, who emphasizes the structure of a subject matter, Doll works to capture the whole *being* of a subject through the notion of "spirit." In-depth understanding of a subject in its own patterns through interplay between teacher/student and the subject matter leads to greater appreciation of the wonder, awe, and vitality of life. Such a broader understanding of spirituality seems to be unusual, but it turns a static notion of knowledge into a moving force of knowing, experiencing, and living that embeds curriculum in the imaginative, the creative, the existential, and the aesthetic as well as in the intellectual. Fascinated by the patterns of nature and life since his childhood, Doll has sustained the role of playing with the patterns of a subject—playing with its spirit—in curriculum and teaching. Integrating science, story, and spirit, Doll's approach to curriculum is simultaneously intellectual, cultural, ecological, and spiritual.

In short, William Doll's curriculum theory and practice challenge taken-for-granted assumptions and ask us to rethink the meanings of play, engagement, and difference in keeping knowledge alive and enabling personal growth and communal inquiry. Although for the convenience of analysis this essay discusses different dimensions—intellectual, social, and spiritual—of Doll's playful engagement with difference, these dimensions are necessarily intertwined in a complex and nonlinear manner.

Doll's play is simultaneously intellectual, social, and spiritual. A playful child, a playful educator, a playful scholar, William Doll's legacy lies in *"the fascinating imaginative realm where no one owns the truth and everyone has the right to be understood"* (Kundera, quoted in Doll, 2012, p. 144; italics in the original). May we all be inspired to play with difference to reach deeper and fly higher, embracing the complexity of life and of education.

References

Aoki, T. (1990). Inspiriting the curriculum. In T. T. Aoki (2005), *Curriculum in a new key* (W. F. Pinar & R. L. Irwin, Eds.) (pp. 357–365). Mahwah, NJ: Lawrence Erlbaum Associates Publishers.

Bateson, G. (1988). *Mind and nature*. New York, NY: Bantam Books. (Original work published in 1979)

Doll, W. (1993). *A post-modern perspective on curriculum*. New York, NY: Teachers College Press.

Doll, W. (1998). The spirit of education. *Early Childhood Education, 31*(1), 1–7.

Doll, W. (2002). Ghosts and the curriculum. In W. E. Doll, Jr. & N. Gough (Eds.), *Curriculum visions*. New York, NY: Peter Lang.

Doll, W. (2012). *Pragmatism, post-modernism, and complexity theory: The "fascinating imaginative realm" of William E. Doll, Jr.* (D. Trueit, Ed.). New York, NY: Routledge.

Doll, W. (2003/2012). Modes of thought. In D. Trueit (Ed.), *Pragmatism, postmodernism and complexity theory: The "fascinating imaginative realm" of William E. Doll, Jr.* (pp. 103–110). New York, NY: Routledge. (Original work published in 2003)

Doll, W. (2013). An exploration of "ethics" in a post-modern, complex, global society. *Transnational Curriculum Inquiry, 10*(2), 64–70.

Egéa-Kuehne, D. (1995). Deconstruction revisited and Derrida's call for academic responsibility. *Educational Theory 45*(3), 293–309.

Fleener, J. (2002). *Curriculum dynamics*. New York, NY: Peter Lang.

Gadamer, H.-G. (1998). *Truth and method* (2nd ed.). New York, NY: Continuum. (Original work published in 1960)

Hershock, P. (2012). *Valuing diversity*. Albany, NY: SUNY Press.

Miller, J. (2010). Communities without consensus. In E. Malewski (Ed.), *Curriculum studies handbook* (pp. 95–100). New York, NY: Routledge.

Pinar, W. (2016). Introduction. In H. Wang (Ed.), *From the parade child to the king of chaos* (pp. ix–xxiv). New York, NY: Peter Lang.

Wang, H. (2014). *Nonviolence and education*. New York, NY: Routledge.

Wang, H. (2016). *From the parade child to the king of chaos: The complex journey of William Doll, teacher educator*. New York, NY: Peter Lang.

Ziarek, E. P. (2001). *An ethics of dissensus*. Stanford, CA: Stanford University Press.

10 A Recursive Path to Infinity

Lixin Luo

For more than a decade, Bill Doll[1] has walked with me through a recursive path. My reflection over the past here allows me to exemplify Bill Doll's significant contributions in teaching, theorizing, and complexifying curriculum through a fractal (Mandelbrot, 1967) approach—seeing the whole in parts. Weaving my personal stories and re-interpretations of Bill's works together, this essay elaborates how Bill's teaching opens space for me in personal, professional, and academic development. It aims to provide a glimpse into Bill's fascinating world, in which he dances between simplicity and complexity occasioning educational experiences that can lead one to a space of infinite possibilities.

Entry

It was June 2003. I sent Bill an anxious email inquiring about his summer graduate courses at the University of Victoria, knowing little about him. Bill's swift reply brought me something different, something warm and lively. I was hooked immediately once I started reading Bill Doll's (1993) *A Post-modern Perspective on Curriculum*. Bill's contemplation on curriculum through examining the history of science and its influence on education, combining multi-disciplinary scientific and philosophical arguments together, spoke to me.

Bill's teaching[2] centers on chaos, complexity, and their educational implications. Chaos in living systems, Bill says, is not randomness without order. There lies invisible order in seemingly chaotic living phenomena.

---

1. Dr. William E. Doll, Jr. is referred to as Bill or Bill Doll in this essay. The quality of my relationship with Bill demands a personal tone that honors Bill's long-term commitment to relationality.
2. Bill's ideas take root in the works of Whitehead, Piaget, Dewey, Bruner, Prigogine, Bateson, Mandelbrot, and other chaos-complexity theorists, such as Capra and Kauffman. Hence, what Bill taught me also include some of these authors' ideas. It is beyond the scope of this essay to differentiate Bill's ideas and these scholars' works. Most ideas Bill taught me can be found in Doll's (1993) book unless specified otherwise.

It takes time to observe them holistically rather than analyzing them as individual parts: the whole is bigger than the sum of the parts. Living systems are open systems that constantly interact with their environment and are capable of self-organization, so they can conserve a current status yet also co-evolve with their environment. The being of a living system is affected by its process of becoming; the development of a living system results from self-making, occasioned by natural selection. Thus, the future of a living system cannot be imposed externally; it is highly sensitive to the system's initial conditions. This sensitivity and unpredictability of living systems is reflected well in "the butterfly effect,"[3] which refers to the phenomenon that a subtle change in a living system's status at one time can have an amplified effect later. Given the impracticality of knowing a living system's detailed initial conditions to infinite precision, a long-term prediction of the system is impossible (Kauffman, 1995). Considering learners as living systems, Bill rejects pre-set measured curricula and proposes *a* post-modern transformative curriculum that cherishes chaos. Chaos is needed for learning as living systems transform and evolve at the edge of chaos, which is far from equilibrium: "In open systems, a great deal of dissipation must be developed if transformation is to take place" (Doll, 1993, p. 104). Learning, as a process of breaking and re-establishing equilibrium, cannot happen without a stage of disequilibrium, or chaos.

Bill's teaching touched me profoundly. My summer study with Bill was exactly what I had longed for: a meaningful learning experience in which thinking is enjoyed for its own sake and through which the learner's mind and soul are changed. Besides forming a non-dualistic worldview, I began to appreciate confusion, chaos, and uncertainty in education and life. I had been lost long before meeting Bill: I had been shaming myself for lacking knowledge, contribution, and stability in life goal and identity. Chaos theory inspired me to reframe my past as a chaotic one with hidden order(s). I became more patient with myself. Bill's call to keep knowledge alive (Doll, 2005) prompted me to re-appreciate my former education through its contribution in cultivating thinking habits. I felt less insecure for having difficulty in conserving knowledge. Bill's emphasis in interaction and relation helped me understand quality as a property of relationship rather than an internal property. I found it easier to stop regretting the past and not cling to a stable goal or identity. I started to attend more to building constructive environments to bring forth something good from myself and other people. Understanding the butterfly effect also calmed me down so I could do small things to change myself and the world gradually, rather than being paralyzed by not bringing about rational changes quickly. My

---

3. The butterfly effect is told in a metaphorical story: "a legendary butterfly flapping its wings in Rio changes the weather in Chicago" (Kauffman, 1995, p. 17).

disappointment towards myself and disillusion about the society faded; I was hopeful again. Looking through these transformed perspectives of world, education, self, and life, I saw vast implementations of Bill's ideas in education and beyond (Luo, 2004).

The change Bill occasioned in my thinking was nothing but subtle, yet it would take me much longer time to enact this level of change. As the intense summer study with Bill subsided, I entered a recursive journey of re-encountering complexity and its accompanying chaos and hopeful transformation.

Looping

> 02/17/09 Lixin: Today's class [G12 Advanced Functions] was terrible. . . . I failed to get a sense of wholeness and smoothness before the class started. All I had was many parts. . . . I could not make them flow smoothly from one to another.
>
> I wanted students to see many different features of polynomial functions, but had not enough time for them to investigate one by one. . . . In this lesson, I was restricted by my concerns about pace and time; no one could flow . . .
>
> 02/18/09 Bill: The art is—and this may take more than one teaching of a course—is to take the linear ordering a syllabus/textbook uses and rearrange it in a nonlinear manner. Time now is no longer linear but rather nonlinear in its recursiveness. One looks at the whole semester/block as a system and sees in a system or grid a number of ways to move. Which way is chosen depends upon the class and where it is at on a given evening/lesson.
>
> One example here: When I worked with the red and white discs and turned them Into R's and W's we began to move into both combinations and permutations and algebra. So exploration at one level becomes foundational for study at another level and coming to such study later one recurses back to work done earlier.
>
> Finally trying to cover all (linear in itself) leads to feeling and being stretched. Underneath any set of operations are some basic ideas—Whitehead calls these "big ideas." These need to be focused on and shown to appear in various forms in different lessons.
>
> I hope my general comments can help your particular situations. There is a whole/part relation here.
>
> (W. Doll & L. Luo, personal communication,
February 17–18, 2009)

After my master's program, I taught secondary math. Believing in growth through interaction,[4] I kept in touch with Bill. I shared the highs and lows

---

4. "Both Dewey and Piaget have pointed out, it is interaction that forms the heart of growth" (Doll, 1993, p. 63).

in my personal and professional life with Bill via emails and annual visits. Bill maintained a swift speed in replying to my emails and an everlasting caring and enthusiastic attitude during our conversations. Bill became my mentor, continuously cheering, supporting, and provoking.

Having learned from Bill about the necessity of inventing locally fit curricula with openness towards emerging possibilities, I was liberated rather than restricted by my limitations in teaching strategies, math knowledge, and teaching materials—my first teaching assignment was to teach a new G12 math course without textbook. Using what I learned from Bill (e.g., his four R's—richness, relations, recursion, and rigor, the four criteria for Bill's post-modern curriculum) as guiding principles, I worked as both a student and a teacher, creating one lesson at a time. This led me to experience loops of re-learning and re-teaching: By choice and chance, I ended up teaching the G12 course six times and its related G10–11 courses several times in four years. I tinkered and redesigned course materials when re-teaching. This "reinventing the wheel" (Doll, 1981) process was educationally beneficial: it allowed me to re-learn and re-visit what I had seen before and see something new, pedagogically and mathematically. This generativity kept my spirit high in the cycles of re-teaching and re-learning. As my teaching flexibility increased and my appreciation of mathematical ideas' interconnectedness deepened, the practical space for Bill's ideas, particularly relations, enlarged. Many new teaching strategies emerged.

I included more math ideas—learned in the past, present, or future—in one lesson to show their relations. Students were introduced to categorize questions without solving them in order to encourage holistic thinking (for examples, see Luo, 2014). More lesson examples were generated in class by modifying a previous example slightly yet significantly (e.g., $y = x^2 - 2x$ becomes $y = x^2 - 2x + 1$; see Luo, 2015) to prompt students to connect different types of problems (i.e., $y = ax^2 + bx$ vs. $y = ax^2 + bx + c$). Whenever possible, I reordered textbook content (sometimes across grades) and created lessons where students could revisit general patterns in later lessons.[5]

With Bill's ideas taking more concrete practical forms and more math contents coalescing into a few core ideas, I improvised more and experienced more flow in class. Time and pace became less uniform. Bill's idea of transformative curriculum that encourages teachers and students to dance rather than march (Doll, 1993) seemed possible.

Nevertheless, recursion remained puzzling for me. Considering recursion as iterative reflection and a process of thoughts looping back to thoughts and seeing something new from what one has seen before (Luo, 2004), I implemented recursion through reflective sessions/tasks (e.g., journaling) and re-tests. I was unsatisfied, yet little did I know that I was

---

5. E.g., investigate the patterns for general functions' transformations sufficiently before studying special functions' transformations that follow the same general patterns.

already approaching a recursive curriculum while emphasizing mathematical relations.

Re-entry

My confusion with recursion and my interest in relations formed a gravitational pull for my doctoral study, in which I re-studied complexity and Bill's works. My understanding of complexity started to move beyond chaos theory into a broader field of complexity thinking.

Complexity thinking is a way of thinking and acting assuming a complex universe (Davis & Sumara, 2006). Complexity thinking studies complex systems, which include systems made of conscious or unconscious agents and the phenomena brought forth through the interactions of these agents. Thus living systems, swarm robotic systems, culture, economy, math understanding and cognition are all complex systems. Recursion, an iterative self-referencing process, is essential for creating and sustaining complex systems: a complex system's development follows a recursive path; its being is affected by its becoming (Davis & Sumara, 2006).

My renewed understanding of complexity helped me see something new in Bill's recursion. Subtly yet saintly, my focus shifted from "reflection" to "recursive," which, based on complexity thinking, suggests recursion more as a continuous generative looping back movement. The question in recursion, then, is not just how to reflect, but also how to loop back. Meanwhile, with its association to hermeneutics (Gadamer, 2004) and *currere*,[6] Bill's recursion is more than reflection: it is a continuing and repetitive reflecting, interpreting, and experiencing process (Luo, 2014). Recursion rejects the closure of interpretations and supports contingent interpretations that are personally relevant and meaningful. Recursion invites learners to make their individual learning processes unique rather than universal. Recursion's openness towards newness makes it generative rather than reproductive. Undoubtedly, recursion lies at the heart of Bill's post-modern curriculum: It is through the process of recursion that one can see relations among isolated topics and understand richer and deeper, hence recursion brings forth the other three R's in Bill's transformative curriculum (Luo, 2017).

With this new interpretation, I re-considered the curricular implications of recursion, stressing practices with a structure of looping back. Reviewing, in which students go over what they have learned before, logically came to focus (Luo, 2014). Yet, what kind of reviewing can afford recursion? More generally, how can educators design looping back processes that help students build connections and see something new

---

6. *Currere*, a notion developed by Pinar and Grumet (1976), emphasizes curriculum as a running process rather than a course to be run and calls for a learning experience that connects to learners personally.

from what they have encountered before? Or, what might a recursive curriculum be?

To answer these questions, I embarked on a hermeneutic inquiry.[7] I sought inspirations to understand reviewing, recursion and recursive curriculum differently through re-interpreting multiple texts, such as teaching documents, conversations with experienced teachers, and my personal reflection. This study turned out to teach me recursion more through offering me recursive learning experiences.

Initially I treated the teacher participants as a collective other to provoke my thinking. Thus teachers could join an individual meeting or group workshop once or multiple times, despite that each session was shaped by its prior one(s). After experiencing difficulty to see something new in a few sessions, I realized that working with the same participant(s) repeatedly is organic for a hermeneutic study of recursion—an unfamiliar word for many people. This repetition affords the building of familiarity needed to enable conversation to flow and deepen, and more importantly, possibilities for something new to emerge.

This understanding quickly found support in my work with a teacher who attended all six workshops. By the third workshop, we had repeated so much that we did something new and unplanned: we did math and got stuck together. Upon reflection, this spontaneous activity taught me so much about math, recursion and recursive curriculum that a third dimension unplanned in my workshops suddenly appeared: working back and forth between reviewing recursion and re-designing math curriculum inevitably invites the participants to review the same math ideas. Thus, focusing on math events in a workshop helped me learn both math and math curriculum. Upon realizing this, I reinterpreted the previous two workshops' texts and finally saw something new. My experience above demonstrates the affinity between hermeneutics and recursion: the generativity of a hermeneutic learning process is inseparable with its recursiveness.

My re-interpretations of my experiences or stories in this inquiry are often an answer for a call to be heard. These experiences obsessed me, without me knowing why, and demanded to be understood. This being addressed by a story or experience is where hermeneutic work starts, as "[i]t is always something that happens that awakens our interest in pursuing interpretations" (Jardine, 2015, p. 238). Through this study, I learned to listen better to my personal experiences and stories. This willingness to be led by one's personal experience and to answer its call is exactly what a *currere*-oriented curriculum promotes—one needs to make sense of one's experience and make personal experience educational. This is opposite to

---

7. The process and the results of the inquiry presented here are included in my dissertation in preparation (Luo, 2017).

making given knowledge one's own; this is treating one's experience as the beginning and the spring of one's inquiry and repeatedly going back to understand what it tries to teach. In this sense, we learn from ourselves reflexively. So being hermeneutic, recursion is inevitably *currere* oriented.

I have understood recursion differently. With the recursive learning experiences afforded by my inquiry, in math, curriculum, and even mental health, I was actually re-transformed. Now, designing towards a recursive mathematics curriculum, for both teachers and students, and for mathematical, educational, and personal growth, is clearly significant and possible.

Looping Backward and Forward, to Infinity

In the same spirit with Bill's works, my striving to envision a recursive curriculum is not to prescribe a model for teachers to follow. It is to provoke and inspire teachers to think about recursion differently and invent their locally fit curricula; it is to "seed" (Doll, 1993, p. 102) a recursive learning process.

Like his four R's, Bill's words are often concise and general. For some, they may be too condensed, thus fuzzy, and too general, thus impractical. Yet, it is in this seeming simplicity and fuzziness wherein complexity lies. Grounded in diverse cross-disciplinary research, Bill's works are so rich that they invite readers to revisit over time. It is during this revisiting that novelty might emerge. For me, the fuzziness of Bill's works, contrasting against the complexity of his works' foundations, often puzzles me enough to invite me revisiting his works. Every revisit affords me possibilities for new interpretations and implementations. In this sense, Bill's works are both theoretical and practical.

Bill's significant contributions in theorizing and complexifying curriculum cannot be overstated. For me, Bill is more than a curriculum theorist: he is a teacher, a teacher who has embodied what he teaches; he is a mentor, inspiring, and full of life. Through teaching a few big ideas thoroughly without prescribing methods, Bill has led me to a land of creativity and imagination. Bill has invited me to join his dance between simplicity and complexity. Through the recursive movements of making complexity simple and making simplicity complex, we have entered a fascinating world where boundaries[8] become heuristic and newness becomes inevitable. Most impressively, despite me being a student who seems chaotic and somewhat frustrating, Bill has cherished my complexity and patiently worked *with* me with care. Besides complexity, relations, and recursion, Bill had taught me patience and faith.

---

8. E.g., between new and old, between personal and professional, between practical and theoretical, between self and other.

Bill is also a fellow student. He has remained cheerful and excited about playing with ideas and learning along with others. He has kept the conversation going as Rorty (1980) teaches. He has convinced me that it is possible to enact complexity thinking and occasion educational experiences that can lead oneself and others to a space of infinite possibilities. Bill has kept the knowledge alive!

References

Davis, B., & Sumara, D. (2006). *Complexity and education: Inquiries into learning, teaching, and research*. Mahwah, NJ: Lawrence Erlbaum Associates Publishers.

Doll, W. (1981). The educational need to re-invent the wheel. *Educational Leadership, 39*(1), 34–35.

Doll, W. (1993). *A post-modern perspective on curriculum*. New York, NY: Teachers College Press.

Doll, W. (2005). Keeping knowledge alive. *Journal of Educational Research and Development, 6*, 27–42.

Gadamer, H. G. (2004/2013). *Truth and method* (Reprint ed.). London, UK: Bloomsbury Academic.

Jardine, D. W. (2015). On hermeneutics: "over and above our wanting and doing," In K. Tobin & S. R. Steinberg (Eds.), *Doing educational research* (2nd ed., pp. 235–254). Rotterdam: Sense Publishers.

Kauffman, S. (1995). *At home in the universe: The search for laws of self-organization and complexity*. New York, NY: Oxford University Press.

Luo, L. (2004). Letter to my sister about Doll's 4R's. *Transnational Curriculum Inquiry, 1*(1).

Luo, L. (2014). Recursion in the mathematics curriculum. *Philosophy of Mathematics Education Journal, 28*.

Luo, L. (2015). Repetition as a means of encouraging Tall's met-betores. *Delta-K, 52*(2), 15–17.

Luo, L. (2017). *Towards a recursive mathematics curriculum*. Manuscript in preparation.

Mandelbrot, B. (1967). How long is the coast of Britain? Statistical self-similarity and fractional dimension. *Science, 156*, 636–638.

Pinar, W., & Grumet, M. (1976). *Toward a poor curriculum*. Dubuque, IA: Kendall Hunt Publishing Company.

Rorty, R. (1980). *Philosophy and the mirror of nature*. Princeton, NJ: Princeton University Press.

Part III
Of Play, Praxis, and Pedagogical Grace

In Wang's (2016) text on Doll's pedagogy, not only is his pedagogy the central focus of the work due to its most arresting and recognizable "grace"—virtue, elegance, and beauty, and that which bestows beauty, charm, good will, mercy, praise, celebration, favor, esteem, etc. (*OED*, 1989)—but also *play* is highlighted as the first of the seven P's[1] of the signature pedagogy of this "Parade Child" and "King of Chaos." Of course, with laughter comes play—or in the least they are companions; and grace is a gift of God, as it were, involving unconditional love—the echo of God's laughter, Doll fond of imagining curriculum through this image of Kundera (1988) as such. Such speaks to something pleasing, uplifting, and honorable that is freely lent or given, and thus also to *gratus*, gratitude, hospitality, generosity, and the giving of thanks.

We could say, then, here, that scholars in this section—albeit certainly not limited to such—in some way or other illuminate such respecting Bill as a teacher, their teacher, seeking to describe something of the fascinating art of his teaching. While "pedagogy" historically, and even etymologically, invites a number of negative connotations, if we take it in terms of *agogos*, "leader," from *agein*, "to lead," from *ag*, to "draw out or forth, move" and *paidos*, "child," or student, as such has come to mean (*OED*, 1989); we can certainly speak of Doll's art in drawing out and forth and leading and moving students and colleagues to their deepest, broadest, most expansive potentials and possibilities. And this, oft, via play, and praxis—practice, exercise, experimentation, doing, action, activity; thoughtfully engaged. Here, play is christened, too, by reflection, recursion, reflexivity. In embedded thinking and doing—embodied thought and reflection in action—and a dance of reflective thinking and doing again and again, contemplating questions of worth respecting knowledge and living, we partake in the reconstruction of experience that is genuinely, tranformationally, dynamically educative.

---

1. See Wang (2016) and footnote 11 in Quinn's introduction in this collection for more on the seven P's of Doll's pedagogy.

104 *Part III: Of Play, Praxis, and Pedagogical Grace*

Doug McKnight reflects upon his experience of Bill Doll as a teacher, and some of the ways in which he was transformed therein and influenced in terms of his own thought and pedagogy. Here he accentuates the significance of a curriculum of hermeneutic play, of the interpretative play of language and ideas wherein infinite meanings and possibilities may be explored—as we "wander about in wonder" together, new patterns and paths—and knowledge—are born; in a social act of creation, wherein we entertain questions of worth developed in community. As inspired by Doll, he evokes Hermes for us too, mischievous messenger of the gods (in kinship with "the echo of God's laughter"; Kundera, 1988), who resists final meanings—questioning objectivity and truth, critiquing mechanisms of control, and makes possible the articulation of difference and actualization of the new. McKnight notes: "the playful interaction between teacher and student is the process by which knowledge emerges. It is a dance. And every time William Doll appeared in our classroom, Hermes appeared alongside him, each dancing with the other and inviting us to join in the play by creating our own new ways of knowing."

In "A Life with Bill Doll," Stephen S. Triche, too, contemplates the ways in which knowledge emerges through play, and by Doll's play—also via language with concepts and words—self-organizing, part and parcel of his moving curriculum beyond the limiting logic imposed by method toward a more complex, dynamic, ensemble logic: alive, relational, and transformative. Likened to jazz, this feature of Doll's pedagogy counters method's effort aimed at the shortcut, and emphasis on speed; it is a professional ethic, integrally tied to his praxis—deeply thoughtful and reflective, careful and authentically lived—as also to a patience, akin to grace by which Triche has been powerfully supported, affected, and moved: involving deep listening, faith and care, and personalized attention too.

"His thoughtfulness sustains his interpretive and reflective intelligence, intuitiveness, sensitivity, and openness to students' subjectivity. It permeates," says Jung-Hoon Jung of Bill Doll as his teacher. He speaks here, too, of Doll's commitment to play, to precision and to patterns too, in ever seeking to keep knowledge alive; as well as maintain his posture as one who is ever learning. He describes Doll, in this way, as a *susung*—who like Confucius, possesses the heart of a learner, this capacity and desire and love for learning; wherein such is integrated into one's being: one does what one teaches, one is what one teaches; and such a one demonstrates for us, too, how to study, how to be, how to be human. Doll shines forth here as *susung*, especially in a context casting a curriculum predicated on functionality and predetermined ends, awakening, and enlightening us to ethics, care, community, responsiveness, and responsibility: the significance of relationship, and of pedagogical relationships.

> The teacher is a knowledgeable other in the culture of conversation, playing-with curriculum in relation to students. The emergence of

learning occurs in the moment of chaotic play that is scientifically rigorous, richly storied, and spiritually related.

(Pratt)

Sarah Smitherman Pratt, playing with Bill Doll's pedagogical creed, focuses here on his attention to the significance of stories (and as integral to curriculum): of our relatedness together—humanizing, stories tell us, and transform (reframed ongoingly), who we are; and also of our ideas, those behind our scientific truths and understandings. In theorizing Doll's art and vision of teaching—concerning the import of self-organizing networks of relations in play, and playfulness, opening up space for the emergence of something new (neither progressive, nor linear) through which indeterminacy, reflection, and inquiry are honored; she hones in on the "S" of story in Doll's three S's (see footnote 12, Quinn, introduction), ensuing through "complex conversations." Such, she claims, is rooted in an epistemology of difference, thought, and action dependent on responsiveness to those differences that make the difference (from Bateson, 1972), wherein learning can't be determined beforehand, the introduction of something quite small can affect much, recursion is more than repetition and *poesis* than reproduction; and by which knowledge is renewed and advanced.

References

Bateson, G. (1972). *Steps to an ecology of mind: Collected essays in anthropology, psychiatry, evolution, and epistemology*. Chicago, IL: University of Chicago Press.

Kundera, M. (1988). *The art of the novel* (L. Asher, Trans.). New York, NY: Grove Press.

Oxford English dictionary (OED) (2nd ed.). (1989). (J. Simpson & E. Weiner, Eds.). Oxford, UK: Clarendon Press.

Wang, H. (2016). *From the parade child to the king of chaos: The complex journey of William Doll, teacher educator*. New York, NY: Peter Lang.

11 Learning the Play of Language
Hermeneutic Acts of Interpretation While Watching Bill Doll Dance

Douglas McKnight

In the fall of 1992, I attended my first curriculum theory class at Louisiana State University (LSU). I did not really consider curriculum as much more than a bunch of course content and information to be processed and mastered. I was confused why the word "theory" was connected to the term "curriculum." Why was there a requirement to take a doctoral course on how to organize information? Such an act was self-evident, a linear collection of facts. Right? I had a lot to learn. I was trained in cause and effect, chronologically ordered facts of historical events. Schooling taught me to accept blindly claims of objectivity and truth. Notions of "interpretation" and different "theoretical lenses" were foreign to me. I did not know it, but I was about to experience a paradigm shift. The fragile edifice of disciplinary superiority crumbled when in walked this tall, thin, gangly, bespectacled man with wispy white hair and a bow tie, a Dickensian character come to life in the halls of LSU.

He went by the name of William Doll. And he offered something that was strange yet seductive, a concept of curriculum that challenged years of schooling. Dr. Doll on that day gave me a gift, a curriculum of hermeneutic play, of playfulness, of keeping knowledge in play as opposed to being packaged and delivered as dogma. Not until later did I realize that Dr. Doll embodied an archetype that to this day guides my own thinking as a curriculum theorist—Hermes. Let me explain. Dr. Doll ambled to the front of class and held in his hand a rolled up, flag-sized, tie-dyed cloth that when unfurled revealed a colorful design of spirals within spirals, one producing another in an infinite pattern. As he lifted the cloth for the class to see, he gave a quirky laugh and uttered four words that changed everything—"This is your curriculum." Veterans of his classes smiled to each other. My brow furrowed in concern, which soon transformed into utter joy.

Doll was researching complexity (chaos) theory (1993) as a kind of post-modern curriculum framework to create favorable conditions for knowledge to emerge as a social act rather than as highly controlled form of information disposal to students. Doll used the metaphor of fractal patterns in constant motion and state of change, sensitive to any new disturbance that might shift the flow of the pattern toward something different—a new path opened to explore. The new pattern may produce new knowledge or it may die out as others thrive. That was the whole point. Not only does his curriculum theory serve as a critique of the modern curriculum, which functions as a control mechanism for information delivery and as such impoverishes the act of creation, but also approaches curriculum as a fluid framework allowing for multiple ways of understanding and knowing.

The brightly colored cloth Doll held demonstrated that a curriculum could begin with a few basic guiding principles ("play" being the most significant), if allowed to interact and change according to the rules of nature rather than by any external pressure to control the outcomes. Instead of delivering an arbitrary, intensely regulated, and scripted framework of information, Doll demonstrated how a teacher and students could play with the curriculum by beginning with a few basic concepts and combining them in as many different ways imaginable. As the process is set in motion, new patterns, new meanings from old ideas emerge, forcing students each time to reevaluate the meaning of what the patterns produce. I believe for Doll the key is for teachers and students to set aside the drudgery of dogmatic memorization and instead play with the ideas. An idea will either blossom into something new or dissipate and die if it does not hold up to the rules of the game.

As he stood in front of class holding his unfurled flag of swirling colors and patterns, he explained that modern curriculum has created a situation in which we have forgotten how to play and allow knowledge to emerge and evolve. Instead, the official curriculum of schooling in the U.S. has laid over students an oppressive blanket of rules, boring content, uninspired teaching, assessments, and high-stakes tests. We had succumbed to the desire for and delusion of "imposed control" (2002, p. 295), as opposed to emergent self-regulation that occurs as patterns—of thought, behavior, actions, etc.—developed into complex systems (Doll, 1993, 2002). Instead, the human impulse for "imposed control" led schools to measure, assess, and quantify each child to see who fit and did not fit into the acceptable, normative categories of the dominant culture. For Doll (2002), this hidden curriculum of desire for control was a modernist dream turned into a child's nightmare. Doll looked to loosen this grip by demonstrating the damage done because of the wrongheaded belief that a child would learn the desired information by imposing educational theories dependent upon Western philosophical principles of linear, developmental progress in which learning was a self-contained, individual act of remembering as opposed to a social act.

Doll applied the principles of complexity theory to illustrate how—if given the right conditions and adult guidance—curriculum would become an active rather than passive notion that encouraged the child's inherent capacity to interact with the world through basic playful curiosity.

Children want to figure the world out and more often than not, they do so together rather than alone. Modern curriculum gets in the way of this. Doll (1993, 2002) was clear that his vision of a curriculum of play was not about allowing children to be "free-range," doing whatever they wanted when they wanted, because that form of frivolous play, which could be a good thing once in a while, would eventually lead to the same result as the overly controlled curriculum. Doll's form of play was purposeful in that it was attached to a guiding principle and question provided by Herbert Spencer in the title of his 1884 book: "*What Knowledge Is of Most Worth?*" Knowledge is a moving target, popping up here and there, always partial, always unexpected, and sure to work one moment and not the next. But at the same time, knowledge was something that each community, each classroom, had to develop together in order for the community, and each individual within that community, to flourish.

I interpreted Doll's curriculum theory as providing a space for a community of children and teachers, who must be prepared to give a gentle push here and there, to create the conditions in which natural curiosity would blossom rather than wilt. In Doll's take on curriculum, as pulled from complexity theory, each classroom did not need administratively determined rules and regulations of behavior in a classroom. The classroom community would naturally self-regulate a condition in which the children and teacher would find a pattern of existing in the classroom sustained by activities that worked best for that particular class. In other words, the teacher had to be the "lead" player in the game of curriculum. For a curriculum of complexity, though, to survive the weight of the modern technocratic desire for control depended upon the teacher's understanding of the nature of language as fluid wherein meanings are constantly in play.

The significance of the play of language, which must always include the act of interpretation, in a curriculum of complexity became evident as he introduced us to the philosophy of hermeneutics. We read Hans Georg Gadamer's tome, *Truth and Method* (1989). Through the reading of Gadamer, Doll modeled for us what it meant to think hermeneutically, which ultimately helped me become aware of how language is more than a vehicle for a one-to-one correspondence between word and thing. Instead, language conceals even as it reveals and discloses possible meanings, forcing the interpreter to engage in the play of interpretation when interacting with a text as well as with other individuals. I began to realize that this act of interpretation was a product of play because it precluded any final determination of ultimate meaning and forced the interpreter to move beyond binary, either/or thinking and into both/and thinking, which was something Doll worked to help us understand. Suddenly, I could no longer think in terms of reading as an act of determining an author's meaning, but as an act in which I participate in a spirit that animates human life, what the Latin description calls *homo ludens*—man

[sic] the player, the one who plays (Huizinga, 1968). In other words, instead of treating language as something to consume, it became something with which to create (and destroy).

I became obsessed with the notion of hermeneutics as the interpretive play of language with an infinite variety of possible meanings to be explored (think infinite fractal patterns, which Dr. Doll employed effortlessly). Doll introduced me to hermeneutics and helped me learn to use a significant tool of this philosophical mode of interpretation—etymological tracing, an act of following the history of a word to see how the first identifiable impulses of describing and articulating the world shifted and changed over time. My turn to present in class was coming up quickly so I threw myself into the etymological dictionaries to not only trace out meanings of important educational terms, but to create a narrative of how I believed education should be understood. I began my task with the word "hermeneutics" as a lark (one had to begin somewhere). And it all began to fall into place: "Latinized form of Greek *hermeneutikos* of or for interpreting . . . from *hermeneuein* to interpret (foreign languages); interpret into words, give utterance to . . ., considered ultimately a derivative of Hermes, as the tutelary divinity of speech, writing, and eloquence" (www.etymonline.com/index=hermeneutic).

That is how I was introduced to Hermes. And this is how I came to believe Dr. Doll had been joyfully dancing with Hermes from the beginning. Hermes is the ultimate player, the creator of language and messenger of the Gods. Hermes understands that for humans to survive and even flourish, language can never be monolithic. Instead, language is ambiguous and resists any attempt to pin down one final meaning or understanding. Humanity is forced to seek understanding and to reconcile the difference at the heart of language that creates tension and pushes meaning into new territories. While this condition of language makes communication a challenge, it also enables the experience and articulation of difference, the creation of something new, the destruction of something old, as well as the possibility of nuances being revealed in a way that can prevent dogma from condemning a teacher and student to impoverished thinking and a dulled humanity easily manipulated and controlled (which apparently is what is taking place in the current xenophobic, nationalistic, fearful, and hateful political milieu of the U.S.). For Doll, which of these potentialities language reveals depends upon the human capacity to make connections across seemingly unrelated concepts and discourses. Dr. Doll's gift to us was the desire to wander about in wonder and willingly set aside any preconceived notions of what is and what is not possible. Doll (2006, p. 231) borrowed a quote from Milan Kundera (1988) to reveal this spirit of openness: "There exists a fascinating imaginative realm, born of the echo of God's laughter where no one owns the truth and everyone has the right to be understood."

The beauty and frustration of hermeneutic etymological play at the time was that once you begin to trace the branches of a term you realize that for every branch you identify, four more appear. Language is an infinite regress with no original word or thought except recognition of difference. Hermeneutically, each word and concept contains traces of all others, leading to a basic hermeneutic principle that in the particular is the whole and in the whole is the particular. That is what makes the tracing of the term "knowledge" (as I began to try to make sense of that question, "What knowledge is of most worth?") so illuminating and illustrative of how language not only makes play possible but is the ultimate field of play in which one hunts down connection after connection to build some meaningful form. To do so is a visualization of what Doll meant in using complexity theory as a basis for curriculum. While the term "knowledge" tends to indicate something permanent, unmoving, ahistorical, even transcendent, some of the antecedents challenge such assumptions.

In fact, while tracing the etymology I stumbled upon a trace of the term that made me shake my head in wonderful amusement and truly understand what it means to make connections between unlikely and even dissimilar conditions:

> Knowledge (nol'ej),n., knaw leche . . . knaw.lache, etc., knaw + -leche, assibilated form of -leke, KIcel.-leikr, -leiki = Sw.-lek, . . . -lác, in wed-lác, wedlock . . . identical with läc, play, gift: The term -leche became assimilated through -lache, to the suffix -age. 1. The state of being or of having to become.
>
> <div align="right">(<i>Century Dictionary</i>, 1899)</div>

I read that to say that knowledge is a form of play, a gift, a state of being and becoming. God's laughter echoes loudly as Hermes plays with words and helps us understand. Hermes disrupts any binary, something the Greeks had to acknowledge even as their philosophy wrongheadedly imposed on Western thought a foundation of binary thinking from which we create categories of existence, then privilege one category over the other. One of the more problematic binaries created that is being challenged mightily in the present age is male/female, a socio-cultural appointment rather than a biological essence.

For instance, the Greeks placed the male principle, along with all the qualities attached to that principle, within Apollo, God of music, poetry, art, medicine, sun, light, and knowledge. Apollo is all about rationality and reason. Aphrodite and Demeter were deemed to encompass the most female of Greek principles, representing nurturing and caring, but also irrationality, lust, duplicity, and so forth. As inheritors of the Greek mindset, we forced those—society has determined male or female to function within one principle or another, even if our personalities and inclinations favor other characteristics. For instance, if a teacher who is deemed female by the dominant culture, yet possesses and is most comfortable in enacting characteristics that are male, attempts to deny her sense of herself and instead attempts to appropriate qualities at the other end of the gender spectrum, because society expects the teacher to act according to the gender assigned at birth, she is left somehow to navigate the inevitable tensions that will certainly result in a kind of psychological damage and impoverished existence within the classroom. Simply, she will become fractured and fall into despair because she believes she is one thing and is forced to act as another. However, the Greeks offered a third way, if you will, that institutional schooling has forgotten to include. In other words, to have to make such a choice is a false act.

Greek Mythology inevitably recognized this and made space for something different, something "other." In the Greek and Roman paean of gods, each is designated male or female, except one—Hermes, who played with and made fun of the arbitrariness of society's gendered norms. Everything about Hermes is in *play* and *playful*, but not in the sense of silliness. Hermes' play has a purpose. Hermes has multiple roles—prankster, one who guides through difficult terrains, creator and translator of language, as well as the god who delivers important messages. In fact, Hermes' first act was the prank of sewing such ambiguity and difference into the very structure of language (already a contradictory notion given structure must depend on a center that exists arbitrarily despite the metaphysical claims of structure allowing for no play but only finality). This ambiguity has been a nagging frustration for Western philosophers and scientists for millennia. However, without this play, without the space for movement and change, there would be no disciplines, no curriculum theory, no new and interesting ways of concepts coming together to creating surprising patterns and formations.

Hermes disrupts all that is conventional, all that attempts to control, all that attempts to claim final knowledge as well as exposes that no metaphysical center can hold, organize, and give structure to a viable certainty. In terms of gender qualities, Hermes does not care whether humans locate/divide human capacities into male or female. For Hermes, all qualities apply to all humans. Hermes (whose offspring was Hermaphrodite, of course) acts upon what humans designate as a feminine principle when it serves the circumstance and vice versa. More accurately, Hermes operates within the spaces between, where ambiguity (Latin root *ambigere*, "to dispute about" and "to wander about, lead about") reigns and disrupts any decision (Latin, *decidere*—marking off) that there is one side or the other. Simply, Hermes knows how to play with all of the possible voices that identify us as living, social animals who gather into tribes and communities. Hermes draws upon the ambiguity (and hence, the play) to teach humans that the world is more complex than any one method or perspective suggests, perpetually frustrating those who desire dogma and a monolithic ideology to give them a sense of control.

That is why Hermes made play the beginning principle rather than a fixed point of reference, a way of thinking that Doll spent so much time modeling. Hermes is the ultimate teacher who constructs a multiple choice test in which all answers are right and all are wrong, with the student and teacher left to negotiate what meaning will prevail in that moment in time and space. Hermes understands that the playful interaction between teacher and student is the process by which knowledge emerges. It is a dance. And every time William Doll appeared in our classroom, Hermes appeared alongside him, each dancing with the other and inviting us to join in the play by creating our own new ways of knowing.

References

Century Dictionary: Encyclopedic lexicon of the English language (Vol. 4). (1899). New York, NY: Century Publishing.

Doll, W. (1993). *A post-modern perspective on curriculum.* New York, NY: Teachers College Press.

Doll, W. (2002). Curriculum and the concepts of control. In W. E. Doll & N. Gough (Eds.), *Curriculum visions* (pp. 295–323). New York, NY: Peter Lang.

Doll, W. (2006). Looking forward. In D. Trueit (Ed.), *Pragmatism, postmodernism, and complexity theory: The "fascinating imaginative realm" of William E. Doll, Jr.* (pp. 228–231). New York, NY: Routledge.

Gadamer, H.-G. (1989). *Truth and method* (rev. ed.). New York, NY: Continuum.

Huizinga, J. H. (1968). *Homo Ludens: A study of the play element in culture.* Boston, MA: Beacon Press.

Kundera, M. (1988). *The art of the novel.* New York, NY: Grove press.

On-line etymological dictionary. Retrieved from www.etymonline.com. (*hermeneutic*, www.etymonline.com/index.php?allowedin_frame=0&search=hermeneutic).

Spencer, H. (1884). *What knowledge is of most worth?* New York, NY: J. B. Alden Publishers.

12 A Life With Bill Doll
A Journey in Praxis, Patience, and Play

Stephen S. Triche

As I dwell upon my life with Bill Doll, for whom I have a deep affection and owe so very much, my first thought is: *How do I unpack twenty-five years of personal and professional experiences as well as love and affection?* So many things come to mind above and beyond the academic categories of pragmatism, post-modernism and complexity—things like "Friday Friends" and Bergamo, Curriculum Camp and the parties, method and Peter Ramus, Wittgenstein and history, his teaching and the dissertation process, and much more.

Those of us who love Bill Doll know of his love for word play. In this essay on his influence on my life and work, I will focus on three P's: praxis, patience, and play. I believe that Bill Doll's praxis (for Doll, his scholarship and teaching practices always appear to be thoughtful and reflective), as both a teacher and a scholar is best described by his "pedagogic creed" (Doll, 1993b) in which he asks students to join him in a close community of learners that calls upon his students not to naively accept the teacher's authority. The teacher reciprocates by agreeing to be readily confrontable by the students. By so doing, students agree to join the teacher in reflective inquiry. They agree to reveal their struggles with new ideas to one another, and, most importantly, to suspend their natural tendency to disbelief of these new ideas as their taken-for-granted assumptions are challenged. I have included a version of Bill Doll's "pedagogic creed" in my various syllabi during my entire university teaching career. I have worked hard to live up to it, sometime succeeding, but often failing. It has also served as a basis for my own scholarship, as I have attempted to question taken-for-granted assumptions about curriculum history and curriculum theory.

Bill Doll's praxis, too, is fundamentally linked to his patience as a teacher and a scholar. There is no doubt that, as my professor and mentor, he exercised great patience with me. As such, his patience has had a profound impact on my own relationship with my own students. I try to take time, both in and out of class, to be with them and to listen to their situations. Because of Bill Doll's example, I tend to be empathetic to the needs of my students, sometimes overly so. For example, my due dates for assignments are less deadlines than datelines. I don't penalize late work, as long as the student is communicating with me about why she or he is struggling. At Nicholls State, where I teach, we have over seventy percent of first-generation college attendees. As such, many of my students do not arrive enculturated into an academic culture. Whenever I meet with advisees for the first time, I ask them to tell me about themselves, where they grew up, their hobbies or what they are reading, if anything. Not only do I want to know their plans for teaching, but their hopes, their ideas and their passions. This is what I like to call, "being Bill." Many live at home where they continue to have family responsibilities. They also work, often at full time jobs, in order to pay for school. To their credit, few of my students attend college on student loans. More than a few care for their own children as single mothers (sometimes for two or more as a nineteen- or twenty-year-old undergraduate). It is difficult for me not to have patience for their non-academic needs, especially given Bill Doll's example of patience with my own idiosyncrasies.

As Bill Doll's "pedagogic creed" asks, I work at suspending my disbelief when students present their ideas and interpretations in class discussions and in their writings. This is an important source for my own continued education as a teacher and curriculum theorist. I dislike lecturing. I am interested instead in my students' ideas concerning the topics and readings in the class. As such, I organize my classes so I obtain feedback from students on the readings. This, then, enables me to talk about their ideas in light of the concepts we are covering. I have learned, perhaps surprisingly to some, that it is important that teachers listen to students to see how they are using concepts and ideas in their discussions so they can use their students' discourses to teach. Additionally, I also learned from Bill Doll that students' ideas can be a great source of new ways of thinking about and looking at a situation, especially when it comes to everyday teaching practices occurring in schools.

In his scholarship, too, Bill Doll's patience has influenced me. He carefully and thoughtfully works through ideas, asking for constant feedback from both colleagues and students. One of the most biting criticisms he can give to another's work is that a person is not a "careful scholar."

This would include his ongoing critique of *method* and his attempt to offer a way beyond the constraints on teaching imposed by method (Doll, 2002/2012a). It is this work on method and on method's "inventor," Peter Ramus, a 16th-century arts master at the University of Paris, that influenced me to study the medieval art of dialectic (logic). Ramus's use of curriculum from John Calvin's use of "curriculum vitae," to describe a course of study transformed formal education into an intellectual "shortcut" (Doll, 2002/2012a; Triche & McKnight, 2004). Ramus scandalized the academic world of the 16th century by refining the trivium and the art of dialectic (logic) as he tried to make teaching of the liberal arts course of study in the Middle Ages more efficient. Ramus's purpose in making the study of the trivium more efficient was his desire to move students through the trivium more quickly. In so doing, he turned over the five-hundred-year tradition of the liberal arts course of study in medieval logic. Out of his refinement of the art of dialectic, Ramus would eventually develop his method as a way of arranging evidence into an argument. Through this process Ramus developed method, first as a form of deduction, which he would later merge with a form of induction that became a single ladder of logical method (Triche & McKnight, 2004; Triche, 2009).

It was Ramus's refinement of the art of dialectic into method that led to his use of the concept of curriculum. Method enabled Ramus to depict the medieval art of dialectic in the form of a logical diagram (the concept map of today) that could depict any discourse from a general concept to its specific example and back again. One such diagram Ramus created was a map of Cicero's academic life, to which Ramus applied the term "curriculum," using it as an example of a shortcut to a course of study in the liberal arts. It is in this way that curriculum becomes a condensed organizational form of education born of method's limited logic (Triche & McKnight, 2004).

In this way, Bill Doll's critique of method is also a critique of Ramus's use of the concept of curriculum, and the changes to formal schooling that it wrought. While the reconceptualization of curriculum theory has generally focused on the first half of the term curriculum in the appearance of *"currere"* (Pinar, Reynolds, Slattery, & Taubman, 1995), Bill Doll's critique of method can also be understood as a critique of curriculum, and in particular the Latin suffix, *"culum"* (which is a diminutive or limiting modifier), the second half of the term *curriculum*. I have only come to fully understand the nature of this critique recently because Bill Doll does not make this critique explicit in his work. It is, instead, implied in his critique of method and of Peter Ramus.

It is generally accepted that Ramus's use of the term curriculum as a way to describe Cicero's academic life was an adaptation of John Calvin's use of curriculum vitae to describe a believer's life of coming to salvation. But Ramus was not a Calvinist. And while he may well have been aware of Calvin's use of curriculum, it could be legitimately suggested that Ramus, who has been described as one of the most important Latin language scholars of his day, must have fully understood the etymology of the Latin suffix *"culum,"* and, thus, how he was applying the term curriculum to describe an abridged and more efficient (at least in his mind) course of study in the liberal arts *trivium* of the late Renaissance. From this perspective, curriculum is a logic born of method and always will be, by its nature, a limited way of understanding schooling as an educational enterprise.

Much of Bill Doll's work has been about moving curriculum beyond the limited logic imposed by teaching method. His use of post-modernism influenced my own work in curriculum history by showing me that any history of curriculum needs to bring together a complexity of thought within which a curriculum is situated. He helped me recognize that the dynamic nature of curriculum has to be presented within an "ensemble logic" (Janik & Toulmin, 1973). It should not be organized linearly or from a singular theoretical perspective.

What I took away from Bill Doll's post-modernism, including his work on complexity, is that he is trying to situate curriculum thinking within a complex system of concepts organized around ensemble logic. It is this ensemble logic that imbues curriculum with an alternative to the logic that was born out of Ramus's method. Furthermore, I would suggest that Bill Doll's curriculum theory is no longer a theory of curriculum as such because it is an attempt to jettison the educational shortcut by which schooling has been constrained for the last five hundred years. What is needed, then, is a new term to describe what and how we educate other than curriculum. What this term could be is beyond this work. I would suggest that any new concept be framed by Bill Doll's four R's: richness, recursion, relations, and rigor (Doll, 1993a). Using his four R's, Doll critiques both method and curriculum by asking us to see schooling not as a shortcut or racetrack, which organizes the school curriculum along a logical ladder. Instead, he asks us to keep any educational situation as a whole in our view in order to see any given teaching situation in all of its complexity. This ensemble perspective allows us to see the richness of the existing relationships. Such a way of seeing requires patient and thoughtful study that avoids having to pull the situation apart in order for it to be analyzed. This is a way of seeing teaching and learning that promotes a rigor of multiple connections, thereby optimizing the opportunity for, what Doll (1993a) describes, as the "playing with concepts" (p. 182).

From Bill Doll's perspective, the concept of play would have to be included in any new term that we might want to invent to replace the term of curriculum (Doll, 1979, 2003/2012c, 2005/2012b). That the concept of play would be a key aspect of Bill Doll's praxis should not be surprising to anyone who knows him or has read his work. Moreover, his sense of play has certainly influenced my scholarship as well. Play is a most serious aspect of Bill Doll's professional ethic. His sense of play can be found in his own self-description. The example, I believe, that best demonstrates this is the way he identifies his religion as being Catholic, but always adds that his Catholicism is a bit heretical as well. For instance, when he goes to mass, he goes on Monday rather than Sunday. His sense of the heretical, if you will, never allows Bill Doll to leave any idea alone. He is always, as he says, "playing with" ideas (Doll, 2005/2012b). This is the core of his post-modernism, of his sense of complexity. As such, his praxis is grounded in what I have described as a "dialect of play" (Triche, 2009) that became more complex over time as he moved, always non-linearly and recursively, back and forth between and among Dewey, Piaget, Bruner, Jenks, Prigogine, Whitehead, Serres, and Wittgenstein, so forth and so on, as each philosopher and theorist informs, reinforces and critiques the other. It is in his use of so many scholars and their manifold theories and philosophies that we see Bill Doll's use of an "ensemble logic" at work. It is a logic of both causal and concomitant relationships that play with and play off one another as do jazz musicians.

For Bill Doll, play is the ground out of which knowing emerges. While the scope and sequence of most school curriculum is based upon the belief that learning moves from the known to the unknown, this cannot be true of first learning. It is through play, both solitary and with others, that children construct their first knowledge of the world. Through play children engage in a rudimentary form of induction that can be understood as a "natural dialectic" (Triche, 2009). It is from this natural "dialectic of play" that children generalize about the world—their immediate environment. This natural dialectic is an example of an ensemble logic at work as it includes not only sensual experience, but language development as well.

Children at play is a communal action—a natural praxis—because it requires children to engage in extemporaneous thought and reason. There are no rules in this form of play other than those that the children create for themselves. Strictly speaking, the knowledge of how to play is not learned because it is not taught in a formal setting; it is, instead, acquired by way of its natural dialect. No one would generally tell a child for instance: "play with the box this way." It emerges within and through a self-organizing environment, rather than an environment created for instruction—an environment that builds wisdom as well as knowledge.

Doll's concept of play has offered curriculum theory a way of thinking about philosophical practices outside of Aristotle's concepts of: *techne'* (the study of making or craftmanship), *praxis* (the study of doing or action), and *theoria* (the contemplation of truth) (Aristotle, 350 BC/1952). Doll raises play to a serious philosophical construct. A dialectic of play is both impractical and nontechnical, engaging in an open-ended, generative activity related to the unrefined induction presented by a synoptic way of seeing-as—an inexact, pragmatic, momentary, and contextualized holistic way of understanding that questions not only modern philosophical theories but pedagogical practices as well (Triche, 2009). Let us call this philosophical concept *paizo* from the ancient Greek term for play. This form of play cannot be methodized. Nor can there be a theory of play because a theory carries with it a set of practices that serves correctness in using the theory. Play cannot be technologized because it cannot be systematically planned for or implemented. How does a teacher write a lesson plan for looking at clouds or playing with a box without fundamentally altering the very nature of the activity? The imaginative and creative aspect of the activity?

If we try to live Bill Doll's "pedagogic creed," we will never stop searching and playing with our theories and practices. Just as important, as teachers, we will never stop getting our students to stop searching and playing with ideas as well. Through play, teaching praxis is also patient. It stops, if only momentarily, the rush toward the test because it does not require students to get the "right" answer straight away. The teacher has to wait for students to acquire new ways of knowing at their own pace and in their own time. It requires the teacher to have a different type of presence in the classroom. Teaching can move away from the narrowness of "effective" practice (as defined by the test) and once again reclaim a sense of good teaching. Good teaching and good scholarship has been at the center of my life with Bill Doll as he consistently seeks to avoid what Whitehead famously described as "inert ideas" (Whitehead (1929/1967; Doll, 2005/2012b). Instead, Bill Doll has shown me that good teaching deepens upon good scholarship by helping both faculty and students create new ways of knowing and new ways of seeing by presenting the world through new similes that promote learning that refreshes the soul.

References

Aristotle. (1952). Nicomachean ethics. In R. M. Hutchinson (Ed. & Chief), *Great books of the western world* (No. 9). Chicago, IL: Encyclopedia Britannica. (Original work published in 350 BC)

Doll, W. (1979). Play and mastery: A structuralist view. *Journal of Curriculum Theorizing*, 2(1), 209–226.

Doll, W. (1993a). *A post-modern perspective on curriculum*. New York, NY: Teachers College Press.

Doll, W. (1993b). Curriculum possibilities in a "post"-future. *Journal of Curriculum & Supervision*, 5(4), 272–292.

Doll, W. (2002). Ghosts and the curriculum. In W. E. Doll & N. Gough (Eds.), *Curriculum visions* (pp. 23–70). New York, NY: Peter Lang.

Doll, W. (2012a). Beyond methods. In D. Trueit (Ed.), *Pragmatism, post-modernism, and complexity theory: The "fascinating imaginative realm" of William E. Doll, Jr.* (pp. 81–97). New York, NY: Routledge. (Original work published in 2002)

Doll, W. (2012b). Keeping knowledge alive. In D. Trueit (Ed.), *Pragmatism, post-modernism, and complexity theory: The "fascinating imaginative realm" of William E. Doll, Jr.* (pp. 111–119). New York, NY: Routledge. (Original work published in 2005)

Doll, W. (2012c). Modes of thought. In D. Trueit (Ed.), *Pragmatism, post-modernism, and complexity theory: The "fascinating imaginative realm" of William E. Doll, Jr.* (pp. 103–110). New York, NY: Routledge. (Original work published in 2003)

Janik, A., & Toulmin, S. (1973). *Wittgenstein's Vienna*. New York, NY: Simon and Schuster.

Pinar, W., Reynolds, W. M., Slattery, P., & Taubman, P. M. (1995). *Understanding curriculum: An introduction to the study of historical and contemporary discourses.* New York, NY: Peter Lang.

Triche, S. (2009). *Reconceiving curriculum: An historical approach, using Wittgenstein's later philosophy to disrupt the Ramist methodological underpinnings of the modern school curriculum.* Saarbruken, Germany: VDM Verlag Dr. Muller Aktiengesellschaft & Co. KG.

Triche, S., & McKnight, D. (2004). The quest for method: The legacy of Peter Ramus. *History of Education, 33*(1), 39–54.

Whitehead, A. (1967). *The aims of education.* New York, NY: The Free Press. (Original work published in 1929)

13 An Extraordinary Pedagogical Figure
Bill Doll as a *Susung*

Jung-Hoon Jung

Not only in Korea, as I have experienced, but also in the U.S., where I have studied, education has been suffering from curriculum development discourses predicated primarily on functionality. While the two contexts carry different historical and cultural backgrounds—Hakbeolism in South Korea (see Jung, 2016) and Tyler's rationale and others in the U.S. (see Pinar, 2015)—what the educational systems in the two nations have in common is that they have been predominantly systematized, objectified, and today, virtualized. This pseudo-education starts with "predetermined and externally imposed ends" (Doll, 1972, p. 309) and ends with assessment. In this condition teachers become scapegoats and teaching becomes implementation. In the worst case, the classroom becomes bad theater. Teachers in Florida, for instance, are told to "stay to a script . . ., to teach the exact same thing in every single classroom" (Hernandez, 2016, para. 10). I am indescribably sorry for them.

It is more timely than ever, I think, that we, educators and teachers, reaffirm our ethical conviction that we must provide our beloved students with educational experiences that help them navigate through, and hopefully find their own ways of engaging with, the world. To do so requires us to raise questions about what teaching and what being a teacher means under this tyranny of standardization, corporatization, and virtualization and how we can resist the dehumanization process of pseudo-education. I am amazingly fortunate to have been engaged with an extraordinary teacher of our time, one with unfailing excitement, generosity, hospitality, and thoughtfulness—William E. Doll, Jr. In this chapter I juxtapose his being as a teacher, narrated through my autobiographical stories with the Korean concept of *susung*, which I studied in Confucius' teaching, and relationships with his students.

Susung is a Korean concept that can be translated in English as *teacher, mentor*, or *advisor*. The concept carries significant historical connotations with regard to its association with Confucianism, whose ideas have sustained the ideals of education in Korea (Chi, 2011). In *The Book of Rites*,[1]

---

1. *The Book of Rites*, also called *Liji*, is a collection of texts that describes the social forms, administration, and ceremonial rites of the Zhou dynasty. *Li* means all the traditional forms that provided a standard of conduct (Legge, 1967).

a susung is defined as "a person who teaches, enlightens, or awakens one to *de* (virtue, ethics, morality)." *De* is about how to be a human being. Thus, a susung is a person who provides teaching (or learning opportunities) for reaching or achieving *de*. In this sense, *susung* has the rather broad meaning of anyone who leads others to better lives. Confucius, who is worshiped as the Model Teacher for Ten Thousand Ages, said that a "susung is not an exclusive or fixed figure" (Chi, 2011, p. 19). In this sense, it is possible for one to have multiple susungs, not limited to those in institutional structures. Susung as a concept expresses a certain kind of learner agency that allows potential susungs to be other students in one's class, friends, family members, and even one's own students. Yet the concept of susung should not be understood as undermining the centrality of the teacher in education: instead, it expresses the significance of pedagogical relationships between teachers and students.

Pedagogy of Thoughtfulness

With his white hair reflecting the light of the classroom, Bill Doll stood near the door for a moment looking at each of us one by one with a serious gaze. Then he said, "HELLO! Let's make a circle." So we did. After explaining the goals and structure of the course, Bill asked us what we wanted to study. We spent half of the first class talking about who we were and what we were interested in. Bill watched attentively, listened actively, and carefully formed questions for clarification and elaboration. Bill's way of being in the conversation can be conceived as what Ted Aoki calls "pedagogical thoughtfulness" (Aoki, 1992, p. 196). Neither a science nor a behavioral code, it cannot be taught formally; it is an intuitive sense of doing and being in concrete personal embodiment. Bill Doll's thoughtfulness, combined with his wholehearted presence, makes personal growth possible. His thoughtfulness sustains his interpretive and reflective intelligence, intuitiveness, sensitivity, and openness to students' subjectivity. It permeates the classroom, though not necessarily in speech or action. The energy of thoughtfulness expressed through one's genuine being reaches far beyond verbal exchanges. It works as a kind of invitation for student disclosures, which makes the classroom conversation authentic and, most importantly for this section, it is what "[keeps] knowledge alive" (Doll, 2005, p. 27).

In "Keeping Knowledge Alive," Doll (2005) tackles the biggest challenge educators and curricularists face today: that the knowledge we expound is "dead, inert, useless, lifeless, barren, and full of mental dry rot" when it is "disconnected, atomistic, isolated" (p. 28). It is inert when it is not related to "the practicalities of life, an individual's own interests, and to the field in which they exist" (p. 28). Doll elaborates what teaching and learning are through Whitehead's triumvirate of romance, precision, and generalization—in Doll's words these are "play, precision, and patterns (or principles)" (p. 39)—which intertwine and are continuously interrelated. I personally have experienced and observed multiple times how the triumvirate plays out in Doll's teaching, which he has articulated in his academic work. He seriously studies the content he teaches, plays with the knowledge, and helps students find connections (or patterns) between the content and students' lived experiences, thoughts, and imaginations.

What Confucius says about being a teacher and how a master teaches in *The Book of Rites* provides thoughtful and useful contents for us to think about what it means to be a teacher. About the *de* of a susung, the virtue of being a teacher, Confucius said:

> He who gives (only) the learning supplied by his memory in conversations is not fit to be a master. Is it not necessary that he should hear the questions (of his pupils)? Yes, but if they are not able to put questions, he should put subjects before them. If he do so, and then they do not show any knowledge of the subjects, he may let them alone.
> (Chinese, 2006–2017a)

In the same chapter about teaching is the following:

> When a master (or a susung) knows what makes teaching successful, and what causes it to fail, he can become a teacher of others. Thus in his teaching, he leads and does not pull; he strengthens and does not discourage; he opens the way but does not lead the learner to the end without the learner's own effort. Leading and not pulling produces harmony. Strengthening and not discouraging makes attainment easy. Opening the way and not leading to the end makes the learner thoughtful. He who produces such harmony, easy attainment, and thoughtfulness may be pronounced a skillful teacher.
> (Chinese, 2006–2017b)

What Doll shares with being a teacher in *Liji* is a teacher's care for his or her students along with understanding the students, sensitivity to what goes on in students' lives, and the ability to make pedagogical decisions and judgments. Pedagogical thoughtfulness means delivering knowledge without forceful imposition, guiding without coercion, and strengthening without disheartening. Such teaching is rare. Of course, there is a risk in this pedagogical thoughtfulness, the risk that a teacher might fail to identify what students need, fail to catch an appropriate moment for intervention, or fail to notice something valuable in students. Yet it is a necessary risk, perhaps a "beautiful risk" (Biesta, 2013) that lies between our teaching and students' learning. This necessary risk, a space that is not manageable, controllable, foreseeable, or measurable, should be filled with pedagogical thoughtfulness, our trust in students, and our care and love for them.

Pedagogy of Being a Learner

The reading materials for my four courses with Bill Doll (in one, I was a student and for three, a teaching assistant or TA) were always different. Although there were quite a few "returning students" who had been "captured" by his teaching, perhaps a more important reason is that Bill wanted to remain interested, curious, and excited about the materials he taught. Institutionally, Bill Doll was the instructor, but intellectually, he was also a student in the course. The class participants were all asked to write reflections on the weekly readings, and Bill unfailingly wrote his reflections and shared them with us. Not only was it a way to teach his thoughts about the course materials, his reflections also taught us how strongly he wanted to remain a learner.

In the *Analects of Confucius* (Eno, 2012), the word *learning* (學) appears at least sixty-four times. Confucius proudly says, "In a town of ten households, there will surely be one who is as loyal and trustworthy as I. But there will be none who loves learning as much!" (p. 23). Confucius also says to love learning and to defend the good *dao* (道, the evolved moral and cultural patterns of the past eras of sage governance) until death (Eno, 2012, p. 38). Confucius teaches us how important learning is for a teacher: "A person who can bring new warmth to the old while understanding the new is worthy to take as a teacher" (Eno, 2012, p. 6). The desire and ability to be a learner, for Confucius, is a necessary part of a teacher's character. Learning, for Confucius, is not merely obtaining or regurgitating knowledge or skills; it includes living aligned with what is learned, as he explains with regard to *junzi*, an ideally ethical and capable person:

> A *junzi* [君子] is not concerned that food fill his belly; he does not seek comfort in his residence. If a person is apt in conduct and cautious in speech, stays near those who keep to the *do* and corrects himself thereby, he may be said to love learning.
>
> (Eno, 2012, p. 3)

Confucius was especially ashamed of those whose words did not align with their actions, with their knowledge. Confucius was deeply worried about failing to apply his learning into his being and living. Learning for him was a way to become a *junzi*, one who loves learning not for its functionality, from which education in many places around the world has suffered, but for the intrinsic value of learning that may guide one to be a *junzi*. A susung struggles to be a *junzi* through learning. Being an example of a permanent learner, an irreducibly important quality of Doll's teaching, is scarce in institutions where students become customers and teachers become suppliers. In my experience, Bill Doll always expresses his strong desire to learn from the texts and from the students as well. He teaches how to study by making himself an example of a learner.

Pedagogy of Caring Relationships

As time passed and the relationships among individuals in Bill's courses developed, a sense of caring emerged among the members. Sharing professional and private, often highly sensitive, parts of our lives, we became intimately acquainted with one another. As the relationships grew, the members truly cared for one another. Of course such relationships cannot be attributed solely to Bill Doll nor am I convinced that they were the result of his direct instruction. I think the students sensed and responded to how Bill Doll treated them—not as consumers of the course, but as family members about whose development and well-being he truly cared. Bill Doll and Donna Trueit lived on Victoria Island, which meant that the trip to the UBC campus took more than six hours, and they had to leave their house before 6 a.m. for Friday's classes. However, the fatigue he may have felt from traveling failed to weaken his enthusiasm in teaching. Before class started, Bill Doll usually met with a couple of students, sometimes individually, and gave individual advice.

During the class and afterward, he was always available for questions, insights or reflections that enabled the members of the course to stay constantly connected, and not the virtual connectedness that is often promoted by the internet and cell phones; these exchanges always carried the "orality" (Pinar, 2011, p. 176) of the individuals. If Nel Noddings had observed Bill's teaching, I believe that she would have described it as a "pedagogy of caring." The sense of belonging and connectedness, I argue, planted the sense of caring and family within the relationships of the class members. Molly Quinn, the editor of this volume, has confirmed that I am hardly alone in believing this: in her email inviting me to this exciting project, she said, "Any kindreds of Bill's are kindreds of mine." "I agree, Molly." The power of Bill Doll's being overcame the institutional and geographical limitations. The relationships developed through his efforts made the class a familial learning community.

Lee and Lee (2011) praise the relationship between Confucius and Yan Hui (顔回), one of Confucius' notable students. They describe the situation when Confucius and his group were in danger in Kuang (匡) village because the people of the village misunderstood Confucius, believing him to be their enemy. At that time Yan Hui fell behind the group, and Confucius was much worried about him. When Yan Yui finally rejoined them, Confucius said, "I thought you had died." Yan Yui said, "While you are alive, Master, how would I dare to die?" (Lee & Lee, 2011, p. 54). Lee and Lee (2011) understand that their relationship went beyond the teacher-student relationship to that of father and son. Yan Hui considered Confucius not only a teacher, but also his father, whose blood he shared. And Confucius also considered Yan Yui his son, to whom he had given birth. When Yan Yui died, Confucius' followers said, "Your grief is excessive!" "Is it excessive?" replied Confucius. "If I am not to mourn bitterly for him, for whom should I mourn?" (Lee & Lee, 2011, p. 55). Confucius grieved because he was not able to look after Yan Hui as a son.

I am writing this chapter in the small city of Sacheon near the southern coast of South Korea, thousands of miles from Victoria Island. While Bill Doll and I cannot talk as much as we did when we lived closer, my sense of connectedness with him never decreases; it gets stronger as my desire to be with him grows. I cannot prove this connectedness scientifically, but I argue that I truly feel it and I am together with him. The fact that he was there and he prayed for my well-being reminds me of the caring relationship between a susung and a student.

In this chapter, I have attempted to think about what a good teacher, a susung, looks like by studying two pedagogical figures, one who lived thousands of years ago in the East; one who just recently was living in the West. The three aspects of Bill Doll's teaching (pedagogy of thoughtfulness, pedagogy of being a learner, pedagogy of caring relationships) are, however, illustrative and cannot be instructive guidelines for the everyday practices of teachers. I do not intend to mimic the characteristics of Confucius and Bill Doll as teachers. Instead, I want to—and suggest that you—think about what teaching truly is, as an effort to reorient ourselves to overcoming the functionality-oriented notions of our profession.

Thinking of a good teacher I have had, and you have had, and allowing him or her to be present in front of you can be a way of becoming the kind of teacher we want to be, and need to be. Yes, there are lists of qualifications, characteristics, and moral and behavioral codes for teachers. But, we should try to remember the immeasurable, sometimes indescribable mode of being a teacher that memorable teachers in our lives have shown us. Sometimes it goes beyond institutional obligations and confines. Under the tyranny of standardization, corporatization, cybertization, and accountability, thinking about what it means to be a susung becomes our professional and ethical obligation—for us, for our students, and for the education we care about.

References

Aoki, T. T. (1992). Layered voices of teaching: The uncannily correct and the elusively true. In W. F. Pinar & W. M. Reynolds (Eds.), *Understanding curriculum as phenomenological and deconstructed text*. New York, NY: Teachers College Press.

Biesta, G. J. (2013). *The beautiful risk of education*. Boulder, CO: Paradigm Publishers.

Chi, C. H. (2011). The position of teachers and the desirable image of teachers as seen through traditional cultures. *The Journal of Korean Elementary Education, 22*(2), 15–32.

Chinese text project. (2006–2017a). Dictionary. Confucianism -> Liji -> Xue Ji -> 9. Retrieved from http://ctext.org/dictionary.pl?if=en&id=10109

Chinese text project. (2006–2017b). Confucianism -> Liji -> Xue Ji -> 14. Retrieved from http://ctext.org/dictionary.pl?if=en&id=10107

Doll, W. (1972). A methodology of experience: An alternative to behavioral objectives. *Educational Theory, 22*(3), 309–324.

Doll, W. (2005). Keeping knowledge alive. *Journal of Educational Research and Development 1*(1), 27–42.

Eno, R. (2012). *The analects of Confucius: An online teaching translation.* Bloomington, IN: Indiana University.

Hernandez, L. (2016, February 1). Florida's teachers stressed out. *Miami Herald.* Retrieved from http://wlrn.org/post/floridas-teachers-stressed-out

Jung, J. H. (2016). *The concept of care in curriculum studies: Juxtaposing currere and Hakbeolism.* New York, NY: Routledge.

Lee, G., & Lee, K. (2011). The modern meanings of features of the master in the analects of Confucius. *Journal of Secondary Education, 23,* 49–65.

Legge, J. (1967). *Li chi: Book of rites.* New York, NY: University Books.

Pinar, W. (2011). *The character of curriculum studies: Bildung, currere, and the recurring question of the subject.* New York, NY: Palgrave Macmillan.

Pinar, W. (2015). *Educational experience as lived: Knowledge, history, alterity.* New York, NY: Routledge.

14 The Pedagogical Complexity of Story

Sarah Smitherman Pratt

Stories are what humanize our world. In the telling and re-telling of stories, we create, imagine, connect, and convey our thoughts and ideas. It is the act of articulating these ideas that reify or alter who we are. Stories are an integral part of the curriculum.

William E. Doll, Jr., believed in the significance of stories. In his intellectual journey, he embraced this, which he first described as "complicated conversations" but later renamed "complex conversations" (reasons to be shared later). His presence was an open, inviting persona, ready to engage in playful dialogue that is rich in content. He truly embodied his pedagogic creed, introduced in 1993, with an emphasis on inquiry, indeterminacy, and reflection:

> In a reflective relationship between teacher and student, the teacher does not ask the student to accept the teacher's authority; rather, the teacher asks the student to suspend disbelief in that authority, to join with the teacher in inquiry, into that which the student is experiencing. The teacher agrees to help the student understand the meaning of the advice given, to be readily confrontable by the student, and to work with the student in reflecting on the tacit understanding each has.
>
> (Doll, 1993, p. 160)

Doll showed the centrality of inquiry, indeterminacy, and reflection articulated in this creed throughout his intellectual journey. The pedagogic creed was his way of paying tribute to the works of John Dewey (e.g., Dewey, 1897) yet making his voice known. In the creed, Doll (1993) invoked recurring themes from Dewey's theorizing, especially the notions of inquiry, indeterminacy, and reflection in the activity of teaching and learning.

Particularly important to Doll was a Deweyan resistance to categories and to dualities. During his journey into the post-modern era, Doll (1993) sought to point out the "paradoxical dualism" of modernism and post-modernism:

It is time to do more than re-form our methods and practices. It is time to question the modernist assumptions on which these methods and practices are based and to develop a new perspective that simultaneously rejects, transforms, and preserves that which has been.

(p. 11)

As Doll himself concluded, "the past will not disappear but will be reframed continually in the light of an ongoing, changing present" (p. 157). Inquiry, indeterminacy, and reflection played an important role in this reframing.

For example, Doll (2000/2012b, 2002/2012a, 2005/2012c) formulated a way to "keep knowledge alive," by interplaying the three modes posed by Whitehead (1929/1967)—romance, precision, and generalization (as cited in Doll, 2005/2012c, p. 114). Doll's interpretation came from a complex perspective in which life is sustained and where there are networks of relations and space for emergence, not prescriptions to be followed or linear steps of progression. Moving beyond the two modes of thought created by Bruner (1986) of the paradigmatic and the narrative and as attempt to more richly depict the irreducible nature of these two modes that could be interpreted as dualisms, he formed the heart of his ways of learning and teaching in "Modes of Thought" (Doll, 2003/2012e). His intention in this essay was to keep knowledge alive—in classrooms and in life. He incorporated Wittgenstein's (1953) notions of *playing-at*, *playing-in*, and *playing-with* and concluded with his own modes of thought—the three S's: science, story, and spirit (Doll, 2005/2012c). He described science as logic or reason; story as culture or person(s), and spirit as life or breath. He focused on science, for knowledge is important; story, since culture can be conveyed in nuanced ways through narrative; and spirit, because there is the ineffable quality, an emergent awareness yet to be discovered. The image he created of the three S's was an open heart, purposefully left open to invite adaptability and change—an image that depicted his interests in inquiry, indeterminacy, and reflection.

While he presented three modes of thought, of science, story, and spirit, here I chose to focus on story. Using concepts within complexity and chaos theories, I emphasized how Doll's works, and specifically his pedagogic creed, bring forward key ideas of inquiry, indeterminacy, and reflection. This project conveyed the complexity of story and considerations for fostering emergent thinking in a community of learners. Through it all, I built upon my own lived experiences of being a student who suspended disbelief and joined William Doll in regarding complexity theory and education research. I invite you into this interrelated complex conversation of story.

Attention to Story

Doll (1993) once said that "a good story, a great story, induces, encourages, challenges," and includes just enough "*indeterminacy*" (p. 169).

The analytic mode of communication is explanatory, while the narrative is interpretive—and where meanings are constructed through dialogue, a dialogue that is transformational. Stories allow for this open form of narrative.

Story and Inquiry

Story is about the exchanging of ideas, where learning and understandings are formed. As Doll (1993) stated, "learning and understanding are made (not transmitted) as we dialogue with others and reflect on what we and they have said—as we negotiate passages between ourselves and others, between ourselves and our texts" (p. 156). It is in the dialogue, the exchange of ideas, the conversation, that learning and understandings are formed, not in the telling. The stories are shared as parables, fables, rich in description and ripe for divergent interpretations.

Importantly, story and science are interwoven throughout history. As Doll (2005) demonstrated in his chapter "The Culture of Method," he was as interested in the stories behind ideas as he was in the science of them. With eighty-five endnotes in this chapter, he outlined how a modernist ideal of hierarchies shaped and informed the ways that we currently view curriculum and how we employ methods. As he narrated the story, he revealed that often there are ideas that take hold in a culture, and this becomes a challenge when others wish to suggest changes.

Story and Indeterminacy

Indeterminacy is integral to story. Dewey (1960) argued that scientific concepts are formed with starts and stops, ebbs and flows, but, as he pointed out, science is not taught in this way. Doll (1972/2012d, 2002/2012a) took this even further to apply to methods in general. Though educators can have insight and influence, learning occurs as the activity ensues. Looking back on the experience, a story can be shared about what was learned, but what is learned cannot be determined beforehand; in other words, it cannot be predetermined.

Bateson's (1979/2002) research supported this planned but not predetermined perspective. He stated that feedback informs the system and impacts future actions, yet the feedback and actions cannot be predetermined, asserting that "*information* consists of differences that make a difference" (p. 92). Just like in story, an emergence is just on the horizon, not to be controlled or predicted. In nonlinear dynamics, a chaotic system is one in which patterns can be understood in retrospect.

Highlighting the shift from oral traditions before the printing press where stories could be fixed, Trueit (2005) examined the "premodern (re)presentation of '*poiesis*' (to create)" (p. 79). The impact of the printing press led to the mimetic tradition, one of copying and re-producing.

Instead, as in the oral tradition, *poeisis* involves re-presenting, re-telling of a story that is both the same and not the same. The power is in the story, in the aesthetic experience—the embodiment, the inflections of words, the other senses integrated—as well as in the words in and of themselves. Both verbal and non-verbal are part of the story. In the story there is spirit.

Story and Reflection

Story is also about recursively reflecting. Recursion is not the same as repetition; it is the act of doing again but looking for a difference based on initial conditions. Doll (1993) drew from Dewey as he described recursive reflection, "every ending is a new beginning, every beginning emerges from a prior ending. Curriculum segments, parts, sequences are arbitrary chunks that, instead of being seen as isolated units, are seen as opportunities for reflection" (p. 178). This notion of recursive reflection is in the act of telling the story of curriculum and allowing for a looping back and moving forward to strengthen connections among ideas. Recursively reflecting is part of the starts and stops, ebbs and flows.

Additionally, story is a reciprocal relation of interactions. Story is a dance of mutual reciprocity in which the context, the conversants, and the topics help shape and influence the story. This is significant, for the networks of relations and playfulness all impact the dance when teachers and students engage in the act of learning. Maturana and Varela (1987) explored this reciprocity in their investigation of epistemology. Their work resonated with Doll's (2010/2012f) "epistemology of education based on difference" (p. 182), to which he credited Gregory Bateson with the development of this idea. The actions, interactions, and reactions all serve to form the differences in and among teachers and students.

A Story of Inquiry, Indeterminacy, and Reflection

One example of this play can be found in Doll's "Thinking Complexly" (2010/2012f) in which he described possible paths of thinking related to triangular numbers and patterning. His flow of thought with first-grade students and red and white chips began with simple addition, yet it eventually led to a discussion of the Fibonacci sequence and the golden ratio. This story displayed the beauty and emergent potential in conversations, and it suggested how inserting an idea can make a difference and depicting how a small change can make a big difference—a key idea in chaos and complexity theories. In this tale, Doll (2010/2012f) shifted from the closed set of addition or subtraction to fluidity between the two and a connection to other structures such as the Fibonacci sequence and the golden ratio. His argument was not for teachers to follow his strategy verbatim but rather embrace opportunities to move between and among concepts; in fact, he concluded his story with the importance of teachers knowing "their discipline well enough to understand the artificial boundaries that de-contextualize them" (p. 180). Doll loved to tell stories, especially about right triangles; Doll's playfulness with numbers that was storied yet again emerged.

Pedagogical Complexity in Complex Conversations

Stories invite complexity into the classroom and the curriculum. The term "complex conversations" has a particular meaning and can be found in the writings and presentations of Doll's students (Smitherman & Trueit, 2006; Smitherman, 2006; Pratt, 2008). The concept has been used by Bill Doll, Sarah Smitherman Pratt and Donna Trueit to describe learning and teaching that moves away from the mode of "teaching-as-telling" toward an embodiment of thinking this world together. Inasmuch, the concept is itself an emergent idea that resulted from a complex conversation.

Complex conversations couple the science of complexity theory with the culture of conversation to facilitate a poetic/poietic dance of mutual relations that invite opportunities for emergence of ideas. Complex conversations are situated in open systems, ones that require feedback loops to continually consider changes. Aoki (1996/2005) calls this type of systems of relations "a space of conjoining and disrupting, indeed, a generative space of possibilities, a space wherein in tensioned ambiguity newness emerges" (p. 318). In complex conversations participants "ask questions, but not questions to which one already knows the answer" (Pratt, 2008, p. 125). The interpretations for each word "complex" and "conversation" are provided, not to discretely separate complex from conversation, but to describe how each in turn enriches the other aspect.

Complex conversations involve nonlinear moves toward a self-organizing network of relations rather than a controlled, predicted, cause/effect dialogue. They rely on inquiry, indeterminacy, and reflection to facilitate constructions of meaning and sense-making. Furthermore, they include academically rigorous, conversationally rich, filled with relations among ideas and histories, and can move recursively in meaningful ways. Teachers can facilitate complex conversations where the teacher listens for differences (Davis, 1996) to draw out multiple perspectives and representations.

Drawing on Doll's triangulation of ideas for what it means to learn and to teach, I return to his pedagogic creed. Transforming his creed into a more complex network of relations, I wish to offer an altered version, one that I strive to embody in my own instruction as a way to demonstrate my interpretation of Doll's pedagogy, based on my interactions with him. I draw from the work that we began together (Smitherman, 2005). While words are not sufficient to convey the spirit of his *being-with*, his open heart of three S's, I hope that through my attention to story shared above and the terminology included below, I can convey a complex pedagogy that both connects with and diverges from the creed of 1993:

> In dynamic conversations among a community of learners, the teacher and students join together to investigate meanings and the making of meanings. The act of understanding is not a position of knower/knowee but rather a shared understanding that is both individual and collective knowledge. The complex conversations that occur are planned but not predetermined by the teacher, and the stories that enter the dialogue enrich and recursively relate to what is both known and unknown. The teacher is a knowledgeable other in the culture of conversation, playing-with curriculum in relation to students. The emergence of learning occurs in the moment of chaotic play that is scientifically rigorous, richly storied, and spiritually related.

References

Aoki, T. (2005). Imaginaries of "east and west": Slippery curricular signifiers in education. In W. Pinar & R. Irwin (Eds.), *Curriculum in a new key: The collected works of Ted T. Aoki* (pp. 313–319). Mahwah, NJ: Lawrence Erlbaum Associates Publishers. (Original work published in 1996)

Bateson, G. (2002). *Mind and nature: A necessary unity*. Cresskill, NJ: Hampton Press. (Original work published in 1979)

Bruner, J. (1986). *Actual minds, possible worlds*. Cambridge, MA: Harvard University Press.

Davis, B. (1996). *Teaching mathematics: Toward a sound alternative*. New York, NY: Garland Publishing.

Dewey, J. (1897). My pedagogic creed. *School Journal, LIV*(3), 77–80.

Dewey, J. (1960). *The quest for certainty*. New York, NY: Putnam. (Original work published in 1929)

Doll, W. (1993). *A post-modern perspective on curriculum*. New York, NY: Teachers College Press.

Doll, W. (2005). The culture of method. In W. Doll, J. Fleener, J. St. Julien, & D. Trueit (Eds.), *Chaos, complexity, curriculum and culture: A conversation* (pp. 21–76). New York, NY: Peter Lang.

Doll, W. (2012a). Beyond methods. In D. Trueit (Ed.), *Pragmatism, post-modernism, and complexity theory: The "fascinating imaginative realm" of William E. Doll, Jr.* (pp. 81–97). New York, NY: Routledge. (Original work published in 2002)

Doll, W. (2012b). Classroom management. In D. Trueit (Ed.), *Pragmatism, postmodernism, and complexity theory: The "fascinating imaginative realm" of William E. Doll, Jr.* (pp. 222–227). New York, NY: Routledge. (Original work published in 2000)

Doll, W. (2012c). Keeping knowledge alive. In D. Trueit (Ed.), *Pragmatism, postmodernism, and complexity theory: The "fascinating imaginative realm" of William E. Doll, Jr.* (pp. 111–119). New York, NY: Routledge. (Original work published in 2005)

Doll, W. (2012d). A methodology of experience, part I. In D. Trueit (Ed.), *Pragmatism, post modernism, and complexity theory: The "fascinating imaginative realm" of William E. Doll, Jr.* (pp. 49–65). New York, NY: Routledge. (Original work published in 1972)

Doll, W. (2012e). Modes of thought. In D. Trueit (Ed.), *Pragmatism, postmodernism, and complexity theory: The "fascinating imaginative realm" of William E. Doll, Jr.* (pp. 103–110). New York, NY: Routledge. (Original work published in 2003)

Doll, W. (2012f). Thinking complexly. In D. Trueit (Ed.), *Pragmatism, post-modernism, and complexity theory: The "fascinating imaginative realm" of William E. Doll, Jr.* (pp. 172–188). New York, NY: Routledge. (Original work published in 2010)

Maturana, H., & Varela, F. (1987). *The tree of knowledge: The biological roots of human understanding.* Boston, MA: Shambhala.

Pratt, S. (2008). Complex constructivism: Rethinking the power dynamics of "understanding." *Journal of Canadian Association for Curriculum Studies*, 6(1), 113–132.

Smitherman, S. (2005). Creating holes and wholes in curriculum. In W. Doll, J. Fleener, J. St. Julien, & D. Trueit (Eds.), *Chaos, complexity, curriculum and culture: A conversation* (pp. 153–180). New York, NY: Peter Lang.

Smitherman, S. (2006). *Reflections on teaching a mathematics education course.* Unpublished Doctoral Dissertation, Louisiana State University, Baton Rouge, LA.

Smitherman, S., & Trueit, D. (2006, May). *Complex conversations in education: Our need to move away from teaching as telling.* Paper presented at the tri-annual meeting of the International Association for the Advancement of Curriculum Studies. Tampere, Finland.

Trueit, D. (2005). Watercourses: From poetic to *poietic*. In W. Doll, J. Fleener, J. St. Julien, & D. Trueit (Eds.), *Chaos, complexity, curriculum and culture: A conversation* (pp. 77–100). New York, NY: Peter Lang.

Whitehead, A. (1967). *The aims of education and other essays.* New York, NY: The Free Press. (Original work published in 1929)

Wittgenstein, L. (1953). *Philosophical investigations* (G.E.M. Anscombe, Trans.). New York, NY: Macmillan.

Part IV
Of Method, Mystery, and Visionary Magic

Historically, so much of curriculum, as method's child, has been defined by questions or the lack thereof concerning method. Given method's profound influence here, and its situatedness in a larger intellectual history and dominant epistemological (ontological, axiological, cosmological) paradigm, Doll has done much in his work to illuminate the history and culture of method, and its interest in and impact upon—constituting place in—curriculum (e.g., 2005, others), as well as in wrestling to reimagine such, "seeking a method beyond method" (2015). If curriculum as "a course for running" has involved the avid pursuit of identifying, articulating (mapping out), implementing, establishing, assessing, and legitimizing or officiating a prescribed path of/to knowledge (for students—and we should add, teachers—to take); then method has promised to show us the way (e.g., Latin, *methodos*, following after, in pursuit of, about or after, expressing development concerning, the way or manner or system, of doing, saying, taking, etc.; the road, journey, or track) (*OED*, 1989). Historically bound up with the pursuit of knowledge, power of teaching and prescription of disease in medicine via systematic scientific inquiry, method hardly conjures up notions of mystery, magic or vision. Yet, in Doll's strange and marvelous world, fascinating imaginative realm, it does.

From mystery's history in *misterium*—trade, handicraft, and *ministerium*—service, and mastery (*mastrie*); to contemplate method's mystery, in this way, is perhaps to speak to it not only as an art form, but also an act of service, wherein one may be initiated (*myein*) into "a way beyond" (*methodos*). Through such, mastery indeed may be achieved, yet also hidden, secret or as yet unseen meanings (*mystere*) illuminated, and new truths revealed, and this as an ongoing interpretive practice, before which we also stand in awe and wonder (*mysterium*). Through this Dollian lens, there is magic to method, as well, then, or might be—capacity, alchemy, power (*magh*)—by which events are influenced and marvels produced, hidden natural forces emergently engaged. Bill Doll as magician (*magos*), Merlin, as well as King of Chaos? Curricularists as *magi*—learned priestly alchemists and healers, testifying to, taking up and teaching toward, the mysteries? Perhaps such is a bit of a stretch, but Doll has spoken of ghosts (unseen forces, spiritual influences) and of visions (Doll, 2002) respecting curriculum. And he is indeed visionary (e.g., pertaining or belonging to vision—*videre*, to see—that which is seen in the imagination or supernatural, sense of sight, presence, dream, *OED*, 1989) in his insightful and imaginative exploration of it. This section highlights, in many ways, Doll's visionary, magical, mystical, and methodological contributions to the field, in acknowledgment too of an abiding mystery, and in/for the life and work of others.

Kathleen R. Kesson explicitly highlights in her essay the visionary nature of Bill Doll's person and work, to whom she was immediately drawn upon meeting—as part of a kindred tribe of mystics, dreamers, stargazers, and adventure seekers; and whose revolutionary thinking has enriched us in innumerable ways, and is sorely needed (perhaps now more so than ever) in a world of escalating complexity, uncertainty, vulnerability; and for the future—the new metaphors, languages and ways of thinking required to approach such faithfully and fruitfully. She locates Doll, upon whose "very tall shoulders" we now stand, within the Reconceptualist movement of the '60s, which by the emergence of many new ideas—from East and West, the humanities and sciences—expanded upon radical, experimental ideas and practices through deep and expansive interdisciplinary theoretical exploration. Via a concise and compelling composite of the field concerning the unfolding development of its dominant epistemologies, ontologies, pedagogies, she notes Doll's work—challenging us through the emerging quantum sciences of chaos and complexity, in concert with art, philosophy, and theology—in advancing our understanding of curriculum from that of information accumulated to meaning generated, as a process not of transmitting the known but rather of exploring the unknown, questioning our fundamental understandings. Doll, she continues: "though not professing a commitment to any particular form of spirituality, was wonderfully open to the multiplicity of ways that people expressed their own soulful commitments. In this, he was a model for how we might embrace difference in a post-modern world, in which truth can no longer be spelled with a capital T."

Doll's "spiritual" influences and gifts to us Ugena Whitlock discusses further in her essay, that also plays with this idea of not knowing, the inspirited dance of the unknown with the known in cultivating our growth and understanding—the *mysterium tremendum* (see Whitlock's piece, as well as Fleener's [and Quinn, 2001], for more on this concept). There is an acknowledgment here, too, of the significance of presence and of process—and such as Doll embodied in his person, as also in relation to curriculum study and studies. His presentation style itself as process, by which he invites his listeners to his own journey into chaos, complexity, arriving at illumination, is meaningfully reflected upon; as well as his "contemplative search for fascination," his deep listening and responsiveness, the spirit he brought to every relationship and encounter.

Nicholas Ng-A-Fook extends such attention, theorizing further, in conceptualizing curriculum as inspired letter, gleaning much, too, from studying Doll studying. He reflects on his recent visit to China, and writes to Doll of how through his influence, the focus there has turned to living with depth, honoring complexity: countering the anesthetizing effects of standardization and high stakes testing, in schools in China they are seeking to live curriculum also as inspired community (rooted in Doll's three S's and the *mysterium tremendum*; see footnote 12, Quinn, introduction). As Ng-A-Fook—grateful to be among those who have studied and lived Doll's teachings—returns to and moves through Doll's early works, he speaks of his "generous criticism" and insight in terms of historical "post-it notes" we now sorely need: curriculum theory as a productive intellectual site for transformational change; and, a form of love in action, human interaction and community of utmost import. He notes:

> What I witnessed in Wuhan, at that school, and in our conversations, is that your intellectual work continues to provide a reflective window for us to rethink, our approaches to "life and our activities in life, including teaching and curriculum design, in a way that allows the spirit or soul of these activities and of ourselves to come forth."
> (Doll, 2012, p. 166)

"Undoubtedly, Doll has become one of the most influential contemporary scholars among Chinese educators," adds Jie Yu. She discusses here the significance of his post modern pedagogy in China, and of his four R's (see footnote 9, Quinn, introduction)—neither Western imposition nor emulation, but rather initiating cross-cultural conversations through complexity, chaos and the third space or middle way; honoring local place, culture, and history; engaging differences generatively in ways that foster transformative growth for all. Grounded in her experiences with Doll in China, she recounts, too, his delight in the traditional myth of the Monkey King—his vision and art at odds with lifeless rules and rigid methodologies; and of being so dubbed "The King of Chaos."

References

Doll, W. (2002). Ghosts and the curriculum. In W. Doll & N. Gough (Eds.), *Curriculum visions* (pp. 23–70). New York, NY: Peter Lang.

Doll, W. (2005). The culture of method. In W. Doll, J. Fleener, J. St. Julien, & D. Trueit (Eds.), *Chaos, complexity, curriculum and culture: A conversation* (pp. 21–76). New York, NY: Peter Lang.

Doll, W. (2012). Revisiting Aoki's "inspiriting the curriculum." In N. Ng-A-Fook & J. Rottmann (Eds.), *Reconsidering Canadian curriculum studies* (pp. 165–174). New York, NY: Palgrave Macmillan.

Doll, W. (2015, May). *Seeking a method beyond method*. Unpublished Manuscript, IAACS Keynote, Ottawa, Canada.

Oxford English dictionary (OED) (2nd ed.). (1989). (J. Simpson & E. Weiner, Eds.). Oxford, UK: Clarendon Press.

Quinn, M. (2001). *Going out, not knowing whither: Education, the upward journey and the faith of reason.* New York, NY: Peter Lang.

15 Circling the Known

Kathleen R. Kesson

> There once was a man name of Doll
> Who was fair of hair, lively, and tall
> Who expounded with Glee
> On Complexity,
> Chaos, and the Modernist Fall.
>
> With Rigor he argued, with Richness he drew
> Upon quantum mechanics and poetry too
> For you see he was truly just like me and you
> Forever Recursing, Relating and stirring
> A flavorful *Currere* stew.

A giant icy planet is thought to circle slowly around the fringes of our solar system in an elliptical orbit 100 billion miles away from the sun at its furthest point, making its solar revolution about once in fifteen thousand years. No one has actually seen it yet, but the evidence is accumulating that Planet Nine may soon replace Pluto, recently demoted to mere plutoid status.

I liken my friend and colleague Bill Doll to Planet Nine, circling the known world of educational theory in his own orbit, his revolutionary ideas slowly manifesting as adventurous seekers begin to infer the presence of something of enormous import just outside our range of perception. Post-modern theories of curriculum, embodying as they do notions of uncertainty, relationship, complexity, indeterminacy, self-organization, chaos, and transformation circle far beyond the known orbits of modernist curriculum, teaching, and learning practices. Professor Doll, with telescopic vision, has helped to bring the unknown closer into the orbit of the known, enriching our lives and our thinking in multiple ways.

I entered the academic field of curriculum theory at a moment in time when the star of the Reconceptualists was ascendant. Too late for the inception of these ideas in the late 1970s, I nonetheless benefited from the comfortable orbit that was established by the mid-1980s for theoretical experimentation and exploration at the expanding edge of the known. Bill Doll graciously brought me into the planetary fold, embraced my wildly speculative thinking and assured me that there was, in fact, a home for mystics and futurists and dreamers and poets and stargazers and explorers in this field we call "curriculum."

Chaos and the Curriculum

Those of us who have inhabited the scholarly field of curriculum throughout the latter part of the 20th century and into the 21st have been witness to major shifts in how teaching and learning are understood. The pre-Reconceptualist, behaviorist model of learning inherited from Bobbitt (1918), Charters (1923), Tyler (1949) and other founding "Fathers" of curriculum presents a view of the learner as a "closed system." In a closed system, such as a rock or a log, there is no internal transformation of energy. This old paradigm of learning, which finds expression in such models as mastery learning, competency-based instruction, and outcomes-based education proposed a narrow range of predictable learning outcomes, specific behaviors as both means and ends of those outcomes, limited and controlled inputs of information and an emphasis on educational products (memorized facts, right answers, reports). That paradigm has proved remarkably successful—at turning students into rocks and logs. At the core of this technical approach to education is the ontological belief that human nature is wild, uncontrolled, and chaotic, hence its efforts to impose order on human thinking and behavior.

A modest corrective to the behaviorist paradigm is constructivist theory, grounded in the historical ideas of Dewey, Piaget, Vygotsky, and Bruner, which sees knowledge not as something static that can be transmitted whole cloth from teacher to learner, but as something "constructed" through interactions, or as Dewey called them, "transactions" with the environment. It's a more active understanding of knowledge as something "made" not something acquired. We see, we hear, we touch, we interact, and we reflect on these activities, and through such sensual engagement with the world, we come to an understanding of how the world works. And these understandings are constantly under revision as we incorporate new perceptions and understandings into our existing "schema" or blueprints in the brain.

Behaviorism and constructivism are ideologies that embody assumptions about what it means to be human (ontology), how we come to know things (epistemology) and importantly, how teaching and learning should take place (pedagogy). In the behaviorist ideology, the world is thought to be objective and real, consisting of stable and predictable things and events outside of ourselves. Knowledge is the corresponding relationship of our mental processes with those external things, an imperfect reflection of what is in the outside world. Our brains collect and register information, which allows us to form pictures of reality, and with diligent observation, predict and control this reality. Teaching and learning, in

Circling the Known 141

this paradigm, consists of regularized inputs and outputs—information in/information out—and what is highly valued is the ability to memorize and regurgitate. Teaching and learning is akin to conditioning, which is driven by the idea that behavior changes (i.e. learning something) can best be shaped by reinforcement, repetition, and rewards.

The constructivists take a different view of how learning occurs, which is more dynamic and accounts for human agency. Dewey, by many considered a founder of constructivist thought (though he did not use that word), challenged traditional assumptions about the objective nature of reality and thought: "his analyses of the transaction of organism and environment can be perceived as an account of the construction processes that underlie all human activity" (Vanderstraeten, 2002, p. 233). Knowledge, for Dewey, represented "not an external, mind- or organism-independent reality, but rather the relationship between the activities of the organism and the consequences these activities bring about" (p. 238). Piaget, like Dewey, understood the development of mental schemata to be the result of cognitive disequilibrium in the face of novel environmental circumstances, and the resulting accommodation and assimilation that provided for adaptive changes. Vygotsky, with his emphasis on the social nature of learning and language, shares fundamental assumptions with other constructivist ideas, though his theories are often seen as a corrective to Piaget's cognitive model, which focuses more exclusively on the individual. Bruner saw the learner as an active agent, building knowledge through dialogue, reflection, and discovery. All of these historical ideas are at the root of contemporary educational practices such as cooperative learning, inquiry-based learning, discovery learning, scaffolding, and guided learning, though many practitioners are not familiar with the historical foundations of their everyday practices.

Bill Doll stood on the shoulders of these giants of constructivist thought and peered into the far horizon of the known. In that vast distance, he saw the emerging sciences of chaos and complexity as having the power to push our understandings of teaching, learning, and curriculum into entirely new spaces. He understood, in a profound way, how our ontological assumptions about the nature of Being drive our educational decisions. And he pointed us towards a reconceptualization of this human nature, or Being, in terms of the new understandings in complexity theory, understandings with the potential to reorient our thinking.

Chaos theorists speculate about the nature of mind, expanded beyond the simple input-output model:

> At the pinnacle of complicated dynamics are processes of biological evolution, or thought processes. . . . In the development of one person's mind from childhood, information is clearly not just accumulated but also generated—created from connections that were not there before.
> (Packard, in Gleick, 1987, pp. 261–262)

Doll suggested that in the new model of reality generated by chaos theory, curriculum might rightly be conceived as a process, "not of transmitting what is (absolutely) known but of exploring what is unknown" (1993, p. 155). Echoing Bruner, he reminds us that learning and understanding are constructed rather than transmitted, through dialogue and reflection, and he suggested that

> curriculum's role, as process, is to help us negotiate those passages (between ourselves and others); towards this end it should be rich, recursive, relational, and rigorous.
>
> (p. 156)

Teachers and students should be free, he suggests, to develop their own curriculum in conjoint interaction with one another, to "self-organize" within their own situational parameters. His vision of curriculum questioned traditional assumptions about ontology, authority, and epistemology, challenging both the "spectator theory of knowledge" (the idea that reality is apart from us and waiting to be discovered) and the analytic mode that governs our epistemology and our pedagogy, and argues instead for a dynamic and fluid constructivist relationship between the knower and the known (p. 168).

What is it about these ideas from the new sciences that so captured the imaginations of many young curriculum theorists, most with backgrounds not in mathematics or the sciences, but in the humanities? For many of us who came of age in the 1960's, our ideas about the world were shaped by the intellectual, cultural, and spiritual big bang that embodied existentialist philosophy, mind-expanding psychedelic drugs, religious teachings imported from Eastern and Southeastern Asia, transpersonal and humanistic psychologies, the new physics, communal life styles, leftist politics, and experimental art and music, among a thousand other "emergences." The ideas that compelled us had been percolating for some time: quantum physics had its roots in the early 20th century, as did existentialism and phenomenology, and Bohemians had been around at least that long as well. But this constellation of ideas only exploded from the margins into popular culture in the 1960s. Our understandings of what it meant to be a conscious human being underwent radical transformations, and with this came new ideas about teaching and learning. It's no coincidence that the 1960s saw the birth of the free school movement, which though short-lived, symbolized a widespread resistance to conformist, mind-numbing forms of education. With the birth of the Reconceptualist movement, the experimental educational ideas of the 1960s were amplified by interdisciplinary theoretical exploration. Bill Doll was an elder of this movement, a bridge between the innovative educational thinkers of the recent past and the experimentalists of the time.

Metaphors and Metamorphosis

Existence has always been an uncertain proposition. Fragile human life is inevitably at the mercy of immense forces: floods and fires, tornadoes and earthquakes, revolutions and invasions, injury and disease. But at this point in time, the sheer magnitude and scope of the images and information flooding our psyches on a daily basis, coupled with the rapidity of change resulting from technological innovation and the looming possibilities of climate catastrophe, ecological devastation, species extinction, economic implosion, and world scale conflict combine to increase our feelings of vulnerability and make our future seem more uncertain than ever. We desperately need new ways of thinking if we are to come out the other end of this long dark tunnel. We need a language of the future, words that might help us imagine livable scenarios and forms of renewal and regeneration. New ways of thinking cannot come about without new language, and new language is characterized by new metaphors, linguistic icons that encode new possibilities of thought and action.

Theorists of metaphor Lakoff and Johnson (1980) famously wrote about the ways that metaphors are central to our individual meaning-making abilities; they affect how we perceive and how we think, thus structuring our models of reality. The new sciences of chaos and complexity are rich in such structuring metaphors, and suggest a sort of Dionysian rejection of old ways of thinking embodied in such Apollonian words as authority, certainty, predictability, uniformity, conformity, and control, words that certainly characterize educational theory and practice through much of the 20th century. Such words embody a particular worldview. They make my own body/self feel stifled, unable to breathe, and doomed to re-enact ancient intentions. The languages of complexity, on the other hand, embody a kind of wild playfulness; I resonate with and feel joy when I hear and speak such words as emergence, evolution, fluidity, paradox, uncertainty, process, relationships, systems, self-organization, synchronicity, parallel universes and the space-time continuum. The images encoded in these syllables suggest freedom, openness, and surprise. They spark my imagination. They give me hope and the courage to confront the novel and the unexpected. They embody a language of the future, a constellation of possibilities.

Many of the books written by scholars about the implications of the new sciences propose fresh understandings of the connections between spirituality and science. David Bohm, a theoretical physicist, in *Wholeness and the Implicate Order* suggests a new model of the universe that seeks to eliminate the fragmentation and alienation that modern ideas of self and perception have wrought. Morris Berman, historian, in *The Reenchantment of the World* points the way toward a more holistic ecological intimacy between humans and the world of "nature." Physicist Paul Davies, in *God and the New Physics* has expanded the context in which issues formerly the province only of theology (Why is there something rather than nothing? What is my purpose? Is there a God?) can be thought about. And Fred Wolf, perhaps the farthest out of all the theoretical physicists writing about the relationships between physics and consciousness, explores mind stretching new connections between matter, mind, spirit, and the quantum world in numerous works. A scholarly overview of these writings by scientists, historians and theologians, which I was fortunate to have the opportunity to carry out in my doctoral studies in curriculum, leads inevitably to questioning the very foundations of what we know not just about how the world works at its most fundamental levels, but how we conceptualize teaching and learning. Most debates about education remain fixed in the ideological orbits of the behaviorists and the constructivists. But if we are to explore the possibilities of human potential opened up by the new sciences—ideas such as synchronicity, self-organization, non-local causality, intuition, connectedness—then we must be brave enough to enter very new territory in our discussions about teaching and learning.

If there is indeed, an "implicate order," what does that imply about how we might learn to access information? Should we foster contemplation and the development of intuition in education? How might we better cope with world events by understanding the "butterfly effect," the idea that tiny changes can magnify into large-scale macro changes, and what might this teach our students and ourselves about mindfulness, about paying attention to the "small things?" How might understanding that everything in the universe is interconnected in tangible and not so tangible ways affect our thinking about curriculum? How might we better understand student learning if we realize that seemingly random interests may indeed have a deep underlying structure? And how might new definitions of spirituality and human potential throw into question the rigid boundaries we have established between matters of religion and matters of education? In a quantum world, where does matter (flesh) end and energy (soul) begin? Bill Doll, though not professing a commitment to any particular form of spirituality, was wonderfully open to the multiplicity of ways that people expressed their own soulful commitments. In this, he was a model for how we might embrace difference in a postmodern world, in which truth can no longer be spelled with a capital T.

Perhaps my most fiercely held educational belief is that everyone possesses within their being a psychic compass that steers them into the development of their potential, and that this manifests differently in all of us as curiosities, interests, and passions. We can call it soul, we can call it spirit, or we can call it an organism's capacity to self-organize, but I believe, with the Romantics, that these inclinations need to be honored and that education really should be a "drawing, or leading out" (ēdūcere) and development of these emergent intentions.

Educational practices do not change easily, and anyone who has engaged in school reform or renewal can testify that genuine transformation is an elusive process. As Bill acknowledges, transforming curriculum from a modern to a post-modern paradigm and shifting our ways of thinking will be neither an easy nor painless transition. My current research focuses on the emergent practices of "personalized learning" (PL)—which some states have legislated and which now has policy support at the federal level. PL has emerged from a consensus that our conventional way of educating students—discipline-based courses, textbooks, standardized tests, and Carnegie units—is not only inconsistent with what we know about how people learn, it is an inadequate template for preparing people for the increasing complexity and indeterminacy of the 21st century. In Vermont, where this initiative is fairly advanced, everything is in place to foster student self-organization and self-direction, to support the increased complexity of the curriculum as students work with self-chosen mentors outside the school walls, and to embrace the novel demonstrations of learning that can happen with the discarding of Carnegie units and grades. Teachers and students *are now free* to develop their own curriculum in conjoint interaction with one another, to "self-organize" within their own situational parameters. And yet, the conversations occurring in some schools revolve less around the rich experiences this makes possible, and more about how to rigorously document outcomes and proficiencies. It is as though the invisible curriculum police are still looking over our shoulders. Even with policy and legislation in place, changing actual practice is not happening easily. It is just so hard to let go of old models and the language of certainty, outcomes, predictability, and accountability, even when we know it no longer serves us well!

Interestingly, the educators I have met in the course of my research who are most eager, most enthusiastic, and most comfortable with the changes have—you guessed it—had a close encounter with the work of Bill Doll. So thank you Bill—for loosening the ties that bind us to old ideas, for introducing some fresh language into our educational discourse, and for providing new ingredients for our flavorful *currere* stew. And for offering your—very tall—shoulders for us to stand on, to gaze into the stellar distance and feed our imaginations with educational possibilities as yet undreamed, and visualize the space/time bridges that might connect the Now and the New, and to approach the infinite and the vast unknown with the awe, and wonder, and humility which it deserves.

References

Berman, M. (1981). *The reenchantment of the world*. New York, NY: Cornell University Press.

Bobbitt, F. (1918/1997). Scientific method in curriculum-making. In D. J. Flinders & S. J. Thornton (Eds.), *The curriculum studies reader*. New York, NY: Routledge.

Bohm, D. (1980). *Wholeness and the implicate order*. London: Ark Paperbacks.

Charters, W. W. (1923). *Curriculum construction*. New York, NY: Macmillan.

Davies, P. (1983). *God and the new physics*. New York, NY: Simon & Schuster.

Doll, W. (1993). *A post-modern perspective on curriculum*. New York, NY: Teachers College Press.

Gleick, J. (1987). *Chaos: Making a new science*. New York, NY: Penguin Books.

Lakoff, G., & Johnson, M. (1980). *Metaphors we live by*. Chicago, IL: University of Chicago Press.

Tyler, R. W. (1949). *Basic principles of curriculum and instruction*. Chicago, IL: University of Chicago Press.

Vanderstraeten, R. (2002). Dewey's transactional constructivism. *Journal of Philosophy of Education, 36*(2), 233–246.

16 An Ethics of Free Responsible Action
Examining Doll's Struggling With Spirituality

Ugena Whitlock

I've never addressed him as anything other than Dr. Doll.

When Molly invited me to contribute an essay to her tribute collection on the life and work of Professor William Doll, I was eager to do so. I had developed an organizing plan around three brief interactions between Dr. Doll and me, episodes, I would call them, since such engagements were the nature of our relationship over the years, first at LSU and then at various national and international curriculum conferences. Except for one one-hour seminar course together, we only ever kept crossing each other's paths at gatherings and conferences, at his 80th birthday parties in Baton Rouge and New Orleans in 2011, for example, or in Finland at the International Association for the Advancement of Curriculum Studies Conference. Despite there being narrative snippets, they are little jewels I continue to hold personally and professionally. That was my first plan, anyway. But, in the way academics sometimes do I adapted my plan to be more expedient—to adapt one project for use toward another, which is particularly ironic, given Doll's critique of our penchant for the expedient in curriculum, pedagogy, and education (Quinn, personal communication, April 10, 2017).

My revised approach was to take his lovely article from 2002, "Struggles With Spirituality," and employ it as a partial frame for my own work on queer theology and Bonhoeffer's concept of ethics (2008). It was a good plan I thought, and it seemed to work. The piece even had a really good name, *An Ethics of Free Responsible Action: Examining Doll's Struggles With Spirituality*. But here's why it didn't work. I had written a piece and added a helping of Doll—not even a very generous one, and that minimized his importance in a way that telling my little stories would not have. Don't get me wrong, I think what I wrote was a really good segment of my larger work on Queer Theology, and engaging with Doll's struggles has helped me move to a very specific discussion I want to have surrounding Christian Sexual Ethics on a topic that I call *Intentional Monogamy* (Whitlock, 2017). One might pose the question as to whether Doll's theology is queer; he is "queer" in the sense of the word my grandmother used, meaning odd or curious or eccentric. Queer with a capital "Q" requires intentionality and has distinct concerns with gender, sexuality, and politics. One must also claim queerness. Regardless, his work is a queering influence as I consider theology and ethics (Quinn, personal communication, April 1, 2017). So, I suppose that is the fourth episode in which Doll has made a lasting impact on my work. Still, I'm going back to Plan A, because it honors Dr. Doll more appropriately, more fully of spirit.

Episode 1: *Mysterium Tremendum*

First theorized by Rudolf Otto to express how humankind fully experiences the transcendent and engages with the holy, he explains the term *mysterium tremendum* as having aspects of awefulness and fascination (1958, p. 13). Doll uses the term in "Struggles With Spirituality" to represent the ever-contriving complexity and creativity in the cosmos. He furthers the concept of tremendous mystery to also hold feelings of repulsion that works together with awe and fascination. Herein is the nature of struggle with our participation in divine life. In our feelings of intense fear and trembling concurrent with ecstatic attraction, Doll reminds us of Tillich's insistence upon "the repulsive function on those who encounter it" (quoted in Doll, 2002, p. 17), and it is here Doll finds the cosmologic, ecological awakening to an awe-some power of the universe. It is to my great disappointment, I never studied more deeply with Dr. Doll, nor did I turn to his work in a significant way to inform my own (until this project, and I am delighted to be able to do so). I was studying with William F. Pinar as part of the Curriculum Theory Project (CTP) at LSU from 2001 to 2005, and to be honest, I only remember two things about the senior doctoral seminar I had with Doll, and neither has to do with curriculum theory.

First, since I worked full time at the Department of Education in Baton Rouge, I had to rush to campus and take the class over my lunch hour, leaving me very envious of my friends holding graduate assistantships who had what I saw as the luxury of going to the weekly lunch immediately following and following up the class with another hour or so of deep contemplation and conversation—and food! My other memory is of Dr. Doll himself, all almost 7 feet of him that was mostly limbs, silken shock of white hair neatly combed, thick eyeglasses, signature bow tie. And the laugh. Everyone who has spent time with Dr. Doll knows it. He laughs with his whole being, throwing his head back and, well, laughs. I actually looked up adjectives to describe laughter and the best fit would, I suppose, be a joyful, howling roar. It is important that the emphasis is on the *joy*. I remember when one of us students were called upon to share ideas about our reading, he would put his hands together, professorially

An Ethics of Free Responsible Action 149

beneath his chin, close his eyes, tilt his head back, and listen. And just at the point where I was pretty sure he was asleep, he would, without fail, give his feedback: "*ahhh, fascinating, can you tell us more please?*" Looking back, I got plenty of curriculum theory from that one hour per week. The contemplative search for fascination.

Episode 2: Growing Where Planted

I was truly privileged to be a part of the CTP at LSU. I was a former English teacher from Alabama. I had never really wanted to be a teacher, wasn't particularly good at it, and wanted an exit strategy; that, paired with a craving for intellectual pursuits that went back to my childhood, led me to LSU. After about a week of studying with colleagues who had come from all over the world to study with Pinar and Doll, I knew where I was, what I was a part of. As doctoral students, we traveled as a pack, seven or eight sharing a hotel room—room, not suite—at conferences, dashing to each other's presentations, clustering in star-struck awe at networking receptions, reception "hopping" to save our food money for the cash bars. It was magical, in no small part because we were "LSU"—part of the CTP and students of Pinar and Doll. Truly, it opened doors of opportunity for us. It was only later that I learned that students in other doctoral programs had not been prepared for the conference circuit—and thus, pre-graduation publications, which put us at an advantage in the job search. Toward the end of my studies, the last Bergamo (Miller, 2010)[1] I attended as a doc student, such was weighing heavily on me in my nostalgic way of missing a place in time rather than being joyfully mindful of it.

Dr. Doll and I were chatting in the large social room with the fireplace and 1980s furniture. We were talking about how wonderfully the CTP prepared its students to go forth into the world of academe. I knew already that one or two of my fellow students had upcoming interviews at prominent research institutions, and I was envious. Why not me, I thought? What's wrong with *me*? This wallowing in pathos was not exactly how I phrased it to Dr. Doll, but he knew what was troubling me. He paused for a second, took a breath, smiled—his contemplative stance, after which you just *knew* something profound was about to

---

1. The Bergamo Conference on Curriculum Theory and Classroom Practice was established by William Pinar and Janet Miller in 1978, along with the affiliated *Journal of Curriculum Theorizing*. Bergamo sprung from the Reconceptualist movement in curriculum theory and brings together scholars of diverse and divergent backgrounds to engage in complicated conversations surrounding curriculum. It is a place safe to build what Janet Miller terms curriculum "communities without consensus" (2009 Bergamo Keynote, *Nostalgia for the Future: Imagining Histories of JCT and Bergamo*, http://journal.jctonline.org/index.php/jct/article/view/181).

come—*Reta*, he said, because my first name had appeared on the course roll, so Reta I was to him for at least two more years—*do not count out teaching universities. That's where I started, and you can grow as beautifully there—often better. For at smaller places, the opportunities may be far greater.* I got a job at a large teaching university in Georgia, and unless the University of Alabama calls me with a professorship AND a coaching assistantship with Nick Saban, I've never been able to think of any where I'd leave for. Do I still get bitten by the prestige bug? Occasionally, yes, and then I try to practice that mindfulness that evaded me at Bergamo those years ago, and I decide to grow right here, where I am.

Episode 3: *Try Prayer*

In 2015, I had the distinct honor of being paired in a keynote session with Dr. Doll at the 5th IAACS Triennial Conference in Ottawa. His talk was on *Seeking a Method-Beyond-Method*, which drew from Sophist, Epicurean, and complexity theorists. Naturally. Although his theorizing is brilliant and provocative—and inspired, probably the one word I remembered from senior seminar—his topic is usually superfluous to me. It's worth the price of a ticket just to see him present, because he walks the audience through his thought processes, itself a journey into chaos and complexity that ends in illumination. My topic was *Currere and Radical Love: Understanding Curriculum as Queer Theological Text*. I asked to go first because there was no way I was following Bill Doll. I didn't do a bad job; it was the first foray into my new-found research pursuit of Queer Theology. I don't know whether it was because the audience had been unusually energized at his presentation, or that there were curriculum rock stars in the audience there to see him that day, but the question/answer session was rich and spirited. Maybe Queer Theology was especially provocative since I had described engagement with the divine as orgasmic. In any case, I was asked about methodology—his topic, recall—and how I proposed to theorize sexual ethics and divine life and our participation in it for curriculum studies. I was stymied. I had posed an objective—a rudimentary one, granted—and had begun framing how to think of it. But what would it look like, and how might I get there, to illumination?

By that time, Dr. Doll had walked over to me. I ruminated out loud until I came around to the conclusion—admitting to the very large crowd of mentors and colleagues—that I just didn't know how to get to the cavernous empty place for connecting with humankind's ground of being. I looked up at him, and he looked down at me. Again, he paused, breathed, smiled, and said, "*Try prayer.*" After a twenty-minute presentation on theology, I had missed the most common tool for the search for the nature of God: prayer. Intellectualizing theology would help bring it to curriculum discussions, but theologizing intellectualism would, by connecting humankind to our ultimate concern, stretch it beyond its limits. Yes, I am talking about transcending intellectual limitations—but not by turning to God in a fundamental, Judeo-Christian way; I am suggesting a *currere* in which there is a bending backward and forward, apart and together, across space and time, in our search—whatever the ground of being, the ultimate concern may be. All that from two words.

In 2005, Dr. William E. Doll, Jr. was awarded the AERA Division B Lifetime Achievement Award. It is the highest honor the organization bestows. My pack of doctoral students—all of us—were about to graduate, and "The Bills," as they were known in Peabody Hall, were leaving for Canada more than a decade after founding the Curriculum Theory Project. In our end was our beginning (Eliot, *East Coker*, V). Dr. Doll rose up to accept the award. Of course, I don't remember a word of his acceptance speech. What I remember was his *presence*, as always. Contemplative, gentle, deliberate. I remember the silence in the room as he towered over the podium with spectacles, bow tie, and shock of hair in tact. I remember feeling envious, again, of my friends who had had the luxury of time spent with him in study. And I am glad to be able to write of that here.

My own mentor and doctoral advisor—and friend—Bill Pinar has been deep friends with Bill Doll for over forty years. Their friendship—to see them together or to read what Pinar writes of him—is powerful and moving. In *The Synoptic Text Today and Other Essays: Curriculum Development After the Reconceptualization* (2006), Pinar writes,

> Bill has always demonstrated a profound concern for me as person, a keen and enduring interest in my career, and an unquestioned commitment to our common cause: a sophisticated field of curriculum studies through which the practice of education might become more complex, more nuanced, more progressive. That commitment has been a reflection of Bill's own pedagogical practice, a practice not confined to the classroom, but extended in highly individuated ways to those of us he has so generously befriended.
>
> (p. 9)

Reading what I've written above, it is not a stretch for me to have turned to *Struggles With Spirituality* (2002) to turn to Doll. In fact, it is critical that I do. My challenge, my struggle, invites theological thinking and frames that will enrich the complexity, nuance, and progressive possibilities for education. I'll keep working and see what illumination comes from my study of it. The contemplation with which he approaches the most ordinary response, the idea of our work as teachers and theorists being in-spirited—being *breathed in* with a sacred spirit of wisdom—and the mindfulness (my word) with which he is present in the briefest of encounters in such a way that they stay with you more than a decade later—if these are all I know of Bill Doll, I know him in abundance.

Note

I owe a special gratitude to Molly Quinn, whose own spirit connects with Bill Doll's in some cosmic way. Thus, her editorial comments served to inspirit this piece.

References

Bonhoeffer, D. (2008). *Ethics 6* (Dietrich Bonhoeffer Works). Minneapolis, MN: Fortress Press.
Doll, W. (2002). Struggles with spirituality. In T. Oldenski & D. Carlson (Eds.), *Educational yearning: The journey of the spirit and democratic education*. New York, NY: Peter Lang.
Miller, J. (2010). "Nostalgia for the Future: Imagining Histories of JCT and the Bergamo Conferences." 2009 Bergamo Conference Keynote Address. *Journal of Curriculum Theorizing*. 26(2), 7–23.
Otto, R. (1958). *The idea of the holy* (2nd ed.). London: Oxford University Press.
Pinar, W. (2006). *The synoptic text today and other essays: Curriculum development after the reconceptualization*. New York, NY: Peter Lang.
Whitlock, R. U. (2017, March). *Intentional monogomy in the age of tinder: Queer theology and re-thinking Christian sexual ethics*. Paper presented at the Southeastern Women's Studies Association Conference, Kennesaw, Georgia.

17 Addressing "Curriculum" as an Inspirited Letter

Nicholas Ng-A-Fook

Dear Bill,

I am on my way back from a trip to Wuhan, China, which is located just over 800 kilometers west of Shanghai. I was fortunate enough to receive an invitation from Dr. Yao to share and exchange knowledge about our teacher education programs at her university, China Central Normal University (CCNU). In 2016, she traveled to Ottawa to visit and study different ways for conceiving and doing curriculum theorizing and life writing research. It was an enriching "reflective" and "recursive" lived experience for the both of us (Doll, 1993). Although she described the beauty of Wuhan in our conversations during her stay here at the University of Ottawa, it did not fully encapsulate the sensual experiences of visiting the complexities and seasonal beauty of its landscape. We strolled across campus, in deep conversation, while multicolored maple leaves sailed gently toward the ground.

Wuhan is Hubei Province's most populous city (10.5 million people). Like other cities here in Canada, it is now an amalgamation of three smaller cities: Hankou (Economic center and port to the rivers), Wuchan (Innovation and Research Hub), and Hanyang (Manufacturing District). By all accounts, it is the historical and contemporary gateway to the rest of China. We were lucky enough to enjoy clear blue skies during our first few days. Dr. Yao's graduate students took us to visit the Yellow Crane Tower and the Hubei Museum of History. While visiting the Yellow Crane Tower, situated on Snake Hill, we learned that it dates back to AD 223. It initially served as a defensive lookout post at its original location, which was closer to the shores of the Yangtze River. The Yellow Crane Tower was also a prominent site of inspiration for Chinese poets to visit, correspond, contemplate, and write poetry.

Timothy Stanley, an antiracist educator and historian of Chinese-Canadian history, also made the trip to CCNU. He shared some thought-provoking lectures on how antiracist education as a pedagogical methodology has failed us. One only has to turn on the television to see news headlines of "White supremacists" and the "Alt-Right." Much like your foundational works and those of Bill Pinar, he asks us to study history, more specifically the history of White Supremacy, in relation to its manifestations in the present, in order for us to reimagine how we might address it in the future both inside and outside the institutional curriculum of teacher education (Stanley, 2006, 2015). We teased Tim, who is fluent in speaking and reading Mandarin Chinese. But, because of his time studying and living in Beijing during the 1970s, he often uses colloquial accentuated terms that no longer exist (but live through him) from that historical era.

On the flight to Wuhan, I read *Curriculum Windows: What Curriculum Theorists of the 1980s Can Teach Us About Schools and Society Today*. I was asked to review it for *Teachers College Record*. The collection, edited by Thomas S. Poetter, Kelly Waldrop, Chloe Bolyard, and Vicka Bell-Robinson (2016), is comprised of a series of chapters that examine key books written within the field of curriculum studies during the 1980s. The collection itself is part of a larger book series. The other edited collections address texts from the 1960s, 1970s, and 1990s. In the introduction, Poetter (2016) tells us:

> It's important to recognize that the metaphor of the window is familiar to us and seems almost natural in terms of its serviceability as a metaphor. Meaning, we have experiences in our own lives of gazing out or into windows (or passing through them), whether they be in homes or cars or elsewhere. Sometimes these are typically present and pleasant memories and actions, tied often to the gift of free time or the opportunity to reflect, dream, ponder, and wonder.
>
> (p. xxvii)

I have been recursively reflecting, on reflecting, about the historical post-it notes you left us on different curriculum windows (Doll, 2012a). Such action of reflexivity has been a gift of free time, to dream, ponder, and wonder. You have created such historical windows with what Sarah Smitherman (2005) calls elsewhere, "*bounded infinity*."

In her groundbreaking chapter, Smitherman (2005) asked us to "imagine all the numbers that exist on a number line between the integers of zero to one" as "a bounded set of an infinite amount of members" (p. 159). The fractal image of Koch's curve, she told us then, is another example "where the area of a triangle remains within the boundary of the circle (the area of the circle remains fixed), while the perimeter of the triangle increases to infinity" (p. 159). During our Friday morning seminars, Sarah and you often stressed that such metaphors, and their complexities, provide only a "glimpse of some ideas that can be produced from a non-linear perspective in the classroom" (p. 162). In many ways you modeled, in non-modeled fashion, a nonlinear course syllabus. Our time corresponding together in complicated conversations about ghosts in the curriculum (Bateson, 1979;

Dewey, 1902/1990; Whitehead, 1929/1967), whether that was in Peabody Hall, or later over lunch at Arzi's, was us, with you, becoming community. For you, of all the five C's—*Currere*, Complexity, Cosmology, and Conversation—Community was the most important. "Community, with its emphasis on both care and critique—an emphasis that requires a high degree of trust—is what helps elevate," as you so often stressed then, "us above ourselves" (p. 50). Whether it was traveling to the zydeco dance clubs with Laura Jewett (2008), or spending American Thanksgiving with Sarah, Mei, Hongyu, Bill, Jeff, Donna, and you at your house, I was fortunate enough to experience as a graduate student, a friend, and a colleague, a familial community during my studies at Louisiana State University. Like Ted T. Aoki (1987/2005) here in Canada, during our courses on those Friday mornings, you called on "us to be aware that even the most seemingly benign educational act is a political act, one with strong ethical implications" (Doll, 2012a, p. 169). To this pedagogical end, we studied and read the differing histories of our fields of study as an inspired educational act, whereby means made no promises to their ends.

For the past several months, I have studied some of the historical windows you framed with different views in mind. During the 1970s, as a graduate student at Johns Hopkins University, you worked on several book reviews. Reading, studying, and critically reflecting on such earlier works, we can (re)view the pedagogical ways you troubled (quite generously) the works of Ryland W. Crary (1969), who in turn, asked: How might we humanize a school? "Crary's basic theme," for you, was "the conflict that exists between humanitarian values and industrial or technological values; professionalism for the college professor has been interpreted within a humanitarian framework, but for the school teacher within a technological framework" (Doll, 1970a, p. 332). You were critical of Crary's (1969a) instruction to teachers, for them to analyze the issues of their times and, in turn, interpret them for youth. Instead, you called on students, to do their own analysis and interpretation of, for example, the Vietnam War (Doll, 2012b). Here the goal of reeducation bothered you, when it became more nationalistic and technological in its "aims" (Whitehead's, 1929/1967), seeking to produce (or indoctrinate) democratic citizens. Although Crary (1969) called for humanitarian values, the language he drew on supported a nationalistic, production-orientated, technocratic education. You also cautioned, that "there is a definite antithesis between the individual's development as a humanitarian being and his existence within that institutional structure called 'school'" (p. 333). You stressed, "Where Crary emphasized the structure and organization of the curriculum I believe he should emphasize the quality of human interactions," or to quote Dwayne Huebner, "a form of love in action" (p. 333). Today technocratic values continue to creep their way into teacher education programs under the guise of professional accreditation. The University of Ottawa, unfortunately, is no exception.

In another review, titled *Schools Are Killing . . . Vital Learning Force Natural to Every Child*, you drew our attention to Dennison's (1969b) main thesis, namely, "for the elementary school teacher, no matter what the classroom size, to involve and commit himself [themselves], not to the teaching learning process, but to the lives of children" (Doll, 1970b, p. 394). For you, Dennison was not a "naïve idealist believing that learning would occur beautifully if society were not corrupt" (p. 393). Nor was he a negativist of his times. Instead, he was "an activist, a doer" (p. 393). Dennison (1969b) introduced you to alternative community-centered curriculum, where the traditional hierarchical institutional structures of the school were removed.

> The First Street School was not "child-centered"; rather, it was community-centered. That is, it was based not upon the children nor upon the adults, but on the interaction between them and on the interaction between both and the environment in which they lived.
> (Doll, 1970b, p. 393)

For Dennison, and you, this was part of inspiring the school curriculum as community. On those Friday mornings, I missed a pedagogical opportunity, to ask about your lived experiences during the 1970s, times when America was at war with itself, the world beyond its borders (in Vietnam), and disenfranchised African-American and Native American youth. In hindsight, I took such missed pedagogical opportunities for granted. Shortly after my arrival to the American south, I witnessed alongside you, and others, the geopolitical, material, and psychic horrors of 9/11. In response, Uncle Sam sent troops, once again, to Iraq and later (with Canada) to Afghanistan. So many children around the world are still suffering the intergenerational violence of differing values both at home and abroad.

In these earlier works, we get glimpses, through small windows, of past political activism . . . like *Why Johns Hopkins Will Terminate Its Department of Education*. "One cannot help but wonder how the university orders its priorities," you lamented then. "And to what degree the narrow view of education as an inferior activity has obscured the potentialities inherent in a thorough study of both the theory and practice of this enterprise" (Doll, 1970c, p. 13). During the 1970s, whether that was at State University of New York, or later as Director of Education at Redlands, you continued to trouble the false dichotomy between theory and practice in relation to the coming of a post-industrial society (Doll, 1978, 2012b). "The word 'post-industrial' refers only to the social organization of society, especially as this organization is determined or influenced," as you wrote then, "by changing economic and technological forces. These techno-economic forces pose problems for the polity and the culture, but they do not control or determine either" (Doll, 1978, p. 334). Drawing

"Curriculum" as an Inspired Letter   157

on Daniel Bell's (1973) work, you observed, "the post-industrial society has been labeled an automated society, a knowledge society, a leisure society, a technological society, a change society, and a service society" (p. 338). In such a society, as you both forecasted, "the prime commodity will be knowledge, but not just knowledge, for the axial principle of post-industrialism is the 'centrality of theoretical knowledge'" (p. 338). Today, how much has changed or stayed the same since Daniel Bell, and you, foreshadowed the curricular and pedagogical implications of centralizing theoretical knowledge in a post-industrial society?

In *Schools in a Post-Industrial Society*, we can study your early imaginings of "a modernist mind-view," "Puritan restraint," "Protestant ethic," "technology of instruction," "theoretical knowledge," and an "alternative methodology." As you astutely put forth then, "the copying pattern used in so much of today's schooling will no longer be appropriate; a new methodology using alternatives, contrasts, anomalies will need to be developed" (Doll, 1978, p. 348). Such alternatives, call for a new social imaginary, a reconceptualized mind-view, "to replace the technocratic" (p. 349). In turn, you stressed that the greatest challenge facing educators come the 21st century, or curriculum theorists more specifically, is in their creative and imaginary capacities "to develop a methodology to express this new mind-view" (p. 350). While visiting Wuhan, I saw different Chinese curriculum scholars committed to reconceptualizing the mind-views that currently inform their public schooling and its respective national curriculum. Such commitments are also present here in Ontario.

During your tenure at State University of New York, you continued to work on reconceptualizing *A Structural View of Curriculum*. This essay begins with a recollection of the 1976 ASCD conference where James Popham and Arthur Combs dueled it out in an ongoing debate that attempted to reconcile behaviorism and humanism (Doll, 1979). Inspired with the ghosts of Dewey (1938) and the debates of his times (traditional versus progressive), you took readers on a journey that navigated the different theoretical and methodological borders of behaviorist, humanist, ecological, and structural models. And stressed, that the field of education, is not yet ready for an alternative model. Despite such lack of readiness, you were optimistic in your tone of conversation.

> I believe our society, particularly in the decade of the 1980s, is about to enter a new revolutionary transition phase much akin to the transition phase it entered approximately one hundred years ago when we passed from an agricultural-mercantile economy to an industrial economy. That transition caused a major upheaval, in America's concept of education and schooling, and I believe this transition will cause just as great a change, but hopefully not so great an upheaval.
> (p. 337)

Once again, as a curriculum theorist ahead of your times, you provided a historical overview of the cognitive, cultural, philosophical, and political underpinnings that informed a behaviorist model and, how in turn, it has dominated 20th century educational theory. In many ways, the ghosts of a behaviorist model are still present. Despite technological and pedagogical advancements, the industrial school bell still tolls for youth. You reminded readers that such models set up their purposes first, and then correlate various activities to them. You warned that such an end-means industrial model limits our capacity to learn from our lived experiences as the school curriculum. Turning our attention back to Dewey (1938), you caution that "not only is it incorrect to separate ends from means, it is even incorrect to see ends as thing-in-themselves," as "things lying beyond activities"; rather, ends should be considered as "end-in-view," as "turning points in activity," as "terminals of deliberation" (p. 337). Such a reductive and segregated model, as you forewarned us then, "translates into an emphasis on skills or 'competencies.' Not as tools for further growth and development, but as ends in and of themselves" (p. 337). Education, conceived within this mind-view, becomes a reductive (accreditation) checklist of exit outcomes one must complete.

Building on such thought-provoking theoretical work (Doll, 1978), the following year you invited readers to contemplate a world beyond a technocratic mind-view.

> First, I wanted to show that the fundamental tenets of behaviorism are by no means indigenous to either America or the twentieth century; rather they are associated with the very nature of industrialism itself, and draw upon a particular branch of Western, scientific rationality—a branch which is strongly committed to the technocratic paradigm.
>
> (Doll, 1979, p. 338)

Frederick Taylor, as you pointed out, was able to apply such scientific rationality to modes of "best practices" within industry. "Taylor believed that via time and motion studies, using pay as an incentive, fitting the men to the job, and removing all planning and scheduling to a new department of planning and scheduling he could set 'scientific' standards for the one best way to do any give task" (p. 338). Here, we can study, you studying, working through, curriculum theorizing a different branch of Western scientific rationality.

In *Prigogine: A New Sense of Order, A New Curriculum*, we are introduced to three different historical paradigms: (1) Classical-Christian view (Aristotle, Ptolemy, and Thomas Aquinas); (2) Classical-scientific view (Newtonian); and (3) Quantum view. You trace the third view to and through the works of Albert Einstein, Niels Bohr, Werner Heisenberg, and Ilya Prigogine. "Fifty years after these debates, Prigogine has," as you point out, "added new dimensions to the paradigm with his investigation of dissipative and self-organizing structures" (Doll, 1986, p. 11). Fascinating! What would it mean to live together, and within schools, as dissipative and self-organizing structures? You drew on these differing paradigms to both trouble and move beyond the reproduction of a measured curriculum. Moving beyond, calls on us to reconceptualize our mind-views, to see "the world, the universe, and reality itself" as a "dynamic relationship between order and chaos and the nature of transformatory (or becoming) change" (p. 13). Curriculum theorizing, with such alternative views in mind, becomes a productive intellectual site (foresight reflecting on hindsight) for transformative curriculum work, where our realities as teachers and students, our lived experiences, are acknowledged as being "multiple, temporal, and complex" (p. 14). My sense is, that the current mind(less)-view of teacher education here in Ontario and elsewhere—as a certain kind of universalized accreditation, of technocratic professionalization—calls on us to carefully recursively revisit the historical post-it notes, you have so generously left, on the frames of our curriculum windows.

In China, I was able to visit the Wuhan Yucai Second Primary School. Three thousand children from grades 1 to 6 attend this elementary school. The average class size is fifty to fifty-three students. The school is part of Dr. Yuan-xiang Guo's (Dr. Yao's doctoral advisor, now colleague) national school-based curriculum research project. The school administration and teachers are collaborating with his research team to reconceptualize, develop, and live an inspired curriculum as a community. It was a fortuitous coincidence, to then see an interpretation of your *3S's Mysterium Tremendum* curriculum on one of the school's poster boards. The school is set up much like John Dewey's (1902/1990) Chicago Lab School. And, the school-based curriculum draws on your initial conceptions of a 3S's curriculum, which seeks to combine "the rigorousness of *science*, with the imagination of *story*, with the vitality and creativity of *spirit*" (Doll, 2002, p. 48). Their interpretations of your reconceptualizations are as follows:

1. **Spirit**: A focus on moral and aesthetic education. Create time and spaces within the school curriculum for students to engage moral and aesthetic education in activities, life and practice. It also includes spiritual experience and aesthetic cultivation. **Courses in**: Chorus, Traditional Drama, Percussion, Theater, Print, Dance, Art, Painting, Conversation, Basketball, Track and Field, and Soccer.
2. **STEM**: Students develop their capacities in observation, problems solving, creativity, and imagination. The curriculum seeks to create time and spaces for students to develop a spirit of innovation and practical abilities. **Courses in**: Robotics, 3D Printing, Coding, Video Production, Animation, and Mathematics.

3. **Social practice**: Students participate in different social activities that seek to enhance their sense of social responsibility by enacting a lived curriculum and reflecting on their respective lived experiences. **Courses in**: History, Culture, and Travel within Wuhan, Travel Studies, Agriculture and Forestry Practices, and Leadership.[1]

During their studies at the school students are able to choose several of these courses as electives. The school seeks, much like the First Street School, to provide a curriculum, not solely focused on learning, "but upon living," where the "quality of living" has "sufficient depth" (Doll, 1970b, p. 393). Dr. Guo expressed, that the national reforms of the Chinese curriculum, the focus on standardized testing (*Gaokao*, the national college entrance exam), and academic achievement have anesthetized the lived curriculum for many students at school. Over our conversations at dinner, he stressed that more creativity as a lived aesthetic-ness is needed across the school curriculum. In response, they are seeking, a different (unified) way of thinking, theorizing, and doing school curriculum.

What I witnessed in Wuhan, at that school, and in our conversations, is that your intellectual work continues to provide a reflective window, for us to rethink, our approaches to "life and our activities in life, including teaching and curriculum design, in a way that allows the spirit or soul of these activities and of ourselves to come forth" (Doll, 2012a, p. 166). To be a small part of the community that studied and lived your teachings, I thank you.

In honor of a friend and fellow poet, Li Bai wrote *Seeing Off Meng Haoran for Guangling at Yellow Crane Tower*. I leave you with his words:

> My friend said goodbye leaving the west from Yellow Crane Tower.
> In the patterned mist of the third month, he goes down to Yangzhou.
>   His lone sail is an image far on the limit of jade green air. I sense only the Long River's flow, interfacing sky.

Until, Nicholas

References

Aoki, T. T. (1987/2005). Inspiriting the curriculum. In W. F. Pinar & R. L. Irwin (Eds.), *Curriculum in a new key: The collected works of Ted T. Aoki* (pp. 357–365). Mahwah, NJ: Lawrence Erlbaum.

---

1. I would like to thank Ma Jingmeng for being our translator while in Wuhan. She also provided the generous liberal translation of the three S's poster. More research, on my part, needs to be done on how Dr. Guo's research team is developing, implementing, and living a three S's curriculum with teachers and students at the different lab schools.

Bai, L. (701–762 CE). *Seeing off Meng Haoran for Guangling at Yellow Crane Tower* (William P. Coleman, Trans.). Retrieved December 12, 2017, from https://williampcoleman.wordpress.com/2008/03/19/li-bai-seeing-off-meng-haoran-at-yellow-crane-tower-on-his-way-to-guangling/.

Bateson, G. (1979). *Mind and nature: A necessary unity*. New York, NY: E. P. Dutton.

Bell, D. (1973). *The coming of post-industrial society*. New York, NY: Basic Books.

Crary, R. W. (1969). *Humanizing the school*. New York, NY: Alfred A. Knopf.

Dennison, G. (1969b). *The lives of children*. New York, NY: Random House.

Dewey, J. (1990). *The school and society*. Chicago, IL: University of Chicago Press. (Original work published in 1902)

Dewey, J. (1997). *Experience and education*. New York, NY: Simon & Schuster. (Original work published in 1938)

Doll, W. (1970a). Humanizing schools: A problem of curriculum or personal relations? *The Phi Delta Kappan, 51*(6), 332–333.

Doll, W. (1970b). Schools are killing . . . Vital learning force natural to every child. *The Phi Delta Kappan, 51*(7), 393–394.

Doll, W. (1970c). Why Johns Hopkins will terminate its department of education. *The Phi Delta Kappan, 51*(1), 13.

Doll, W. (1978). Schooling in a post-industrial society. *The High School Journal, 61*(8), 333–352.

Doll, W. (1979). A structural view of curriculum. *Theory Into Practice, 18*(5), 336–348.

Doll, W. (1986). Prigogine: A new sense of order, a new curriculum. *Theory Into Practice, 25*(1), 10–16.

Doll, W. (1993). *A post-modern perspective on curriculum*. New York, NY: Teachers College Press.

Doll, W. (2002). Ghosts and the curriculum. In W. E. Doll & N. Gough (Eds.), *Curriculum visions* (pp. 23–70). New York, NY: Peter Lang.

Doll, W. (2012a). Revisiting Aoki's "inspiriting the curriculum." In N. Ng-A-Fook & J. Rottmann (Eds.), *Reconsidering Canadian curriculum studies* (pp. 165–174). New York, NY: Palgrave Macmillan.

Doll, W. (2012b). *Pragmatism, post-modernism, and complexity theory: The "fascinating imaginative realm" of William E. Doll, Jr.* New York, NY: Routledge.

Jewett, L. (2008). *A delicate dance: Autoethnography, curriculum, and semblance of intimacy*. New York, NY: Peter Lang.

Poetter, T. S. (2016). Introduction—Curriculum windows of the 1990s. In T. S. Poetter, K. Waldrop, C. Bolyard, & V. Bell-Robinson (Eds.), *Curriculum windows: What curriculum theorists of the 1980s can teach us about schools and society today* (pp. xxix–xxxviii). Charlotte, NC: Information Age Publishing.

Poetter, T. S., Waldrop, K., Bolyard, C., & Bell-Robinson, V. (2016). *Curriculum windows: What curriculum theorists of the 1980s can teach us about schools and society today*. Charlotte, NC: Information Age Publishing.

Smitherman, S. (2005). Chaos and complexity theories: Wholes and holes in curriculum. In W. E. Doll, Jr., M. Jayne Fleener, Donna Trueit, & John St. Julien (Eds.), *Chaos, complexity, curriculum, and culture: A conversation*. New York, NY: Peter Lang.

Stanley, T. J. (2006). Whose public? Whose memory? Racisms, grand narratives and Canadian history. In R. W. Sandwell (Ed.), *To the past: History education, public memory, and citizenship in Canada* (pp. 32–49). Toronto, ON: University of Toronto Press.

Stanley, T. J. (2015). The strong poetry of Won Alexander Cumyow: Rethinking narratives of connections across time and place. In N. Ng-A-Fook, A. Ibrahim, & G. Reis (Eds.), *Provoking curriculum studies: Strong poets and the arts of the possible* (pp. 74–90). New York, NY: Routledge.

Whitehead, A. N. (1929/1967). *The aims of education and other essays*. New York, NY: Free Press.

18 The Pedagogy of the King of Chaos in a Post-modern Era

Jie Yu

A long, long time ago, there was a monkey born from a rock in a big storm at the far end of the East China Sea (Wu, 2003). As one of the most well-known mystery figures in China, this monkey king is famous for his untiring battles against rigid social structure. He is also called the King of Chaos because of both his birth from chaos and his adventures against all dead orders such as the caste system.

When William Doll visited China in 2007, one of the Chinese hosts, a middle school principal, called him the "King of Chaos" after Doll finished a keynote conference presentation on his post-modern pedagogy (Doll, 1993). After the principal explained why he thought of Doll as the King of Chaos, Doll was immediately fascinated by the story of the monkey king and loved his new nickname in China. Later, Doll often would call himself the King of Chaos and celebrate being given such a title.

Like his idol, John Dewey, Doll has since claimed China as his second home country, after the U.S. As his former graduate student, book translator, and conference interpreter, I went to China with Doll and his wife, Donna Trueit, in 2007, 2010, and 2011, presenting in international and national conferences of education, visiting K-12 schools and teacher education programs in colleges and universities, and having conversations with Chinese educators. Following his footsteps in the last three trips across eight major cities[1] in China, this chapter tries to capture those precious moments and conversations Doll, the King of Chaos, had with Chinese educators at multiple levels to explore the significant influences of his post-modern pedagogy in China. I borrow the term *iteration* from chaos theory to highlight the critical incidents in Doll's *currere* during the three trips, along with their significant impacts upon Chinese educational scholars and practitioners: the first iteration in 2007 as the father of post-modern curriculum theory, the second iteration in 2010 as the King of Chaos, and finally the third iteration in 2011 on "a third way."

---

1. The eight cities visited were Shanghai, Beijing, Harbin, Guilin, Xi'an, Hangzhou, Nangjing, and Rugao.

First Iteration, 2007: The Father of Post-modern Curriculum Theory

In May and June, 2007, nine education faculty members and graduate students led by Doll from Louisiana State University (LSU) attended the First International Conference of Teacher Reform in Shanghai, and then presented in East China Normal University in Shanghai, Guangxi Normal University in Guilin, Shanxi Normal University in Xi'an, Harbin Normal University in Harbin, Capital Normal University and the China National Institute for Educational Research in Beijing. In this trip, we also visited local school districts and talked to administrators, faculties, graduate students, school principals, teachers, and students in K-16 schools across the five cities. All of the institutions we visited in 2007 were most interested in the famous four R's (richness, recursion, relations, and rigor) Doll developed in his *A Post-modern Perspective on Curriculum* (1993). This book was translated and published in Chinese in 2000 and soon became a classic until now in the field of education, not merely curriculum studies. It can be said that Doll first became familiar to Chinese educators as the Father of Post-modern Curriculum Theory who developed the four R's as an alternative to the Tyler Rationale.

One of the most frequently asked questions Doll received during this trip was the ways to *directly* apply the four R's to practical classroom situations in the Chinese public schooling system. Doll (2008) carefully warned his Chinese audiences against "a 'models' frame with its emphasis on a universal form to be followed by all" because "a post-modern approach favors local autonomy, with the sense of general direction coming not from imposition, or direction above" (p. 3).

In this trip, Doll also demonstrated a great interest in the unique history and culture of China. Doll (2008) ended his reflection paper upon this trip with the first school we visited in the summer of 2007. He writes:

> I came away from that school inspired as to what can happen in a normal, inner city school. But I also left with a touch of sadness. In the last classroom we visited a play was to be performed. I was most excited, anticipating a play depicting a story from China's ancient and rich culture. Here was something I would never see in the U.S. Alas, it was not to be. The play was based on Western culture. I expect the teacher wished to show a play that we Americans would understand. I, though, so wanted to reach out and touch the glorious culture of China. I was sad the students did not proudly display their culture, so that we could then discuss with them what their culture meant to them and what we from the U.S. saw in that culture. No nation has the depth and richness of culture that China does. I hope on the next visit to see the magnificence of that culture, not only in China's museums, parks, buildings and older sections but also in its

schools. It is the past with all its glories and failures that makes the present alive and vital.

(p. 8)

As a Chinese graduate student studying education in the U.S. at that time, I was impressed by not only the awe Doll had in the brilliant Chinese culture but his hope, a strong desire to see this culture with an over two-thousand-year history still living vibrantly in the contemporary Chinese society among people rather than in the limelight in museums. Later Doll mentioned his visit to that school in Shanghai several times in the following lectures and conversations he had with Chinese educators during this trip. One high school teacher commented after listening to Doll's reflection on the story: "I think what you wanted to tell us is not just keeping knowledge alive in classrooms by utilizing the 4R's, but keeping *our* culture alive in and through schools." Doll's immediate response was a long applause. I choose this story to end the first iteration in 2007 because I think the high school teacher's comment could be a perfect summary of the important message Doll tried to send to his Chinese readers and audiences in this trip.

Second Iteration, 2010: The King of Chaos

As suggested by the title of Doll's last book, *Pragmatism, Post-modernism, and Complexity Theory: The "Fascinating Imaginative Realm" of William E. Doll* (2012b), a collection of his major works from 1972 to 2011, complexity theory has been one of his major research interests since the 1990s. As one of the primary founders of the Special Interest Group of Complexity and Chaos in the American Educational Research Association, Doll has been working closely with a group of committed researchers in complexity and chaos theories in the field of education. The book, *Chaos, Complexity, Curriculum and Culture*, co-edited with Fleener, Trueit, and St. Julien, was first published in the U.S. in 2005 and later translated into Chinese by me and published in China in 2014. It has become now a seminal work for those with interest in complexity theory and education in both countries.

In November 2005, I worked with Doll as his graduate assistant to help organize the annual Complexity Science and Educational Research Conference hosted by the Curriculum Theory Project of LSU in Louisiana. In the fall of 2009, Dr. Hua Zhang, one of Doll's close academic and personal friends in China and my former major professor at East China Normal University (ECNU), cordially invited the Complexity Science and Education Research group to consider Shanghai as the site for the following conference while there was a growing interest in complexity and chaos theories in Chinese educators. Based upon the hard work and close collaboration between the research group and the Department of Curriculum and Instruction at ECNU, especially Doll and Zhang, the annual Complexity Science and Educational Research Conference was held in Shanghai in November, 2010. Over 230 educational researchers, educational commission administrators, school principals and teachers participated in this conference with the theme of "Complexity, Chinese Culture and Curriculum Reform." The participants from five countries discussed a variety of educational themes and topics from their historical, philosophical, and culturally different perspectives as related to complexity and chaos theories in education. As the Chinese educators were able to listen to the keynote presentations by some of the leading educational researchers in complexity theory, the Western scholars also had a chance to look deep into the Chinese culture and educational system. As reflected by Doll (2012a), "The conference was full of dynamic interplay. . . . The insights gathered from each are great" (p. 1). It was in this complex and dynamic process of conversing with the other that new ideas and new ways of thinking emerged.

In this conference, Doll engaged with the multiple Chinese audiences upon both the present and future of complexity and chaos theories in education through academic presentations, conference forums and discussions, personal communications and school visits. He called on Chinese educators to draw on the new sciences of complexity and chaos as a foundation for curriculum design and instructional strategies. After the conference, Doll worked with Barney Ricca, the editor-in-chief of *Complicity: An International Journal of Complexity and Education*, and me for a special issue of the journal, a collection of four papers from Western educators and four from China. All of the papers were from the Complexity conference presentations in Shanghai. Dynamic conversations between the East and West, the ancient, modern and post-modern, theory and practice, local and global, and simplicity and complexity were woven throughout all of the eight articles. The tensioned differences generated in the conversations forms a pedagogical bridging between China and the U.S. As commented by Doll (2012a), "This conference is only the beginning of building a mythical bridge that each group may walk and talk with the other" (p. 1). He began to shine as the King of Chaos in China since this Complexity and Education conference in Shanghai and significantly inspired more and more interests and researchers in Complexity and Education in China since 2010.

Third Iteration, 2011: "A Third Way"

In December, 2011, Doll was invited by the Rugao City Public Schools (RCPS) in the Jiangsu Province as the keynote speaker in one of its most important annual meetings to recruit principals and teachers in the school district. The RCPS director became very interested in Doll's post-modern theory after he attended Doll's presentation in the Complexity and Education conference in Shanghai in 2010 and then invited Doll through Hua Zhang at ECNU. Unlike most of the interactions with educational researchers in academic conferences in previous visits to China, Doll came into direct contact with school district administrators, school principals and practicing teachers in the Chinese public schooling system. If he entered the ivory towers of research at the top of the pyramid of the educational system in China in former visits, this time Doll had a chance to step down to experience the base or foundation of this huge pyramid in Rugao. Doll (2012c) found this unique visit was "a revelation, an epiphany" (p. 1). In our visit to one of the largest urban public schools in Rugao, The An Ding Elementary School, students played ancient songs with traditional Chinese musical instruments in a Confucian temple on campus. When we walked into the building of classrooms, the celebrations of Halloween immediately jumped into our sights. Doll was pleased to feel a sense of diverse cultures in the school.

When he observed the activity-centered curriculum and instruction in Rugao's schools supported by the district, Doll (2012c) was both "intrigued and bothered":

> The intrigue was in seeing activity in the form of conversation about the subject being studied, this was evident and stunning. The bother, to me as a westerner talking about John Dewey, was that the conversation was tightly controlled, orchestrated. My dilemma: How could I offer helpful comments when my educational frame, coming from Dewey, was on having educational goals emerge from activities while I was seeing teacher goals controlling the activities? The difference was obvious, developmental teaching versus authoritarian teaching.
>
> (p. 1)

Then an incident occurred at a dinner in Rugao that gave Doll insights into the dilemma. In that dinner, the mayor of Rugao came to kindly shake hands with Doll at his table. After the mayor left, Doll asked me how the mayor could get his position, and my quick response was, "He was appointed from above." Doll later wrote in his reflections:

> China's cultural heritage has been authoritarian for generations, centuries, millennia. It is only natural for their curriculum planning to start with an emphasis on goals determined before activity. John Dewey, a resident of a country where mayors are elected by the people, where all public officials are elected, would naturally advocate beginning with the student's own activity, letting the goals emerge. While Rugao and its activity teaching and Dewey and his developmental teaching do start from opposite directions they meet over the concept of conversation. . . . Each country can honor its cultural heritage, and know that these heritages and the curriculum which flows from them meet in the "third space" of conversation.
>
> (p. 1)

As Doll encourages educators from the U.S. and China to continue such productive conversations in the middle space between two different cultures, histories, and educational systems, this is what he has been doing for the past almost two decades between the two countries. Through such conversations, he believes the U.S. can learn from China "a sense of the aesthetic, of the beauty and artistry that exists in life, and of the wisdom which flows from such an aesthetic" while China can learn from the U.S. "being creative in teaching [and] using conversation to explore the unknown" (p. 1). Rather than looking to one country for quick remedies to fix problems in the other country, or establishing one country as a model for the other to follow, Doll wants the educators in both countries to focus on the generative differences to tap into the possibilities of learning from and at the same time collaborating with each other. Doll calls this path "a third way," a way the cultural frames of the U.S. and China could "cooperate without losing their integrity" (p. 1).

Postlude

When it came to the end of writing this chapter, I googled "William Doll" and "post-modern curriculum theory" in English and found about 54,900 results, but it was about 383,000 in Chinese. Then I googled "William Doll" and "post-modern" in English, which yielded about 225,000 results, and 2,270,000 in Chinese. Until now three books written or edited by Doll (2000), Doll and Gough (2004), Doll, et al. (2014) have been translated into Chinese and published in China. Based upon the CSSCI (Chinese Social Sciences Citation Index), his *Post-modern Perspective* book ranked 7th in the list of top 10 most-cited academic books by foreign scholars in the CSSCI publications of educational research in the first decade of the 21st century (Su, 2012). This list also includes J. Dewey's "Democracy and Education" (1916), J. Rawls's "A Theory of Justice" (1971), J. Brubacher's "On the Philosophy of Higher Education" (1977), and B. Clark's "The Higher Education System" (1986). Undoubtedly, Doll has become one of the most influential contemporary scholars among Chinese educators. As Doll's former graduate student, I feel honored and proud that I was able to be part of his team in his past three trips to China between 2007 and 2011. During the trips, Doll untiringly conducted productive conversations with multiple audiences, including policy makers from both the local and national Department of Education, researchers from educational research institutes, education faculties from colleges and universities, administrators from school districts, school principals, teachers, and students. On a bridge "which is not a bridge," Doll let the conversations go on between two cultures, countries, and education systems (Aoki, 2005, p. 228).

References

Aoki, T. (2005). *Curriculum in a new key: The collected works of Ted T. Aoki.* Mahwah, NJ: Lawrence Erlbaum Associates Publishers.

Brubacher, J. S. (1977). *On the philosophy of higher education*. San Francisco, CA: Jossey-Bass.
Clark, B. R. (1986). *The higher education system: Academic organization in cross-national perspective*. Berkeley, CA: University of California Press.
Dewey, J. (1916). *Democracy and education*. New York, NY: The Free Press.
Doll, W. (1993). *A post-modern perspective on curriculum*. New York, NY: Teachers College Press.
Doll, W. (2000). *A post-modern perspective on curriculum* (H. Wang, Trans.). Beijing: China Educational Science Publishing House. (Original work published in 1993)
Doll, W. (2008). Experiences of the post-modern in China: Utilizing the 4R's. (J. Yu, Trans.). *Global Education*, 37(11), 3–6.
Doll, W. (2012a). Complexity science and educational research conference, Shanghai 2010: Prolegomena. *Complicity: An International Journal of Complexity and Education*, 9(1), 1–2.
Doll, W. (2012b). *Pragmatism, post-modernism, and complexity theory: The "fascinating imaginative realm" of William E. Doll, Jr.* (D. Trueit, Ed.). New York, NY: Routledge.
Doll, W. (2012c). Reflections on five visits to Chinese schools (J. Yu, Trans.). *Shanghai Educational Sciences*, 2, 1.
Doll, W., Fleener, M. J., Trueit, D., & St. Julien, J. (Eds.). (2005). *Chaos, complexity, curriculum, and culture: A conversation*. New York, NY: Peter Lang.
Doll, W., Fleener, M. J., Trueit, D., & St. Julien, J. (Eds.). (2014). *Chaos, complexity, curriculum, and culture: A conversation* (J. Yu, Trans.). Beijing: China Educational Science Publishing House. (Original work published in 2005)
Doll, W., & Gough, N. (Eds.). (2002). *Curriculum visions*. New York, NY: Peter Lang.
Doll, W., & Gough, N. (Eds.). (2004). *Curriculum visions* (W. Zhang, H. Zhang, J. Yu, & H. Wang, Trans.). Beijing: China Educational Science Publishing House. (Original work published in 2002)
Rawls, J. (1971). *A theory of justice*. Cambridge, MA: Harvard University Press.
Su, X. (Ed.). (2012). *A report on the academic impact of Chinese books in the humanities and social sciences*. Beijing: China Social Sciences Publisher.
Wu, C. E. (2003). *Journey to the west* (W.J.F. Jenner, Trans.). Beijing: Foreign Language Press. (Original work published in China in the 16th century)

Part V
Of School, Society, and the Sacred in Scholarly Tradition

Perhaps, if only implicitly, all study of education writ large entails some address of school, society, and scholarly tradition, and their relations. Curriculum studies—attending to curriculum as the contemporary center through which most of educational experience is organized (Pinar, 2012), and we might suggest also conceptualized, actualized, and assessed—likewise has such in view, in the very least as the background, ground or context from which its work is undertaken, even where such is intentionally set aside to imagine and create new possibilities and alternate views. David Gordon (1988), with others, has further asserted here that education serves "as a text that says something about the things society considers sacred" (p. 446). In curriculum, such is reflected, for instance, in the abiding question of what knowledge is of most worth, as well as in its ongoing critique. All such speaks also to the incredible scope and breadth, and heights and depths, of our work in curriculum. Doll's is no exception here, in fact, rather exceptional—exemplary and expansive in its cosmic curricular concerns.

The heading of this section was meant at first to hearken back to work Doll echoes and advances from Dewey's *The School and Society* (1915/1956), as well as locate Doll's work within and in relation to particular schools of thought and illuminate their through-lines in and transformations of, as well as possibilities for, curriculum studies, some of which was to include potential promising influences in schools as well as societies. These essays, and others in the collection, to a good extent, still achieve such. However, as some authors herein began exploring, as proposed, for example, Doll's work in relation to complexity and school education, pragmatism, feminism, and French poststructuralism, the focus of their essays shifted and tenor changed. We find talk of life and death, conversations with ghosts, pedagogy and poetry, reviving vision and living spirit, wrestling and dancing. And thus the sacred had to be brought in, included, and highlighted here too.

If school denotes the act of educating, disciplining, and even reprimanding, Doll *schools* us indeed, and the field in many ways, for instance,

172   Part V: Of School, Society, and the Sacred in Scholarly Tradition

in the ways we are still wrapped up in the work of control, suppressing vision, intellect, and spirit. If school is a place of learning and instruction, of learned conversation, discussion, and debate, a meeting place for students and teachers, Doll illumines much for us herein as well, particularly how to cultivate and sustain such a place as educationally transformative and life affirming, in critical and caring community. If school, and scholar, from the Greek *skhole*, *scholastes*, is contrasted to work (*OED*, 1989), signifying leisure for learning, one who lives at ease, we have much to learn from Doll here too who has lived slowly, deliciously, playfully, poetically, so well the scholarly life and its traditions herein. Tradition— to give over (*trans-*, over; *dare-*, to give)—here involves that which is presented, handed over, given up, delivered, surrendered, presented to us, concerning generational passing down of ways, customs, doctrines, practices of worth, echoes of a sort we may indeed embrace, keep alive and carry forward . . . legacies even to confirm, ratify, consecrate, sanctify, dedicate ourselves to, make sacred (*sak*, PIE, *sacrare*, Latin, *sacrer*, Old Fr.) (*OED*).

And all herein, is sacred too, perhaps, in the sense that it is undertaken ever in and through society—companionship, association, alliance, fellowship; with the awareness of living and dwelling together in community, cultivating shared purposes (and complex conversations), bound as neighbors, engaging an ethics of relationality, respect, and even reverence (Fr *societé*, Latin *societatum*, *OED*). Doll's work and way reminds us of such, envisioned, yes, in that "fascinating imaginative realm where no one owns the truth and everyone has a right to be understood" (Kundera, 1988, cited in Doll, 2006/2012, p. 231).

Nel Noddings frames her discussion of Doll's work and its promise for us in terms of curriculum that is organized around fundamental concerns, the human search for meaning, and educational practice undertaken in ways that genuinely matter respecting such—human growth, community, and relations. Critiquing present conceptions and practices, as she calls for us to revive the post-modern vision of Doll—also via powerful examples in and for schools, looking at his four R's anew (see footnote 9, Quinn, introduction), she highlights his sense of transforming and transformative education that is rooted in the understanding of change as the essence of life, and of living. Authentic, interdisciplinary study and inquiry may promote the "richness" he advocates. In order to gain a new view, see something from a fresh lens, "recursion," too, is of utmost import, where we not only dig into our "own storehouse of knowledge" again and again, but also remind ourselves and build on what was formerly forgotten. As education occurs in an open emergent system, dynamically shifting and moving in dialogue, to attend well to our cultural and pedagogical "relations" is also essential. "Rigor" we find through continual critical thought, practice, and reconstruction within

Part V: Of School, Society, and the Sacred in Scholarly Tradition 173

the pursuit of meaning—Doll's insight to combine the hermeneutics of interpretation with the complexity of indeterminacy.

Critical, too, of present expressions of curriculum, in the school and society, Eero Ropo and Veli-Matti Värri find much, as well, in Doll's complex cosmological vision and work to recommend in relation to the fundamental problems within/of our global community. Here, their focus on interpretation and indeterminacy in relation coheres around Doll's notion of "ghosts" (Doll, 2002), as narratives in curriculum, and education as a site for illuminating, discussing, attending to, such narratives. In such, we may reckon with these ghosts that haunt and control us, what they describe as/extend to: wicked world problems, hybrid and hyperobjects of cultural and material dimensions, formative narratives, which have become a part of our lives—and through the denial of which, and via an instrumental ontology, curricula dangerously keeps alive. Doll's ghost metaphor, as well as his work around the five C's and three S's (see footnotes 10 and 12, Quinn, introduction) of curriculum—advancing rigor, imagination, and vitality; inspire the new ways of thinking and novel approaches required of us in the face of such pressing human questions and concerns in the world.

Denise Egéa also highlights the new ways of thinking and considerations of the field of possibilities we most need and to which Doll summons and provokes us through his work. She skillfully locates his post-modern critique of curriculum within intellectual history and tradition, and in relation/through a return to the work of Edgar Morin, a kindred thinker by whom he was also challenged. In analyzing method, both men—reaching for a "method beyond method"—saw the order within chaos—emerging patterns, organizing principles, if unpredictable. Both honor complexity (for Doll, gleaning the potential of the paradigms of chaos and complexity, honing in on the criteria of paradox, indeterminacy, self-organization and play, 1993): the generative role disorder plays therein, its transformative influence on our conception of knowledge, the way that to reform our education is to reform our thinking, and vice versa. And how the production of knowledge is integrally tied to its evaluation—the significance of recursivity. "Wrestling with complexity," Doll, too, is seen dancing, devoting his career to education that expands human mind and life, with a livelier sense of method, and sight through multiple curricular moves and views.

The "Provoking Curriculum" Conference of which Carl Leggo speaks in his essay, he admits in fact, was inspired by a query of Doll's: *Can you see another way?* It is where Antoinette Oberg gave tribute to Bill, too, via an Argentinian dance—akin to Doll's own imaginative and mythopoetic dance with chaos and order, "leaning into love with tantalizing hope for the other." The poet laureate of curriculum—as Doll dubbed him, Leggo artfully expresses here something of the essence of Doll's gifts to us, as an extraordinary teacher, scholar, and human being—greatly loved, and grandly loving. Visionary, distinguished, eloquent, exuberant, and playful, he notes, Doll:

> lives with a poet's delight in language, dialogue and questioning. . . . "To write poetry . . . is to enter a long, never-ending conversation" ([Neilsen Glenn, 2011] p. 108). Bill invites us to conversation. His life has been devoted to nurturing the complex relationships of knowing that are possible (and possibly impossible) when *I* and *you* interact.

We are taught by Doll—ever learning, and living in wonder, generosity and humility—not only how to be in the academy, from the heart, listening to self and others; but also the art of living itself, and aging, beautifully and well, holistically embracing all of the energies that influence our lives.

Petra Munro Hendry speaks similarly of Doll's "living the spirit of education," and well, education as spirit, and in such: showing us too how to live, with awe, and open arms; attending to the complex relations in which we are embedded, the ironies and indeterminacies; and as mysterious, dynamic and ever becoming. From her lived experience with Bill, and through the temporal lens and lore of Lent and Easter—and interplay of darkness/light and chaos/order from which the new is born/reborn; she notes how we learn from him, too, the art of being present to life—with vitality, integrity, and truthfulness; which means confronting death as well. She highlights his attention to recursion, the return that is also recognition, reminding us of our interconnectedness and interdependence, to reawaken to reverence and relationship and live beyond ourselves. Education, here, is a living process; knowledge: unpredictable, emergent, regenerative—created with others. His unconditional faith in relationships compels us to view our differences as generative sites for expansion and exploration rather than opposition, for living together in complex conversation and creative transformation.

References

Dewey, J. (1956). *The school and society* (Rev. ed.). Chicago, IL: University of Chicago Press. (Original work published in 1915)

Doll, W. (1993). Curriculum possibilities in a "post"-future. *Journal of Curriculum and Supervision*, 8(4), 277–292.

Doll, W. (2002). Ghosts and the curriculum. In W. Doll & N. Gough (Eds.), *Curriculum visions* (pp. 23–70). New York, NY: Peter Lang.

Doll, W. (2012). Looking forward. In D. Trueit (Ed.), *Pragmatism, post-modernism and complexity theory: The "fascinating imaginative realm" of William E. Doll, Jr.* (pp. 228–231). New York, NY: Routledge. (Original work published in 2006)

Gordon, D. (1988). Education as text: The varieties of educational hiddenness. *Curriculum Inquiry, 18*(4), 425–449.

Kundera, M. (1988). *The art of the novel* (L. Asher, Trans.). New York, NY: Grove Press.

Neilsen Glenn, L. (2011). *Threading light: Explorations in loss and poetry.* Regina, SK: Hagios Press.

Oxford English dictionary (OED) (2nd ed.). (1989). (J. Simpson & E. Weiner, Eds.). Oxford, UK: Clarendon Press.

Pinar, W. (2012). *What is curriculum theory?* (2nd ed.). New York, NY: Routledge. (Original work published in 2004)

19 Post-modern Curriculum
Reviving the Vision

Nel Noddings

In *A Post-modern Perspective on Curriculum* (1993), Bill Doll explores ways in which post-modern thinking might transpose education from a closed system characterized by stability, centers, and equilibrium to an open system in which "change not stability is [its] essence" (p. 14). It would require another, much longer, essay to explore why this vision has failed to become a reality. Here I will look at the four criteria at the center of Doll's vision, ask what remains of them, and point to current developments that might renew our hope. He suggests four R's—richness, recursion, relations, and rigor to replace the older, more familiar three R's of reading, 'riting, and 'rithmetic.

Richness

Doll tells us that the term richness "refers to a curriculum's depth, to its layers of meaning, to its multiple possibilities or interpretations" (p. 176). He counsels the use of "dialogue, interpretations, hypothesis generation and proving, and pattern playing" (p. 177). Today, some of us agree wholeheartedly with him on the idea of openness, and we emphasize choice, dialogue, and collaboration. Our overall aim is to produce better people, but "better" is left open to continuous discussion and development (Noddings, 2013, 2015). The discussion itself contributes to the richness of the curriculum we are trying to develop.

In this way of going at curriculum, large topics or concepts may be predetermined, but sub-topics, related concepts, and methods of tackling them will be decided by teachers and students working together. One of the most promising ideas that pops up as we read Doll's words on richness is a possible emphasis on interdisciplinary work. He does not use the word—concentrating instead on the "historical contexts, fundamental concepts, and final vocabularies" in each discipline—but he does advise us to connect each discipline to the larger culture in which it appears. Today, some thirty years later, many of us follow E. O. Wilson in adopting an interdisciplinary approach to education. In discussing such an approach in biology, Wilson describes a "middle domain" in which disciplines come together to do investigatory work:

The middle domain is a region of exceptionally rapid intellectual advance. It, moreover, addresses issues in which students (and the rest of us) are most interested: the nature and origin of life, the meaning of sex, the basis of human nature, the origin and evolution of life, why we must die, the origins of religion and ethics, the causes of aesthetic response, the role of environment in human genetic and cultural evolution, and more.

(Wilson, 2006, p. 136)

The basic idea promoted by both Doll and Wilson is to organize the emerging curriculum around fundamental human concerns and to connect the concepts and methods of study to those concerns and to each other. Even this initial organization should be open to interests and problems that emerge in continuing dialogue between teachers (across disciplines) and students.

Current education in most of our schools has moved devastatingly far away from Doll's vision. In an early chapter, he looks at the Tyler rationale and, noting its popularity, reminds us that it is reflected in "the behavioral objectives movement of the 1960s, the competency-based education movement of the 1970s, and Hunter model of the 1980s" (p. 54). Where are we now? In what sense are the "standards" established for our schools *standards*? How do they differ from objectives and competencies? In the last section of this paper, on "rigor," I'll return to this topic for a discussion of critical thinking. Here we can agree that the possible richness of a curriculum is largely sacrificed by over-specification.

Recursion

One of the most powerful tools in learning and creating new ideas and methods is *recursion*. When we are trying to learn something new or to create new tools, we loop back to what we already know and ask how we can extend this knowledge or use it to shape a new method. Doll writes: "In a curriculum that honors, values, uses recursion, there is no fixed beginning or ending" (p. 178). This is an essential feature of an open system.

It is hard to over-estimate the value of recursion in education, and it is disheartening to see how nearly we have abandoned it. As an old math teacher, I can testify to its power. In introducing a new concept, we should ask students to consider what they already know that might suggest a way of approaching the new problem. Consider exponential equations. Until this unit of study, students have not seen a variable, say x, as an exponent. How to begin? Well, we all remember how to evaluate an integer, say 2, to the second, third, ... power, and we know how to do this with x raised to a power. So let's experiment a bit. Remember how to picture an equation—to graph it? We then spend some time plotting points—powers of 2. What could be meant by 2 to the zero power? Again we use recursion to remind ourselves that 2/2 could be expressed as 2 to the zero power, so 2 to the zero must be 1. This recursive process is very different from the standard review process, controlled step by step and vaguely motivated by the teacher. The recursive approach invites students to dig into their own storehouse of knowledge and experiment with ways to use that knowledge. If they run into a block, something they need but can't remember, they are urged to use further recursion. What do I know that will help me to restore what I've forgotten?

Not long ago, I talked with some graduate students planning to become administrators. For some reason, they were trying to solve a quadratic equation. They were stuck. They knew there was a formula that would do the trick, but they couldn't remember it. Finally, they decided to "ask Joe," the only math major in the group. It did not occur to them to search their storehouse of knowledge to find a way to *reproduce* the formula.

Incidents such as this should prompt us to rethink our modernist methods of teaching: teacher establishes an objective (say, learn a formula), students learn the objective, apply it to a string of examples, pass a test on it, and forget it. In contrast, when we recognize the power of recursion, we may note that some of the skills and concepts used to develop the formula are more important than the formula itself. We know that (somewhere in our own treasure chest) we have what is needed to reproduce that formula.

"Dialogue," Doll comments, "becomes the *sine qua non* of recursion" (p. 178); dialogue between teachers and students stimulates and sustains recursion. But this sort of dialogue, reflective dialogue, can even be engaged by oneself. Jerome Bruner advised that we should distance ourselves from our own thoughts (Doll, p. 178); that is, we should move away from the immediate problem and dig among our past thoughts to shed light on current ones that might be brought together in a new way to solve the problem. It is connections we seek, and sometimes we have to move away from the object right in front of us to find those connections.

Relations

In his discussion of relations, Doll elaborates on his earlier points about the centrality of connections in developing a post-modern curriculum. *Pedagogical relations* refer to connections among the various elements of subject matter, how they are chosen, and the conditions under which they arise. The curriculum in an open system is not determinate; it is not pre-set before teachers and students have met. This is not to say that *nothing* is pre-established. An algebra course will certainly involve algebra; a course in American history will certainly mention American political leaders, significant events, and national documents. But the day-to-day conduct of lessons will be open to changes in both topic and method, and the changes will be induced by dialogue. Students will speak, not just listen, and some of what they say will re-direct the lesson.

The advice often given to teachers today is to control "dialogue" so thoroughly that the pre-planned lesson will not be disrupted. Keep them on the point stated as today's learning objective. Don't let them distract you! Consider the following account of a vocabulary lesson reported by Elizabeth Green (2014).

Karen (a teacher, critic, observer) has been watching a vocabulary lesson in an elementary school. The teacher had given the class a list of words and then asked them to use each word in a sentence. On the first word, "enjoy," Karen noted that the teacher should have asked the boy who offered a sentence to say more, to elaborate a bit. The next word was *poison*, and a student suggested this sentence: "One day when my uncle came, I made a poison" (Green, 2014, p. 179). Think what you might do with this sentence! But the teacher just said, "Okay, next word." Criticizing the teacher's handling of this, Karen noted that the boy had not demonstrated that he understood the word, *poison*. Worse, "in the process, he'd gotten the whole class thinking about his uncle, rather than the meaning of the word *poison*—and the teacher had done nothing to steer back their focus" (p. 179). This is bad enough, but Karen takes it even worse:

> What are the important words to learn? In the sentence they're using, is that the best way to decide: is that the right word to use or not? If a sentence comes up that takes them off task—well, now there's 18 kids that really want to hear about the uncle making poison, as opposed to deciding what is the word, what does it mean, on we go.
> (p. 179)

There are times, of course, when teachers need to bring the class "back to focus." But there are also times when teachers should change focus, at least temporarily, to consider the connections to real life suggested by a student's comment. It is important to seek *cultural* as well as *pedagogical* relations as we develop curriculum through interaction with our students. Instead of moving on to the next word and leaving all those students wondering about the boy, the uncle, and poison, the teacher might have shown some interest: Tell us more. What poison did you make? And as critical observers, we wonder: Was a murder being considered? Is the uncle a chemist who felt the need to warn the boy about a project he was undertaking? Did the boy mean "puzzle," not "poison"? Or, more likely, had the boy often heard his father greet the uncle with the words, "What's your poison?" Had the boy mixed a gin and tonic? From there, the class might have gone on to a lively discussion about poisons in mystery books, the discomfort induced by poison ivy, other poisonous plants in the area, and the meaning of "poison-pen letter." Nothing of this sort happened. We despair of both the teacher's approach and that of the critic.

The historian Gordon Wood (2011) has remarked that we Americans tend to be all-or-nothing people, and teachers today are too often advised—even coerced—into doing things in one best way. A story such as the one just told should remind us that, although it is often right to restore focus on a specific learning objective, it is sometimes right to diverge along lines suggested by unexpected remarks or reactions. That is part of what we mean when we speak of a post-modern, open curriculum.

Rigor

Doll's fourth R is *rigor*: "In some ways the most important of the four criteria, rigor keeps a transformative curriculum from falling into either 'rampant relativism' or sentimental solipsism" (1993, p. 181). The word, as it is used today in schools, more often is interpreted as *hard, difficult,* and *strictly logical,* and it is used to warn teachers and students that a new unit or curriculum will be more challenging. "Rigorous" is not an adjective that induces comfort and good cheer.

To understand Doll's meaning of rigor, we have to discuss his use of *transformative*. A transformative curriculum is a genuine alternative, not "another variation on the very thing it tries to replace" (p. 181). He reminds us of Dewey's warning on a viable alternative: "This alternative is not just a middle course or compromise between the two procedures. It is something radically different from either. Existing likes and powers are to be treated as possibilities" (quoted in Doll, p. 182). This means that the ideas and methods offered by every rational approach should be examined individually and analyzed with respect to their possible utility in the alternative scheme we are trying to construct.

But we rarely approach things this way. The historian Gordon Wood has said this of Americans: "We seem to be very much all-or-nothing people. It is very difficult for us to maintain a *realpolitik* attitude toward the world. We have to be either saving the world or shunning it" (2011, p. 334). So it is also in education. We always seem to be seeking a perfect solution—one that can be used on everything. Dewey worried that people sometimes went too far even with progressive education. Indeed, he rejected the label "child-centered" for the new curriculum. The child should play a significant role, of course, but Dewey's transformative, democratic approach did not suggest turning everything over to the child. What is there in the old curriculum (the one under transformation) that should be retained? What should be revised? What should be discarded and why? What should be added? How can we bring it all together?

In today's discussion of curriculum, there is great emphasis on critical thinking, although those using the term rarely say what they mean by it. Doll's *rigor* points directly to the facets of critical thinking. The curriculum should be under continual construction through a collaborative project marked by analysis, interpretation, evaluation, recursion, imaginative projection, and experimentation. We do not look at the recently old curriculum and say, "Behavioral objectives? Bah! Throw them out!" Rather, we ask where and for what they might sensibly be used. Similarly, we would not discard standardized tests but examine their place in a more human-centered curriculum. To think critically means to maintain a search for meaning and for ways to apply that meaning to practical matters.

Doll concludes his discussion of rigor this way:

> So, too, rigor may be defined in terms of mixing—indeterminacy with interpretation. The quality of interpretation, its own richness, depends on how fully and well we develop the various alternatives indeterminacy presents. In this new frame for rigor—combining the complexity of indeterminacy with the hermeneutics of interpretation—it seems necessary to establish a community, one critical yet supportive. Such a community is, I believe, what Dewey thought a school should be.
> (1993, p. 183)

I would just add to this that critical thinking or rigor (like richness, recursion, and relations) should be accompanied by—guided by—moral commitment. It is not our intention to produce a generation of highly intelligent critical thinkers who apply their prodigious skills merely to advance their own selfish aims—a whole generation of Professor Moriartys (Noddings, 2013, 2015). Rather, our aim is to produce better people, and what we mean by that is perpetually open for transformative exploration.

References

Doll, W. (1993). *A post-modern perspective on curriculum*. New York, NY: Teachers College Press.
Green, E. (2014). *Building a better teacher: How teaching works*. New York, NY: W. W. Norton & Co.
Noddings, N. (2013). *Education and democracy in the 21st century*. New York, NY: Teachers College Press.
Noddings, N. (2015). *A richer, brighter vision for American high schools*. Cambridge, UK: Cambridge University Press.
Wilson, E. O. (2006). *The creation: An appeal to save life on earth*. New York, NY: W. W. Norton & Co.
Wood, G. S. (2011). *The idea of America*. New York, NY: Penguin Books.

20 Complex Conversations on Curriculum
Ghosts and the Five C's Revisited

Eero Ropo and Veli-Matti Värri

Introduction

Education is not only for knowing, but it also plays a pivotal role in constituting what a person is, what he will be, and how she positions herself in personal, social, or societal life contexts. All those life contexts are interpreted, experienced, and constructed by people themselves. The resulting narratives are sometimes explicit and verbalized, sometimes implicit and unreflected.

One of the most inspiring thoughts in Bill Doll's theorizing of curriculum has been the groundbreaking analyses of ghosts. The ghost is a powerful metaphor, character in a narrative, related to understanding the life world. A ghost is something that intervenes in peoples' actions, thinking, or storytelling. The ghost is typically unrecognized, invisible, able to come and go wherever and whenever it wants to. It is even able to intervene in the educational processes. As such, the ghost is a scary creature, indeed.

After hearing the idea years ago, it sounded strange, but forced us thinking. Ghosts reminded of the fairytales in which spirits sometimes appeared in visible form communicating with people. They were also said to live in certain places or locations. Bill Doll has convinced us that there really are invisible "ghosts," not only in places but in certain processes, objects, and phenomena such as curriculum.

Theoretically we categorize this idea under the umbrella of narrative paradigm in which human knowledge of the world is understood in terms of narratives (e.g. Barthes, 1977; Fisher, 1985). A narrative paradigm emphasizes:

> that even scientific (technical) discourse, which is in a form of literature, is informed by metaphor (and myth), contains "plots," and is time-bound.
>
> (Fisher, 1985, p. 356)

This paradigm aims at giving perspectives and understanding the reasons, or like Fisher (1985, p. 357) says, "good reasons" for the perspectives of texts. Referring to control as one of "the ghosts," Doll, asserts that "control as an operating concept is actually embedded in the history of curriculum from the very first usages of the word in an educational setting" (Doll, 2002, p. 34). Applying the metaphor, the ghost of control seems to exist in many countries in the form of religious or ideological dominance through education (e.g. Azhar, 2017).

By acknowledging the existence of "ghosts" to which Bill has introduced us in his speeches and writings, we will now discuss the ghosts that current curricula should recognize. As a frame, we apply the narrative paradigm described briefly above. Particularly, we want to reflect the perspectives of the five C's Doll proposed.

Ghosts as Narratives in Education

Barthes (1977) and many others have argued that one's life is best understood in terms of narratives, temporally relevant stories having a plot. In this sense narratives are personal, social, and cultural interpretations, constructed from experiences, social interactions, and history. Like many others, we argue that narrative understanding is essential for the complex existential relevance of being in the world (Meretoja, 2014, p. 2). Abbott (2008) describes a narrative as a "representation of an event or a series of events" (p. 13). It can be presented in verbal form or seen as a mental image, like a "ghost of control" in Doll's thinking.

According to Doll (2002, p. 28), we should throw away "the ghosts" acting as controllers and replace them with novel representations, a "livelier spirit of control." Doll refers to a possible need to rename "control" with a new term, but is satisfied with the expression "emergent control" with which he means a milder control (Doll, 2002, p. 56).

It is interesting to speculate what the new spirit of control might be. To us it seems that there are also other types of ghosts, even more scary than the ghost of control. The time we are living can be described as the age of wicked problems. The term was first introduced by Rittel and Webber (1973). Wicked problems are typically hard to formulate and solve. It is even difficult to find out if the introduced solutions are appropriate or working at all. Examples of those kinds of problems are easy to find (e.g. climate change, over-population, waste). To our understanding these "wicked problems" are like ghosts. They control life without us having much power or control over them. Latour's (1993) concept "hybrid object" and Morton's (2010) "hyperobject" both refer adequately to such kind of ghosts.

A "hyperobject" is a strange being, a ghost, we may say, without a strict situation in time and space. It is something we can speak about, but not see or touch. Education and curricular thinking cannot ignore these "hyperobjects" as constituting "elements" of our individual and common life and prospects for future. The border between human creatures, human culture, and nature are mixed in them and thus they are a kind of a combination of nature and culture.

According to Morton's definition hyperobjects are "vicious." This means that we are not able to isolate them or abjure their existence. They have become part of our life and world narratives. The more we try to abjure them the more they will be engaged in our ways of living and affecting our expectations for the future (Morton, 2010, pp. 130–135; Morton, 2011a; Morton, 2011b).

"Hyperobjects" were created as an unintended consequence of our technological culture. Pollution, such as nuclear waste or floating plastic rafts in the ocean, for instance, can be understood as scary "ghosts" causing a reaction of repression and rejection. This collective refusal, and reluctance from considering those phenomena as real, is very ambivalent in our technological civilization. It is evident to us that this "ghost" exists, but we make every attempt to reduce its influence by denial.

Nonetheless, in the context of a technology-driven world, the instrumental ontology with isolated "hyperobjects" seems to be a self—evident basis for the socialization process in civic education. The result is that the socialization process, and the curriculum, maintains and reproduces the unstable and even dangerous order of wicked "ghosts." It is a big problem if curricula keep these kinds of ghosts alive.

The ghosts acting globally, like the above described "hyperobjects," threaten our lives in a lot more serious ways than the "ghost of control" or its milder forms. To save our planet, we need new ways of thinking to create new narratives. Our traditional dualistic and anthropocentric concepts do not reach the "reality" of "hyperobjects." Consequently, Doll's idea of ghosts is phenomenal in opening novel visions for theorizing in the deep "metaphysical" sense of our being in the world.

Is this realistic? Have we experienced this kind of development in our educational systems, from the worldwide perspective? We have no clear answers. We may just say that we have seen both positive and negative developments in different systems and parts of the world.

Curricula and Five C's From the Perspective of Emerging Narratives of the World

We believe that education is the forum to discuss these emerging narratives. Curricula, as the intellectual bases for education, are the main documents or tools to enhance discourses towards new kinds of thinking and understanding. Bill Doll has described the emerging new curricula as something related to acknowledging the importance of relations (Doll, 2002, p. 42). He chose to discuss the novel curriculum concept in terms of five C's, namely *currere*, complexity, cosmology, conversation, and community. We will revisit these C's, keeping the ghosts we have introduced above in our minds.

Currere

Like Doll (2002) mentions, *currere* is the concept Pinar and Grumet (1976) introduced and Pinar developed further in his theorizing (e.g., Pinar, Reynolds, Slattery, & Taubman, 1995). The emphasis in this concept is on the individual progress (running, from L. "to run") of a person based on autobiographical processes (Pinar, 1994, pp. 19–27).

From the societal point, currere is an individual process. Typically, currere is not a content issue in the curricula, but deals with the individually important learning and transformation processes. From the narrativity point of view, it also deals with the ontology of being in the world. In the Finnish basic education curriculum educational goals are divided into the knowledge and performance goals in different subject domains, and those related to personal growth, identity, and citizenship (National Board of Finland, 2016). The objectives related to students' currere processes are not well explicated in the text and are left for the teachers to decide. Partly this may be due to the lack of theoretical understanding of what currere might mean in school practice. To us it means growing into personal understanding of life and world narratives in which wicked ghosts take an increasingly active role. It is also necessary to construct ways to control the power of such ghosts.

Complexity

Typically, curriculum design begins by asking what knowledge is the most worth knowing. Instead of what, we might ask what kind of knowledge. *Complex* is an excellent adjective for the current nature of scientific knowledge. We have realized that the scientific knowledge base is not a coherent entity, but full of often very contradictory "truths." The "ghosts" we have described, are part of this narrative complexity of understanding our common world and life contexts. Theories can be considered as narratives consisting of rules, truths, and also beliefs that are objects for continuous change and evolution.

Personal narratives are typically based on one's own autobiography in which the whole is experienced and interpreted. Socially and culturally shared narratives are created through conversations, which are always complex. The process is never-ending, including continuous reinterpretation. Like we have already written, Doll (2002) refers to complexity when thinking of replacing the original ghost of control with a new type of ghost having less control over children, young people, or people overall. This dominant "ghost" advocates simplicity by casting control on the nature and quality of learning results. Those results are typically considered as quantitative and measurable with the aim of assessing the effectiveness of the education system. This kind of control does not acknowledge the individual meanings based on life experiences or autobiography. Instead of giving space for complex and contradictory meanings (personal, community, or cultural), the "ghost" markets and controls the achievement of clearly defined and verbalized performance goals, violently simplifying both the learning process and the resulting narratives of the studied phenomena.

New types of ghosts—hybrid objects, hyperobjects, and often contradictory narratives created out of them—complicate both our current life, and prospects for the new generations. Our clear vision is the same as Doll's: we cannot and we should not avoid complexity. If we do, the ghosts will take over.

Cosmology

Cosmological perspectives on curriculum are very seldom dealt with in curriculum literature. Typically, they are reduced to subject-specific questions in physics, philosophy, or religion. Scientific cosmology is usually regarded as belonging to physics. Doll has, however, shown that this perspective has many implications in our understanding of life, world, and ourselves (2002, p. 46). He (Doll, 2002, pp. 46–48) discusses cosmology in curriculum by referring to a paradigm change. This shift from a cosmology (including ecology, ethics, epistemology, metaphysics, pedagogy, and worldview) based on the "brute facts" of independent atoms to a process cosmology based on the dynamic flux of entities or occasions, all "complex and interdependent," is a truly paradigmatic shift.

This kind of understanding that everything is related and dependent on other perspectives keeps the knowledge "alive." Particularly, it is the spirit that keeps knowledge alive. Consequently, he proposes a curriculum that combines the "rigorousness of science, with the imagination of story, with the vitality and creativity of spirit" (Doll, 2002, p. 48).

Our descriptions of the new "wicked ghosts" as parts of emerging world narratives, threatening and limiting the prospects of life, indicate that even more serious problems must be encountered and solved in the future. We believe that solutions cannot be reached without following the cosmological model Doll has suggested.

Conversation

Conversation is a process in which people share thoughts, ideas, and information. It is typically spoken communication, interchange of information, experiences, and meanings related to them. Conversation and negotiation are close concepts—both deal with discourses and understandings between people. Negotiation aims at agreement whereas conversation has no such a goal. Instructional conversations have a special purpose of enhancing students' construction of socially shared and accepted narratives, whatever they are in different social communities and societies. Some are based on research and facts, some on beliefs and ideologies. Although instructional conversations deal with meanings, it is evident that meanings like beliefs are often created through autonomous and unconscious processes. Doll (2002, p. 50) emphasized the importance of respect and honor between the partners of the conversation. He also mentions the importance of respecting "otherness" of other people and texts in which the ways of thinking can vary.

In education and instructional conversation, referring, for instance, to classroom conversations, there are typical "topics" that the conversations focus on. Yrjänäinen (2011) studied classroom discourses in junior high and high school science classes. She recognized four types of discourses, namely, science and scientific, the school subject matter, pedagogical—related to teaching and learning—and the curriculum. This all shows that educational reality includes all types of knowledge from scientific to social and contextual, facts, beliefs, and attitudes, to mention a few. Narrative construction of personal, social, and cultural knowledge takes place in different discourses, some of which are based on exactly defined concepts, some on loosely described beliefs or opinions.

If the purpose of school learning is to acquire only measurable learning outcomes, the classroom conversations become artificial. The metaphysical or cosmological perspective, the reason to be at school, disappears, like Doll (2002) might say. Realizing that the "ghosts" have not left us, but that there seems to be more "ghosts" than ever before, makes the school context more equal for teachers and students. We all have the same problems as citizens and learners. Constructing solutions requires myriad conversations, new ways of thinking, and creative narratives to the challenges and threats of the "ghosts" we have created by our own culture and technology.

Community

We agree with Bill that community may be the most important of the five C's (Doll, 2002, p. 50). Doll refers to the concept of identity in respect to belonging to a community. If identity is a narrative, constructed and negotiated through conversations in relations, then other people, communities, and cultures are crucial for understanding who I am and who we are. Without others, we converse only in our own minds, intra-individually, with silent speech or phrases, typically re-enforcing our limited interpretations of meanings related to ourselves, others, knowledge, or "ghosts."

In those conversations, narrative construction and reconstruction of personal, social and cultural identity stories are the main processes (cf. Yrjänäinen & Ropo, 2013). Those narratives are also applied when we decide our positioning as teachers or students, citizens, members of different communities, or individual persons. Like Jansen's (2009) book has showed, communities are strong in maintaining the ontological and epistemological narratives about themselves and others.

Community conversations are important in creating common interpretations and meanings shared through narratives. Those narratives are, however, often limited. They omit important facts or phenomena, sometimes because of political purposes, sometimes because of history and traditions. Certain types of narratives, which are rich in beliefs and poor in facts, are delivered to new generations without revision or criticism. Attitudes separating cultures, communities, and people, are built into the narratives that children adopt as true knowledge. Communities and cultures also seem to be selfish in the sense that ugly "ghosts," knowledge or facts not supporting the way of understanding life, can be totally ignored, often until they begin to limit and interfere with the adopted way of life.

In the time of globally affecting wicked "ghosts" it is important that thinking about communities is expanded from local to global. We are part of the global community whether we recognize it, or understand what it means. Conversations we participate in must be globally motivated and themed. Globally affecting "ghosts" bring the signs of wicked problems into our vicinity in the form of objects or global social problems. Waste, unemployment, or masses of refugees are all signs of "ghosts" that cannot be ignored from education and the curricula anywhere in the world.

Concluding Remarks

We conclude the discussion with the same recommendation as many other researchers in this field have done before us. Continue the complex conversation! As humankind, we are more aware than ever of the threats, challenges, and problems facing us all. Believing mostly in positive development we seem to ignore many of them from the everyday conversations in our ontologically and epistemologically separated communities, cultures, and nation states. Communities are necessary for identity construction, but they have weaknesses. Typically, they collect only similarly thinking people into the conversations. If the curricula are based on community narratives and values, education does not integrate; it separates. The more we know as humankind, the more we need conversation to understand, integrate and respond to the global and societal problems involving our relations to the universe, nature, and each other. "Ghosts" are myriad and they have not left us!

How do we respond to the challenges in education, as curriculum theorizers? Is this the end of common education and beginning of self-serving learning communities? If local is global, are the learning communities better able to respond to locally and globally acting "ghosts"? Are we happy with locally valid curricula in which local goals, permanence of communities, societies, and their traditions are maintained? Or do we need a global curriculum, something that responds to the very basic needs of the whole humankind, to develop global citizens, transform people towards universally positioning thinkers, and to help them grow into responsible agents, willing to serve the universal good, equity, equality, and democracy? Maybe we also have to introduce a new PISA test promoting the common understanding of the world and ghosts we have with us.

This is the legacy from Bill Doll. Thank you Bill! Is it time to start the work, together?

References

Abbott, H. P. (2008). The Cambridge introduction to narrative. Cambridge: Cambridge University Press.

Azhar, K. (2017). *Human agency in a curriculum: An analysis of Indonesia's 2013 curriculum for primary level*. MA Thesis, University of Tampere. Retrieved from https://tampub.uta.fi/handle/10024/101688

Barthes, R. (1977). Introduction to the structural analysis of narratives. In S. Heath (Ed.), *Image—music—text* (pp. 79–124). New York, NY: Hill and Wang.

Doll, W. E., Jr. (2002). Ghost and the curriculum. In W. E. Doll, Jr. & N. Gough (Eds.), *Curriculum visions* (pp. 23–70). New York, NY: Peter Lang.

Fisher, W. R. (1985, December). The narrative paradigm: An elaboration. *Communication Monographs, 52*, 347–367.

Jansen, J. (2009). *Knowledge in the blood: Confronting race and the apartheid past*. Cape Town: UCT Press.

Latour, B. (1993). *We have never been modern*. Cambridge, MA: Harvard University Press.

Meretoja, H. (2014). *The narrative turn in fiction and theory: The crisis and return of storytelling from Robbe-Grillet to Tournier*. New York, NY: Palgrave Macmillan.

Morton, T. (2010). *The ecological thought*. Cambridge, MA: Harvard University Press.

Morton, T. (2011a). Sublime objects. *Speculations, 2*, 207–227.

Morton, T. (2011b). Here comes everything: The promise of object-oriented ontology. *Qui Parle: Critical Humanities and Social Sciences, 19*(2), 163–190.

National Board of Finland. (2016). *National core curriculum for basic education 2014*. Helsinki, Finland: Finnish National Board of Education.

Pinar, W. F. (1994). *Autobiography, politics and sexuality: Essays in curriculum theory 1972–1992*. New York, NY: Peter Lang.

Pinar, W. F., & Grumet, M. R. (1976). *Toward a poor curriculum*. Dubuque, IA: Kendall Hunt Publishing Company.

Pinar, W. F., Reynolds, W. M., Slattery, P., & Taubman, P. (1995). *Understanding curriculum*. New York, NY: Peter Lang.

Rittel, H., & Webber, M. (1973). Dilemmas in a general theory of planning. *Policy Sciences, 4*, 155–169.

Yrjänäinen, S. (2011). *"But, really, are we the right sort of people for this?" The puzzle of subject teacher education and the teacher student's professional practical capabilities*. Academic Dissertation, University of Tampere (in Finnish, English summary). Retrieved from http://tampub.uta.fi/handle/10024/66701

Yrjänäinen, S., & Ropo, E. (2013). From narrative teaching to narrative learning. In E. Ropo & M. Huttunen (Eds.), *Conversation on narrativity in teaching and learning*. Tampere University Press (in Finnish). Retrieved from https://tampub.uta.fi/handle/10024/95533

21 "Wrestling" With Complexity
Bill Doll's "Dancing Curriculum"

Denise Egéa

"Wrestling" was one of William Doll's favorite words and endeavors, be it with a text, an author, or a concept—an approach he constantly fostered among his students. Like Edgar Morin, he did not subscribe to the "paradigm of simplicity," and wrote about his "method/beyond-method." After recalling Bill Doll's "dancing curriculum," I propose to revisit Edgar Morin's texts, and push further the exploration of complexity, working toward a better understanding of its "field of possibilities" (Morin, 2006, p. 25) for curriculum.

Bill Doll's New Perspective on Curriculum

In 1993, Doll published a book titled *A Post-modern Perspective on Curriculum*, in which his goal was not to propose developing a curriculum based on a post-modern philosophical approach, but to raise our awareness and "generate concerns about existing curricular practices and assumptions" (Stuever, 2009, p. 87).

What Doll appreciated most in what, at the time, was a philosophical trend still developing, "still too new to define" (i.e., post-modernism; Doll, 1993b, p. 158), was its capacity to "provoke" (another one of Doll's favorite words) the profession into a new way of thinking, more appropriate to a rapidly changing world. The traditional and assumed tenets and values held throughout the previous decades, and still too often taken for granted, were no longer valid in our increasingly complex environment. In the late 1980s and early 1990s, Doll found himself and the profession "caught between paradigms" (1993b, p. 62). He saw the necessity to "develop a new paradigmatic frame" (p. 62) and realized that "these [then] contemporary movements [could] help us" (p. 62) do so.

Doll objected to the education system's linear, sequential, and deterministic structure which paced students along a preordered progression through a rigid and closed system whose goal it was to "transmit and transfer" (Stuever, 2009, p. 88) some pre-established knowledge. This system, mostly unchanged and unchallenged since the 19th century (de Marrais & LeCompte, 1999), was reaffirmed by the Tyler Rationale

(1949), which had a tremendous impact at the time, and on which the educational profession relied heavily (and still does to an extent). The so-called modernistic approach to knowledge and understanding was based on, even deeply rooted in, the 17th-century Enlightenment's very specific view of the world further developed, especially since the mid-20th century, due to the rapid advances in sciences and technologies.[1]

Doll pointed out that the Cartesian tradition emphasized knowledge based on a discovery of "that which already exists" (Stuever, 2009, p. 88), that which is already known. With the industrial revolution in the late 19th and early 20th centuries, that approach "answered America's needs [and the whole Western world's] in a rapidly changing society and provided a methodology for the future" (Doll, 1993b, p. 51). However, our world has been—still is to an even greater extent—undergoing some never before witnessed increasingly rapid changes, and the effect of the lightning speed at which sciences and technology advanced, and their remarkable successes, have had a "dizzying and blinding effect . . . so rapid that epistemology could not keep up" (Egéa-Kuehne, 1998, p. 12); those sciences and technology changed the world and our understanding of it.

Doll's book warned that "radical intellectual, social, and political change" was causing fundamental modifications in our perception of the world (1993b, p. 157). He stressed the need to escape those constraining structures "built on what existed before," with a caution that "the future is not so much a break with, or antithesis to, the past as it is a transformation of it" (p. 8). Doll advocated a "challenging of the status quo and calling into question accepted knowledge and practices" (Stuever, 2009, p. 88).

In summer 1993, Doll also published the article "Curriculum Possibilities in a 'Post'-Future" in the *Journal of Curriculum and Supervision*. In this text, he turned specifically to post-modernism, "a worldview wherein traditional categories, such as order and disorder, are not dramatically opposed or separated but are entwined, each within the other, each reinforcing and sustaining the other" (Doll, 1993a, p. 279). That approach led to some fundamental questioning, a stance which for many was frightening to the extent that they saw it as the collapse of established stability, order, and values. Yet, citing Haynes (1991), Doll pointed out that it does not necessarily lead to chaos, but to a new kind of order: a "chaotic order," naturally found through the universe, as the Hubble telescope has enabled us to see.[2]

1. Descartes's work (*Discours de la Méthode*, 1637) was supported by the so-called miracle of the 1620s scientific revolution, which—in the margin of the theories recognized as official at the time—founded the modern sciences.
2. See Chaisson, 1992; Fienerg, 1992; Maran, 1992. In a footnote Doll (1993) adds: "The newness lies in our perceptions, both conceptual and visual" (n. 16).

"Dynamic chaos" was first hinted at when, in 1903, a French mathematician, Jules Henri Poincaré, entered a contest sponsored by the king of Sweden. The question was to solve the famous three-body problem (the sun, the moon, and the earth), and "show rigorously that the solar system as modeled by Newton's equations was dynamically stable" (see Diacu, 1996, p. 67). The linear framework of mathematics did not lead Poincaré to a solution, but to the conclusion that "Prediction becomes impossible, and we have the fortuitous phenomenon" (Poincaré, 1903, npn).[3] Later, the formulation of chaos theory, complexity theory, and the nonlinear processes could develop with the advent and progress of the computer. One of the foremost contributors was Mandelbrot who, in 1975, pioneered a new geometry, which helped visualize natural patterns. Fractal geometry and the computer helped describe the action of chaos on a screen. The many irregular shapes that make up our natural world at any scale (clouds, smoke, surf, etc.) are not random, but follow some organizing principles. More recently, Doll (2012) pointed out that "it is these two concepts—fractalness and self-organization—that characterize the 'nature' of complexity" (p. 18).

In 1993, in his article and in his book, Doll offered a new vision of education and a set of new curriculum concepts based on four criteria he associated with complexity, and what it means in terms of curriculum: "paradox, indeterminacy, self-organization, and play" (1993a, p. 279).

Indeterminacy

Doll questioned the traditional, sequential linear concept of learning as being solely the result of teaching, this "cause-effect epistemology" (1993a, p. 280) underlying the Tyler Rationale. In this context, the student is merely a receiver of the knowledge bestowed by the teacher (Freire's "banking" approach), a passive subject who "can only discover what already is," not a "creator of knowledge" (p. 280). Such a curriculum "emphasizes transmission, linearity, [reproduction], and measurement rather than transformation, nonlinearity, and creation" (p. 280). Indeterminacy, by removing the limiting barriers of certainty, opens up the possibility of generating meaning and creating knowledge.

Self-Organization

However, a degree of self-organization is necessary for indeterminacy to become a "rich and generative *dissipative structure*" (Prigogine, 1980; emphasized in Doll, 1993a, p. 281). Self-regulation is inherent in life.

---

3. Although Poincaré could not reach a solution, "his work was so impressive that he was awarded the prize anyway" (Peterson, 1993).

In fact, recalls Doll, according to Piaget, "auto- and self-regulation are *the essence of life itself*" (original emphasis; Doll, 1993a, p. 281), the basis of his theory of cognitive development. A curriculum must include perturbation, disturbance, disequilibrium (Piaget, 1971) and dissipation (Prigogine, 1980). In other words, as educators, "We must encourage [our students] to take risks in learning and discovering the other, the unknown" (Egéa-Kuehne, 1996, p. 161). As educators, we must expose students to challenges, controversies, and to a "chaotic" nonlinear curriculum "so that self-organization will be encouraged" (Doll, 1993a, p. 281). This approach to curriculum eschews "precisely defined, well-articulated, pre-set goals" and "competency-based assessment" (p. 281) which consider students as mere recipients of pre-packaged information, as opposed to generators of meaningful knowledge.

Paradox

Paradox is another important factor in Doll's new curriculum. To the Cartesian separation of mind and body, he prefers Foucault's understanding whereby there is no fixed self, no distinction of "I" from the "other," no separation subject/object, but rather relation and interaction. "*Self* is understood only in relation to *other*. Both are needed, each becomes the *sine qua non* of the other" (original emphasis; Doll, 1993a, p. 282). To "the teacher teaches, the learner learns," Doll opposes a "discovery pedagogy" which "provides more flexibility and openness" (p. 282). In this view, based on indeterminacy, openness, and self-organization, curriculum is then driven by dialogue, negotiation, and interaction. For Doll, this is a "transformative curriculum" (p. 283).

Play

Those skills of dialogue, negotiation, and interaction can be developed through what Doll called "play," recalling the shaman, the fool, the jester, or Shakespeare. He acknowledged that "[t]his is not an easy task" (1993a, p. 283), but requires much work and attention on the part of the teacher "to help students develop their play with, and metaphoric use of, ideas, forms, procedures, and patterns to create productive happenings" (p. 283).

Doll's Four R's

In his "dancing curriculum," Doll did suggest some "curricular steps." They are patterned, but inherently unique as they emerge through the interrelation and interaction between "teacher and text, teacher and student, student and text" (1993b, p. 103). This new view of curriculum did require new criteria, still much relevant today. In opposition to

Tyler's famous three R's (reading, 'riting, and 'rithmetic), Doll proposed to base his curriculum not on three but on four R's: richness, recursion, relations, and rigor. It eschewed the rigid, linear, sequential, and deterministic structure of the traditional curriculum, and advocated an open system, which welcomed complexity, indeterminacy, self-organization, paradox, and play, which promoted emerging patterns, and supported creativity and the development of new knowledge.

Edgar Morin and the Paradigm of Complexity

Internationally recognized for his work on complexity theory, Edgar Morin already introduced what later he would call "complex thought" (*la pensée complexe*) in his first book, *L'an zero de l'Allemagne* (1946).

Complexity

Since then, the concept of complexity has evolved and has been given a variety of interpretations according to "epistemologies and methodologies of research sometimes in opposition with each other" (Alhadeff-Jones, 2009, p. 61). Those differences also find their roots in the histories of cultures, of thought, and of academic institutions. The nature of complexity and complex systems became the focus of Morin's work in his six volumes on *La Méthode* (1977–2004) whose introduction to the new French boxed set is titled "Mission Impossible" (2008). In 1996, Myron Kofman wrote:

> Morin's approach is in harmony with a new culture of uncertainty as instanced in the literary and philosophical writings of Derrida, Levinas, or Deleuze. But unlike his fellow travelers Morin has been alone in daring to attempt a method which connects sciences and philosophy through complexity.
>
> (in Montuori, 2013, p. 16)

In Morin's thought, uncertainty and disorder are central concepts. However, they do not lead to nihilism; but, questioning the hegemony of order, certainty, and control, characteristic of modern science (and traditional curriculum), they call for a greater awareness and acknowledgment of the existence of disorder and of its generative role.

The concept of complexity is not new, but it encountered much resistance from "classical sciences, essentially in virtue of three fundamental explanatory principles: . . . universal determinism, . . . reduction, . . . disjunction" (Morin, 2006, p. 1). For classical sciences, the notion of complexity goes strongly against their mission. Unlike, for example, Hinduism or Buddhism which may accept that the "true" reality "is inexpressible and in extreme cases unknowable," the quest of Western sciences is "to search, behind those appearances, the hidden order that is the authentic reality of the universe" (Morin, 2006, p. 2). Morin recalled that, during the 19th century, with the second law of thermodynamics complexity appeared in science "*de facto* before being recognized *de jure*" (p. 2). He concluded: "Thus, the arrival of disorder, dispersion, disintegration constituted a fatal attack to the perfect, ordered, and deterministic vision" of classical sciences (2006, p. 3). Morin also saw the notion of "chaos," another "antinomy of order," ushered in by Darwin's work on evolution (p. 3). In any case, the difficulty comes from the traditional view that order and disorder are incompatible, so are disorder and organization.

Chaos

In his 2006 article "Restricted Complexity, General Complexity," Morin further explained how, in its early development, complexity never made it into physics, biology, or social sciences (p. 5). When the word "irrupted," it was through mathematicians and engineers in the 1940s and 1950s, in connection with information theory (von Neumann), cybernetics (von Foerster), and general system theory (Ashby), work pretty much ignored at the time. Morin also acknowledged Chaitin's work in "algorithmic incomprehensibility," and Jacques Monod's notion of emergence (which Morin called "a conceptual bomb"), and the enduring confusion among "the terms chance, disorder, and complexity" (2006, p. 5).

The breakthrough came from the Santa Fe Institute[4] in 1984, and their study of "Complex Systems," where, according to Morin,

> the word will be essential to define dynamical systems with a very large number of interactions and feedbacks, inside of which processes very difficult to predict and control take place, as "complex systems," where the classical conception was unable to be considered.
> (p. 5)

As the concepts of chaos, fractals, disorder, and uncertainty developed, it became evident that "the word complexity would encompass them all" (p. 6). However, it was not theorized yet; Morin called it "restricted" complexity (p. 5). He wrote: "the word complexity is introduced in 'complex system theory'; in addition, here and there the idea of 'sciences of complexity' was introduced, encompassing the fractalist conception and chaos theory" (p. 5).

Education

From an educational perspective, the complex way of thinking calls for a method of learning which involves human error and uncertainty.

---

4. The world headquarters for complexity science. www.santafe.edu/

Alhadeff-Jones (2009) identified "the critical aim of [Morin's] project": it "fundamentally challenges the ways one conceives knowledge production from an epistemological, psycho-socio-anthropological, and ethical point of view" (p. 62). In this approach, knowledge is not only produced, but, following Morin's familiar pattern of "the recursive loop," or more accurately "the spiral," the process of its production is in turn linked to the process of its evaluation. It means acknowledging the circularities (or spiraling) of production, organization, and evaluation of knowledge based on that knowledge itself.

At the core of Morin's paradigm of complexity is a challenge to what he identified as "the paradigm of simplification" (1982/90, 1990) whereby science privileges unidimensionality, abstraction, and decontextualization. However, Morin's complex way of thinking does not reject traditional scientific approaches, but advocates a dialogical stance whereby an equilibrium between order and disorder is continuously negotiated. This requires a continuous process of self-reflection and questioning, acknowledging doubts, ignorance or confusion, and a willingness to confront them. It means guiding students and prompting them to question, "question again and question the question. . . . The moment we think we know something, we must look at it again, and question it . . . to either recognize its weaknesses . . . or affirm it, build on it, and then question it again" (Egéa, 2018).

The complex way of thinking thus becomes a *cheminement*, akin to the concept of *currere* as developed by Pinar (2004), a journey on the continuous path of learning, of change. For Morin, writing becomes "*open and not hiding its own wandering, without renouncing the fleeting truth of its own experience*" (Morin, Motta, & Ciurana, 2003, p. 19; emphasis by Alhadeff-Jones, 2009, p. 63).

Morin drew on a very rich variety of sources[5]—we already referred to some of them. He "reminds us that every form of knowledge, every theory, and particularly any effort to develop an integrative perspective is a construction" which, despite its limitations due to the choice of sources and historical contingencies, also offers the openness of the creative process, and "the ongoing dance[6] of constraints and possibilities that mark all paths of inquiry" (Ceruti, 1994, in Montuori, 2013, p. 18).

Based on eleven "principles," Morin's paradigm of complexity is both "antagonistic and complementary with the principles framing the paradigm of simplification" (Alhadeff-Jones, 2013, p. 21). In his encyclopedic work, *La Méthode* (1977–2004), Morin insisted that a "reform of thought" was "absolutely necessary" (2006, p. 22). Invited by the French

---

5. E.g., Bachelard, Bateson, Bergson, Heraclitus, Montaigne, Pascal, Rousseau, Spinoza, the Frankfurt School, and others, and the philosophers of science Holton, Lakatos, and Popper.
6. Echoed by Doll's "dancing curriculum."

198 *Denise Egéa*

Minister of Education to propose a reform of the secondary education curriculum, his proposition "to introduce [his] ideas of reform of thought into an educational project" was never implemented. This led him to writing the first book of what would be a trilogy: *La Tête bien faite. Repenser la réforme. Réformer la pensée*, published in 1999, in which he advocates to reform our thinking in order to reform education, and to reform education in order to reform our thinking. It was followed by the proceedings of the seminar organized in 1998 by the French Minister of Education, whose theme was to show that it is possible to respond to two major challenges facing knowledge in the next millennium: globalization and an exponential increase of fragmented knowledge. This second opus that he edited, *Relier les connaissances—The challenge of the 21st century*, was also published in 1999. In the third volume, which he qualified in his Foreword of the "ultimate" one of this trilogy and invited by UNESCO, *Les Sept savoirs nécessaires à l'éducation du futur* (2000), Morin discussed the modifications he deemed necessary in education so that it would respond better, and would be better adapted to, the complexity of the new world. His thought was developed in seven chapters: "Blind knowledge: errors and illusions"; "Principles of a relevant knowledge"; "Teaching the human condition"; "Teaching the human identity"; "Confronting uncertainties"; "Teaching human understanding"; and "Ethics of the human race."

He held the hope, what he called the "necessary idea" (2006, p. 22), to create "Institutes of fundamental culture," which would be "sheltered in a University or independent" institution opened to everyone. For him, "fundamental culture" designates what is currently missing in education (what has always been missing?). He laid it out in the seven chapters (cited above) of the last book of his trilogy, and marked it as "the most vital matter to be taught, the most important to face life" (p. 23).

Concluding Remarks

Both William Doll and Edgar Morin dedicated the decades of their long professional lives to searching how to expand and enrich the human mind and life through education, but an education which relentlessly challenges the rigid, linear, deterministic traditional approaches. Early on, they both saw the potential offered by the new paradigms of complexity and chaos to articulate their respective visions of education.

Although Doll affirmed that he "would not claim a cause-effect relation between studying complexity theory and teaching for 'that yet-to-be-seen'" (2012, p. 27), he nevertheless recognized that "the study of complexity has opened [his] eyes to that which [he] did not see before" (p. 27). He has been eloquent about advocating his new "curriculum informed by complexity," sharing his beliefs that "there does exist a fascinating, imaginative realm where no one owns the truth and everyone has a right to be understood" (Doll, 1993b, p. 155).

Edgar Morin also questioned the ways that knowledge and education were traditionally conceived. He developed his reflection on the paradigmatic level, and challenged what he called the "paradigm of simplification" with the paradigm of complexity. However, he did not reject wholesale the perspectives of "traditional scientific approaches," but advocated a "dialogical combination" (Morin, 2008, p. 62). Over a span of nearly three decades (1977–2004) and a very large number of landmark publications, he developed his major work in six volumes, *La Méthode*. He also produced a trilogy, which he claimed laid out what is for him "the fundamental teaching that can aid the reform of the spirit, of thought, of knowledge, of action, of life" (2006, p. 23).

Both scholars' works and lives are an inspiration for all educators to strive for an education whereby "a complex way of thinking may be understood as a method of learning" (Morin et al., 2003, p. 19), where curriculum would "engage our students [not only] in a quest for knowledge which should take them way beyond the boundaries of their immediate socio-politico-cultural context in space and time" (Egéa-Kuehne, 1996, p. 161), but which would encourage them to become constructors and generators of meaningful knowledge, meaning makers.

I would like to close with a question from Edgar Morin: "The intelligence of complexity, isn't it to explore the field of possibilities, without restricting it with what is formally probable?" (2006, p. 25), to which those words of William Doll's echo: "The study of complexity has opened my eyes . . . to a new and livelier sense of method, one based on seeing more and seeing from multiple perspectives" (2012, p. 27).

References

Alhadeff-Jones, M. (2009). Revisiting educational research through Morin's paradigm of complexity. A response to Ton Jörg's programmatic view. *Complicity: An International Journal of Complexity and Education, 6*(1), 61–70.

Alhadeff-Jones, M. (2013). Complexity, methodology and method: Crafting a critical process of research. *Complicity: An International Journal of Complexity and Education, 10*(1/2), 19–44.

Ceruti, M. (1994). *Constraints and possibilities. The evolution of knowledge and knowledge of evolution* (A. Montuori, Trans.). New York, NY: Gordon & Breach.

Chaisson, E. (1992, June). Early results from the Hubble telescope. *Scientific American, 266*(6), 44–53.

de Marrais, K. B., & LeCompte, M. (1999). *The way schools work* (3rd ed.). New York, NY: Longman.

Diacu, F. (1996). The solution of the n-body problem. *The Mathematical Intelligencer, 18*(3), 66–70. https://doi.org/10.1007/BF03024313

Doll, W. (1993a). Curriculum possibilities in a "post"-future. *Journal of Curriculum and Supervision, 8*(4), 277–292.

Doll, W. (1993b). *A post-modern perspective on curriculum*. New York, NY: Teachers College Press.

Doll, W. (2012). Complexity and the culture of curriculum. *Complicity: An International Journal of Complexity and Education*, 9(1), 10–29.

Egéa, D. (2018). Derrida's archive and legacy to education: Between past and future. In P. Smeyers (Ed.), *International handbook of philosophy of education*. Basel, Switzerland: Springer International Publishing.

Egéa-Kuehne, D. (1996). Neutrality in education and Derrida's call for "double duty." In F. Margonis (Ed.), *Philosophy of education 1996* (pp. 154–163). Urbana, IL: University of Illinois at Urbana-Champaign.

Egéa-Kuehne, D. (1998). Michel Serres's connection through the multiplicity of time: A metaphor for curriculum. *JCT*, 14(4), 8–13.

Fienberg, R.T. (1992). COBE Confronts the Big Bang. *Sky and Telescope* 84: 34–36.

Haynes, K. (1991). *Chaos and order*. Chicago, IL: University of Chicago Press.

Kofman, M. (1996). *Edgar Morin: From big brother to fraternity*. London & Chicago, IL: Pluto Press.

Maran, S.P. (1992). Hubble Illuminates the Universe. *Sky and Telescope* 83: 619–625.

Montuori, A. (2013). *Complex thought: An overview of Edgar Morin's intellectual journey*. MetaIntegral Foundation, Resource Paper.

Morin, E. (1946). *L'an zéro de l'Allemagne*. Paris: Editions de la Cité Universelle.

Morin, E. (1977–2004). *La méthode: La nature de la nature* (1977/1981). Paris: Le Seuil; *La vie de la vie* (1980/1985). Paris: Le Seuil; *La Connaissance de la connassance* (1986/1992). Paris: Le Seuil; *Les Idées: leur habitat, leur vie, leurs mœurs, leur organisation* (1991/1996). Paris: Le Seuil; *L'Humanité de l'humanité, l'identité humaine* (2001/2003). Paris: Le Seuil; *Éthique* (2004/2006). Paris: Le Seuil.

Morin, E. (2006). *Restricted complexity, general complexity*. Proceedings. Colloquium "Intelligence de la complexité: épistémologie et pragmatique." Cerisy-La-Salle, France, June 26, 2005 (C. Gershenson, Trans.).

Morin, E. (2008). *La méthode*. Boxed collection, 2500 pages. Paris: Le Seuil, Collection Opus.

Morin, E., Motta, R., & Ciurana, E. R. (2003). *Éduquer pour l'ère planétaire. La pensée complexe comme méthode d'apprentissage dans l'erreur et l'incertitude humaines*. Paris: Balland.

Peterson, I. (1993). *Newton's clock: Chaos in the solar system*. San Francisco, CA: W. H. Freeman and Company.

Piaget, J. (1971). *Biology and knowledge: An essay on the relation between organic regulation and cognitive processes* (B. Walsh, Trans.). Chicago, IL: University of Chicago Press.

Pinar, W. F. (2004). *What is curriculum theory?* Mahwah, NJ: Lawrence Erlbaum Associates Publishers.

Poincaré, J. H. (1903). *Quoted from essay in Science and Method*. Retrieved September 17, 2017, from www.chaos.umd.edu/misc/poincare.html

Prigogine, I. (1980). *From being to becoming: Time and complexity in the physical sciences*. San Francisco, CA: W. H. Freeman and Company.

Stuever, N. L. (2009). *Review of the book* "A post-modern perspective on curriculum, by William E. Doll, Jr." (pp. 87–90). Retrieved September 17, 2017, from http://ojs.uwindsor.ca/ojs/leddy/index.php/JTL/article/viewFile/1187/732

Tyler, R. W. (1949). *Basic principles of curriculum and instruction*. Chicago, IL: University of Chicago Press.

22 Living Poetically
The Pedagogy of William E. Doll, Jr.

Carl Leggo

In 2015, I co-organized with Erika Hasebe-Ludt the 7th Biennial Provoking Curriculum Studies Conference at the University of British Columbia. Canadian curriculum scholars gathered together in order to examine critically and creatively the meaning of "provoking curriculum" for innovative education. Acknowledging that curriculum studies are always plural and polyphonic, Erika and I invited educators to provoke curriculum studies by attending to the multiple denotations of *provoke*: to stimulate, arouse, elicit, induce, excite, kindle, generate, instigate, goad, prick, sting, prod, infuriate, madden, ruffle, stir, and inflame. The conference was devoted to learning how to live well and wisely in the world by providing opportunities for educators to discuss curriculum studies by focusing on arts-based research, narrative inquiry, poetic inquiry, life writing, and hermeneutics. Inspired by William E. Doll's (2012) question, "I ask of those I am privileged to teach, 'Can you see another way to do/read/interpret what we have just done?'" (p. 27), we invited presentations that asked diverse questions about curriculum studies by engaging with creative, interactive, and imaginative scholarship.

At the conference on February 20, 2015, a circle of curriculum scholars located in Canada were celebrated, including William E. Doll, William F. Pinar, Ingrid Johnston, Karen Meyer, Peter Grimmett, Rita L. Irwin, Antoinette Oberg, David W. Jardine, Terry Carson, and Cynthia Chambers. They are all part of a vibrant network of educators and scholars who not only challenge curriculum studies with provocative questions but also imagine new possibilities for understanding, conceiving, shaping, and practicing curriculum studies. This celebration was an opportunity for conversation among some of Canada's most eminent curriculum scholars as well as emerging curriculum scholars. A highlight of the evening was Antoinette Oberg's tribute to William E. Doll. With Daniel, her partner, Antoinette danced an Argentinian tango—sensual, fluid, lyrical, delightful! Long ago, Antoinette invited Bill Doll to the University of Victoria to teach as a visiting professor. Eventually Bill moved to Victoria. While he had long been esteemed in Canada as a significant part of the circle of creative curriculum scholars that included Ted Aoki, Bill Pinar,

Dwayne Huebner, and Madeline Grumet, Bill's influence in Canada grew with his enthusiastic presence at the University of Victoria and the University of British Columbia, as well as other Canadian universities. Antoinette Oberg's dance represented a kind of love story, and from my perspective that is the story that Bill has lived in Canada among students and colleagues—a story of abiding love. Above all, Bill lives with a poet's delight in language and dialogue and questioning.

I cannot recall the first time I met Bill Doll in person at the University of British Columbia. Long before that first meeting, I was enthused by the anecdotes and references that colleagues like Bill Pinar, Antoinette Oberg, David W. Jardine, and Ted Aoki shared about Bill Doll. When colleagues spoke about Bill, they spoke with a kind of bemused reverence. Bill Doll was loved! When I finally met him, I understood immediately that he is a man of singular charm. Bow ties always breathe with an air of stylish exuberance! Bill lives poetically in the spaces between his primary two names. On the one hand, he is William E. Doll, Jr.—a name with enough gravitas to gain entrance to a prestigious golf club! On the other hand, he is Bill Doll—like a Dr. Seuss play on words, the name reverberates like a bell, a spondee with two stressed syllables, singing out a psalm of delight.

In *The Slow Professor: Challenging the Culture of Speed in the Academy*, Maggie Berg and Barbara K. Seeber (2016) claim that "Slow Professors act with purpose, taking the time for deliberation, reflection, and dialogue, cultivating emotional and intellectual resilience" (p. 11). According to Berg and Seeber, "slowing down is about asserting the importance of contemplation, connectedness, fruition, and complexity" (p. 57) while acknowledging that "distractedness and fragmentation characterize contemporary academic life" (p. 90). William E. Doll was living the conviction of the slow professor long before the concept was invented. Bill teaches us how to live in the academy. He lives with compassion, care, and conscience. Angeles Arrien (2005) asks, "Who have been the teachers of our hearts? What are we learning about love? What do we know about love?" (p. 92). Bill is a teacher of the heart. Bill lives with a commitment to integrity and interrogation and interconnection. Bill is constantly curious, motivated by awe and wonder. As Sandra Finney and Jane Thurgood Sagal (2017) understand, "our teaching flows from the quality of our inner life" (p. 8).

What I admire most about Bill Doll is that he always seems comfortable in his own presence, and therefore comfortable in the presence of others. He is always the host. He is never arrogant, loud, extroverted, self-centred. He is always gracious and generous. He lives with his feet in the earth, the *humus*. He lives with humility. And he lives with his heart, the source of all courage for living well. That is the most important lesson I have learned from Bill—to live well, we need to attend to the earth and the heart. It is a privilege and a joy to live on the earth, but to live well on the earth, we must attend to the heart.

In *Reverence: Renewing a Forgotten Virtue* the philosopher Paul Woodruff (2001) notes that "awe is the most reverent of feelings" because "you feel, when you are in awe, that you are human, that your mind is dwarfed by what it confronts" and "that you had best keep your mouth closed and your mind open while awaiting further disclosure" (p. 147). Bill has lived with awe. He has never lost the child's sense of wonder for the gangly grasshopper or the creation beyond imagination. As Woodruff knows, "the most important example a teacher sets is by learning—by showing the curiosity, industry, and open mind that learning requires" (p. 191). Bill is always a learner. According to Wendell Berry (1990) paying attention is coming "into the presence of a subject" by stretching "toward a subject, in a kind of aspiration" (p. 83). Bill pays attention; he is always a learner; he is always learning.

As a teacher, Bill is always open to wonder. When he and Donna Trueit taught courses in curriculum and pedagogy at UBC, I often heard from students how Bill and Donna created caring and loving communities where everybody took creative risks with language and ideas and possibilities. I have always been impressed with the comprehensive and complex conceptions of curriculum studies that Bill presents in his scholarship. He is one of a small circle of educators who have invested long hours in making sense of post-modern critical theory in relation to curriculum studies. William F. Pinar (2011) notes that "the impoverishment of theory and ignorance of the field's intellectual history have plagued curriculum studies for decades" (p. xi). This is one of Bill Doll's most significant accomplishments. Mary Oliver (1994) reminds us that: "language is a vibrant, malleable, living material" (p. 91). As a poet, she promotes the need for all of us to learn to attend to voice in our writing. Bill's writing and teaching are full of voice—the unique voice that he has honed and sustained in a lifetime of devotion to scholarship and education. One of his lasting gifts is his invitation for us to learn to hear our own voices, especially as we learn to hear the voices of others.

I will next focus on three specific moments in my living stories with Bill, moments that are now cherished memories.

Moment 1

In April, 2013, Bill invited me to the monthly meeting of the Department of Curriculum and Pedagogy at UBC. I am a professor in the Department of Language and Literacy Education, but I collaborate with many colleagues in Curriculum and Pedagogy. When I arrived, Bill asked me to sit in a special chair at the front of the room. He then gave a tender and glowing speech about Carl Leggo, the poet. At the end of the speech, he reached into a bag, and pulled out a beautiful glass award embossed with the words: *Carl Leggo, Poet Laureate of Curriculum and Pedagogy*. The last time I received a trophy was in 1963. I received the trophy for being the most outstanding boy scout in my local troop. Bill's trophy is the second trophy I have received in my life. It is a treasure!

The poet Gregory Orr (2002) thinks that: "somehow something has gone wrong with poetry in our culture. We have lost touch with its value and purpose, and in doing so, we have lost contact with essential aspects of our own emotional and spiritual lives" (p. 1). Bill lives with a holistic commitment to the physical, spiritual, intellectual, and emotional energies that shape our lives. Bill lives heartfully. He is not afraid to laugh loudly. He is not afraid to grieve. He is not afraid to be vulnerable. He lives with the energy of the exclamation point. I claim that we need more exclamation points in the academy.

> Exclamation!
>
> what is the point?
>
> what is the point
>   in exclamation?
>
> what is the exclamation
>   in the point?
>
> are we afraid
>   of the exclamation point?
>
> afraid of the point in the heart
> or learning there is no point?
>
> like we are afraid of clichés of the heart
>   afraid of the heart?
>   prefer the illusion of *sangfroid*
> where cold blood pumps slowly
>
> I am dying
>   in meetings
>
> we meet to
> discuss the budget
> review the department
> review the faculty
> review the department chair
> review the faculty dean
> & one another
>
> we spend so much time reviewing
>   we are always looking backwards
>   with necks like pretzels
>
> we meet to plan
> programs and policies

procedures and processes
productivity and promotion

the academy is a speed dating service
where there is no romance, no seduction,
just reduction and a stupefying trance

we need textual intercourse full of pleasure,
instead of this *coitus interruptus* that leaves us
desiccated, depleted, dry like a dean's dirge
about branding, and random, never randy,
encounters with potential wealthy benefactors

we need to claim more, declaim more
exclaim more, proclaim more
we need to reclaim
        the bold voices of poetry

our poetry needs to startle
    our poetry needs to howl

Moment 2

André Gide (1970) first published his prose poem *Fruits of the Earth* in 1897. It is one of those philosophical and poetic books that I return to again and again. Gide notes that "out of attachment to the past we refuse to understand that tomorrow's happiness is only possible if today's makes room for it" (p. 182), but he also observes "that every wave owes the beauty of its curve to the retreat of the one that precedes it" (p. 182) and "every flower must fade in order to bear its fruit" because "unless the fruit falls and dies, it cannot produce future flowerings" (p. 182). Therefore, "spring itself is founded upon winter's loss" (p. 182). I have been writing about the curriculum of growing older. Bill invited me to speak on November 13, 2015, in a seminar series he was hosting with Donna Trueit and Bill Pinar. The series was titled *Diverse Perspectives on Curriculum and Pedagogy*. I spoke about "The Curriculum of Character: Poetic Ruminations on Growing Old." In *The Force of Character and the Lasting Life*, James Hillman (1999) asks, "why *do* we live so long?" (p. xiii). He then recommends that "the last years confirm and fulfill character" (p. xiii). Hillman describes aging as "an art form" (p. xv). I know nobody who has aged more artfully than Bill. All the decades of his vigorous life, Bill has been growing into his character which as Hillman understands is really his characters: "Character is characters; our nature is a plural complexity, a multiphasic polysemous weave, a bundle, a tangle, a sleeve. That's why we need a long old age: to ravel out the snarls and set things straight" (p. 32). For all the wise and insightful words Bill has generated in teaching, speaking, and writing, the most important gift of wisdom Bill offers us is the wisdom of his aging artfully.

Mary Oliver (1994) writes:

> A mind that is lively and inquiring, compassionate, curious, angry, full of music, full of feeling, is a mind full of possible poetry. Poetry is a life-cherishing force. And it requires a vision—a *faith*. . . . For poems are not words, after all, but fires for the cold, ropes let down to the lost, something as necessary as bread in the pockets of the hungry.
>
> (p. 122)

The most used words in the English language are *I* and *you*. There are about seven billion people on the planet earth. I am in relationship with about seven billion other people, not to mention all the other creatures and non-sentient parts of the creation. Bill seeks to know others. Lorri Neilsen Glenn (2011) reminds us, "To write poetry . . . is to enter a long, never-ending conversation" (p. 108). Bill invites us to conversation. His life has been devoted to nurturing the complex relationships of knowing that are possible (and possibly impossible) when *I* and *you* interact. Bill's devotion is to relationship, to ways of knowing.

Ways of Knowing
(*science—Latin* scio: *to know*)

    aesthetic
    biological
    cultural
    dialogic
    ethical
    fluid
    genealogical
    holistic
    interpersonal
    joyful
    kinesthetic
    linguistic
    mythological
    narrative
    open
    personal
    questioning
    recursive
    sensual
    theoretical
    unique
    vocal

wise
xylophonic
yearning
zesty

Moment 3

In 2013, I saw Bill at the Sixth Provoking Curriculum Studies Conference in Ottawa. He was walking with a cane. I asked, "What happened?" He told me a story about putting on his pants. He said, I inserted one leg. I then inserted the second leg. Unfortunately I tried to put the second leg in the pants leg that already had a leg! It's not easy to put two legs in one pants leg. And in that moment, together, Bill and I almost fell over with laughing.

Walter Brueggemann (2001), the Old Testament theologian, writes that: "the characteristic way of a prophet of Israel is that of poetry and lyric. The prophet engages in futuring fantasy" (p. 40). According to Brueggemann, "the prophet does not ask if the vision can be implemented, for questions of implementation are of no consequence until the vision can be imagined. The *imagination* must come before the *implementation*" (p. 40). I wonder if our imaginations are sufficiently robust, creative, and courageous. Bill Doll lives with imagination. Perhaps you can't put two legs in one pants leg, but you can always try, and you can always count on a good story when you lose your balance.

In Love With the Alphabet
(*for Bill Doll*)

> *The aesthetic imagination is the primary mode of knowing the cosmos.*
>
> (James Hillman, 1999, p. 184)

changing paradigms   changing times
nothing is   stable   simple   solid

modernism received a postcard
from postmodernism: *wish you were here*

but here & there are not so easily rendered
after Descartes & Newton's methodical meddling

tired with Tyler's rationale
& rationalism & rations

Bill sought to see with an owl's eyes
what Tyler saw with an accountant's ledger

CLOSED on the school window
who can learn when the school is closed

we need living systems in evolution
like language speaks our knowing

in both the letters of the alphabet
& the spaces between the letters

the challenge of the biological view:
too logical, tame, domesticated, controlled

chaos & cosmos are one
3S's (Science, Story, Spirit)

4R's (Richness, Relations, Recursion, & Rigor)
5C's (Currere, Complexity, Cosmology, Conversation, Community)

like all my favorite curriculum scholars
Bill Doll loves the alphabet

language, diction, connotation, rhythm
a new sense of cosmos in the wild abundance

Bill embraces a mythopoetic view
knows language points to more

who wants cosmetic curriculum
when the cosmos calls, a cacophony

chaos is not wild & random, instead
inimitably orderly & complex

cosmos & chaos dance
an Argentinian tango

moment by moment in the momentous
composing of living wholeness

like a poem is never closed & controlled
curriculum is emergent & startling

we are not sentenced to linear expression
sitting meekly at desks in tight uniforms

curriculum attends to the spaces between
letters & words & lines where poetry grows

with spell-binding delight in wild possibilities
leaning into love with tantalizing hope for the other

A Final Anecdote

In 2015, when Erika Hasebe-Ludt and I co-organized the 7th Provoking Curriculum Studies Conference at UBC, and we were making plans for the special evening to celebrate a circle of influential curriculum scholars,

I mentioned casually to Bill Doll that I had invited a musician to help us celebrate. I told Bill that I didn't have much money in the budget to offer an honorarium to the musician, but I thought the musician would not complain. Soon after, Bill slipped me an envelope, and said, "This is for the musician." (I doubt the musician has ever been so well remunerated for a gig!) In Bill's typical way, he told me that he was offering the honorarium anonymously. I might be breaking his confidence a little by telling this story now, but we need to know more about the stories behind the stories. I agree with David G. Smith's (2006) conviction that "the purpose of education is to learn how to live well" (p. 39). Bill Doll has devoted his life to learning how to live well, how to live poetically, and by living poetically, he teaches us how to live well, too. May the poetry continue to resonate without end . . .

References

Arrien, A. (2005). *The second half of life: Opening the eight gates of wisdom.* Boulder, CO: Sounds True.

Berg, M., & Seeber, B. K. (2016). *The slow professor: Challenging the culture of speed in the academy.* Toronto, ON: University of Toronto Press.

Berry, W. (1990). *What are people for?: Essays.* New York, NY: North Point Press.

Brueggemann, W. (2001). *The prophetic imagination.* Minneapolis, MN: Fortress Press.

Doll, W. E. (2012). Complexity and the culture of curriculum. *Complicity: An International Journal of Complexity and Education*, 9(1), 10–29.

Finney, S., & Sagal, J. T. (2017). *The way of the teacher: A path for personal growth and professional fulfillment.* Lanham, MD: Rowman & Littlefield.

Gide, A. (1970). *Fruits of the earth.* Harmondsworth, UK: Penguin Books.

Hillman, J. (1999). *The force of character and the lasting life.* New York, NY: Ballantine Books.

Neilsen Glenn, L. (2011). *Threading light: Explorations in loss and poetry.* Regina, SK: Hagios Press.

Oliver, M. (1994). *A poetry handbook.* Boston, MA: Mariner Books.

Orr, G. (2002). *Poetry as survival.* Athens, GA: University of Georgia Press.

Pinar, W. F. (2011). *The character of curriculum studies.* New York, NY: Palgrave Macmillan.

Smith, D. G. (2006). *Trying to teach in a season of great untruth: Globalization, empire and the crises of pedagogy.* Rotterdam, Netherlands: Sense Publishers.

Woodruff, P. (2001). *Reverence: Renewing a forgotten virtue.* Oxford, UK: Oxford University Press.

23 Confronting Life and Death
Reflections on Living the Spirit of Education

Petra Munro Hendry

It is fitting that I should start this essay the day after Ash Wednesday. Ashes remind us that it is from "dust that we came and to dust we will return." Our individual lives are but fleeting moments, temporary spaces we inhabit that are constitutive of a much larger cosmos. In his essay "Struggles With Spirituality" (2012), William Doll poignantly reminds us that it is not only individual human beings who die, but that humanity, our species, will also ultimately return to dust:

> We humans have always known our personal and physical existence to be temporal—we are born, live, die. This is what it means to be an individual human being.
>
> (2012, p. 33)

The temporality of our existence and the world is often difficult to contemplate. Perhaps this is why it has been so arduous for me to write this essay, I write knowing that my dear friend and colleague at Louisiana State University of over twenty-five years, now eighty-five years old, while vibrant in spirit, is grappling with the temporality of his physical life. The Lenten season of the Catholic church requires that we face death—through death, we embrace life. Bill's reverence for death (chaos, disorder) is, I believe, a profound reminder to live life with open arms, to embrace the irony and complexity of the human condition with awe and wonder.

But, of course, this is no easy task. As I have often been reminded in Bill's writings (Doll, 1987, 1993), the modernist frameworks which we have inherited are based on notions of permanence, control, linearity, reason, and method which leave little room for ambiguity, temporality, nonlinearity, play, complexity, and spirituality. Bill's struggles with spirituality, as I understand them, are rooted in this tension between traditional, modernist theology in which God assumes some type of permanence through separation from the human fabric of life. This separation (original sin), in which God is understood as "outside" the human world, as "the" creator and as *the* power, makes God inaccessible and someone to fear. The struggle with this "Christian," anthropocentric, all powerful God is that it makes impossible a cosmology in which all facets of life are seen as part of a dynamic, entangled, generative, and interdependent process that is inherently unpredictable, mysterious, ever changing, and the source of creativity. The season of Lent embodies for me the recursive, cyclical, nonlinear nature of experience which refuses to reduce living to representations/binaries/abstractions and instead suggests an organic process of the cycle of life and death, of order and chaos, reason and spirit (Hendry, 2011). This Lenten ritual is a constant reminder for me of my temporality.

It is this sense of temporality that I will elaborate on in the rest of this essay because it has profoundly shaped my being of and in the world. First is my understanding of curriculum/education as a living, breathing phenomenon that cannot be reduced to a technological endeavor but is always a moral or spiritual one. Understanding education as spirit requires me to be present to the complex relationships within which I am embedded in order to be alive to the awe, wonder, and process of being. Of course, embracing temporality is a challenge for those of us steeped in modernist, humanist notions of subjectivity, agency and change. The tension between acknowledging the indeterminacy of life and my simultaneous desire for a theory/vision/plan for a more just, humane society has been the focus of many animated conversations with Bill over the years. Our engagement/dialogue has taught me much about embracing the temporality and spirit of education.

Education as Spirit

> *Everything that is done in schools, and in preparation for school activity, is already infused with the spiritual.*
>
> Dwayne Huebner (1993, p. 13)

Bill's "struggles with spirituality" remind us that, not only are we intertwined and connected to a larger ecology and cosmos, but also that in the end, our individual lives have little meaning except as part of a much larger whole. What matters is our relationships; to each other, to the worlds we inhabit and to the "spirit" of life. The use of the term "spirit" is not invoked in a strictly religious sense, as in a soul, but as a reminder that we (human and non-human) are intimately interconnected, interdependent, and in fact function as one living, breathing organism. For education, this means that a school, classroom, or community cannot be separated into students/teachers as subjects and knowledge cannot be reduced to an object. This technocratic view of education "kills" the spirit, the living, breathing force of creativity. Spirit, as Bill describes it, as the "breath of life" gives force, passion, and commitment to an event. According to Bill (2012):

> spirit (along with the spiritual, the sacred—not necessarily the religious) is what gives a situation, as George Santanya (1968) points out, not only its vitality but also its integrity, its honesty, its truthfulness.
>
> (p. 22)

To understand education as a sacred or spiritual process in which we are called to be present to life also requires confronting death.

So, now at the start of the Lenten season, I am reminded of how significant this time of year was for William Doll. Experiencing Bill engage with the Lenten season year after year taught me much about his spirit—his humility, self-discipline, doubt, and contradictions. As a heretical Catholic, Bill always went to Mass on Mondays (never Sundays), yet he observed the Lenten season with a great deal of reverence. He observed all the Lenten rituals: giving alms, sacrifice (no meat on Fridays), repentance and confession. The three traditional practices to be taken up with renewed vigor during Lent are prayer (justice towards God), fasting (justice towards self), and almsgiving (justice towards neighbors). I don't believe he did this in the "spirit" of following the "law" of the church. The "law" assumes a type of permanence and stability that defies temporality, complexity and the dynamic nature of the cosmos, and I think Bill would argue, of "God." God is not about law. God is a poet. An understanding of "spirit" as a living, breathing indeterminate process is what the Lenten season signals us to remember, and in order to do so we must confront death.

The forty days of lent, as I believe Bill understands them, are to remind us of our own insignificance. We are constituted as human beings only through our connections to others, and it is hubris to think that we can make it on our own. Sacrifice, penance, self-denial, atonement, and prayer are rituals to help us give-up the "self" or sacrifice ourselves, our egos, our belief in our own self-importance. We are reminded that we are not the center of the universe (that is our sin), that the world does not revolve around us. It was Bill who reminded me that we must embrace death: death of selfishness, death of self-centeredness, death of self-righteousness and death of knowledge. Lent is not blind obedience to laws, but giving up the self to reawaken (like the spring, which is what Lent means) our profound relationship and interconnectedness with all that is. Lent is the astonishing reminder that there is no self, only relationship.

Lent culminates in the Easter Vigil. The first Easter Vigil I ever attended was with my husband John, Bill Doll, Donna Trueit and Philipp Jackson at Sacred Heart Church in Baton Rouge. At the time, it was 2000, I could not have realized the significance of this event in reorienting myself in space and time. It was this shared evening sitting in complete darkness, then bathed in candlelight and returning to the darkness of night that reminds me not only of the temporality of life but that the spirit of life is beyond all comprehension. This ritual is a profound embodiment of

Confronting Life and Death 213

the mystery of life, the never-ending cycle of life and death, and a call to embrace the indeterminacy of life.

The Easter Vigil is an ancient tale or, perhaps, I should say multiple tales, or a palimpsest, a layering of ancient stories. The stories (like the Vigil) begin with/in darkness/chaos/death, invoke prayer/reflection/divination, and end in light/order/life, only to be repeated again and again and again through ritual. While the Easter Vigil is commemorating the life/death and resurrection of Jesus, the cycle of life/death portrayed in this narrative is much older. Stories of death (darkness) and the return to life (light) are not just central motifs in the narratives of Christianity, but as Bill Doll maintains are indeed emblematic of the cyclical, recursive, dynamic, and unpredictable nature of the cosmos. There is a striking parallel between the great myths of the ancient world, as Bill maintains, which embrace chaos as central to the primal mass from which order is fashioned, or as the "continual interplay between created order and the primal mass from which it evolved" (1993, p. 88). Narratives of the cyclical nature of life (as opposed to a linear narrative of progress) are older than Christianity tracing their roots to pagan religions in the Mediterranean whose religious celebration were often conducted at or following the Spring Equinox. As Bill reminds us, "in virtually all creation myths, those of the ancient cosmologies, chaos was the 'messy' primordial source from which all being and organization sprang" (1993, p. 86). In the great myths of the Western world—those from Babylon, Greece, Israel, and Rome—chaos is always present, but understood in multiple ways. For some, chaos is the amorphous mass from which order is fashioned usually by God and eventually science; or as the continual interplay between chaos and created order. Ironically, order, control, and structure result in stasis; in extinction, there is no regeneration, creativity, and play. This interplay of chaos (dark), and order (light) is where creativity occurs. The Vigil reminds us that not only do we need both darkness and light, but that we can never transcend either darkness or light because they are mutually constitutive of each other. The power of this narrative is not only the fact that it still speaks across millennia, but that it requires us to suspend narrative's ability to represent human experience. Instead, the vigil invites us into the ongoing ritual of creation/generation/recursion, the spirit of life, not inevitable progress, knowledge or determinacy.

These narratives of the cycle of life/light/order and death/darkness/chaos remind us as Walter Ong (1982) points out that the world is not an object or paradigm, but is something that is dynamic, chaotic, regenerative, and unpredictable. Embracing this dynamic tension, or spirit, between chaos and order, what Bill calls perturbation/dissonance/vitality is central not only to understanding our temporality, but illuminates an understanding of education as a breathing, living, spirit that surpasses all understanding. In other words, education cannot be reduced to a technology. Education that is rich, recursive, rigorous, and relational (Bill's four R's) emerges from the interplay of chaos and order, dark and light, death and life. Knowledge is not a product; it is process. Like the Lenten rituals which are repeated every year to remind ourselves of our temporality, it is this sense of recursion that I now also understand not only as central to Bill's teaching, but his very vision of education. We return again and again, this iteration is not repetition but a recognition that the dynamic process of education cannot be reduced to a linear story, an objective or method. Perhaps it is fitting that the Lenten season begins with Mardi Gras (another favorite time for Bill) in which the carnival season reminds us of the ironies of the human condition. Each year signals again a reminder not to take ourselves too seriously, that we can control nothing and to embrace the chaos of life.

Keeping Knowledge/Spirit Alive

> *The art born as the echo of God's laughter is the art that created the fascinating imaginative realm where no one owns the truth and everyone has the right to be understood.*
>
> Milan Kundera (cited in Rorty, 1989)

This quote, which Bill referred to often in his teaching, has also become one of my favorites. When I imagine God laughing it is a robust, joyful, and loud laughter that reminds me to not take myself, or my ideas, too seriously. I have often struggled with the self-righteousness that comes with commitment to a particular ideology, with believing that I have found the "truth," the way, and the light. This intellectual hubris has served me well as an academic where one is expected to take up a position, argue, and defend it in the name of positing new, better knowledge. Ironically, this is only achieved at the cost of disregarding or delegitimizing the ideas of others. This form of assault or violence on others, as Bill often reminded me, is paradigmatic of modernism's quest for certainty, control, and order. Western, scientific reason does not allow for everyone to be understood, only some. Education, as we know it, is designed to categorize, sort, rank, label and differentiate into those who know and those who don't. Schools are not designed to facilitate human understanding (ethics), but to indoctrinate students into a particular belief system based on representation/knowledge (epistemology). In other words, education as we know it serves as a form of transmission, not as a transformative process in which we engage in the awe, wonder and spirit of the call of "moreness" (Doll, 2012, p. 175).

And transformation (not resurrection), as I now understand it, in no small part due to my work with Bill, is all about relationships. But it is not just the human relationships that matter. All matter, matters. In other words, human beings are continually being constituted in and through matter. As

Karen Barad (2007) has helped me to understand, "matter is substance in its intra-active becoming—not a thing but a doing" (p. 151). This doing, or always be-coming, reminds us that human beings are not objects, but are continually emerging as part of a network of relations in which we are embedded. As Bill maintains, "we are modes in networks, interconnected to other nodes within other networks: people within cultures, cultures within humanity, humanity within an ecosystem, our ecosystem within our universe, our universe within a cosmos, ever evolving" (2012, p. 176). This dynamic, self-organizing *"relation of relations"* is unpredictable, nonlinear and always in a state of flux (p. 177). Much like the "loss" of self I experience through the ritual of the Easter Vigil, the recursive, indeterminate nature of experience not only reminds me that there is no progress, but that the nature of relationships (both human and non-human) requires not change or improvement, but being present to and embodied in the creative, generative, living, breathing dynamics that constitute being. I believe this is the notion of spirit as pedagogy, a pedagogy that embraces, not limits, "the complexity found in relationships, life, situations" (p. 175). Faith, and I would add spirit, according to Bill (2012):

> should lie not in our personal ability to control through predication, but believe it should lie in what Dwayne Huebner (1999) labels the call of "moreness." "Moreness" has a spirit to it, a spirit which asks us to realize our own finitude, our own ignorance, and calls us to transcend the known, the expected, even the ego and the self.
> (p. 403)

Ironically, it is necessary to give-up the "self" (the unitary, Western, autonomous self) to engage in relations.

I did not realize until many years after starting at LSU the profound impact that Bill's unconditional faith in relationships, whether it be faculty, students, or staff, would have on my way of being in the world. While our politics were radically different—I was a feminist, critical, post-structuralist seeking social change, and Bill was a post-modernist, complexity theorist who sought to embrace chaos; it seemed that Bill never saw our differences as opposition, but as pedagogical spaces to explore multiple sites of meaning, to generate more questions as a way to keep knowledge alive. It was not a matter of who had the "right ideas" or whose theory was more useful in understanding the world. Curriculum, understood by Bill, was a site in which "everyone has the right to be understood." This requires an openness to the other, faith/trust that understanding will emerge, and embracing a spirit of education as a journey with others in which education focuses on:

> our *being*—on our engagement with life as this is manifest in humanity, the world, the universe, the cosmos. . . . This is an education

> which questions the being of all we hold sacred while at the same time manifests a faith that such questioning will lead us to the sacredness of being.
>
> (Doll, 2012, p. 42)

The difference that makes a difference is to be present to that being/becoming. As a curriculum scholar/teacher it is my obligation to engage in an ethics of relationality, what Molly Quinn (2010) has called a "question of hospitality" in which our work as curriculum theorists is understood as an ethical engagement to make room for the *other* (p. 101). However, to do so, as Derrida suggests, is to acknowledge the impossibility of ever "knowing" the other. To embrace the stranger, the other, without seeking to name, represent or understand is a curricular ethics which requires scholars to be troubadours, wanderers, continually in motion to be present in the complicated conversation that is curriculum. Conversation, as Brent Davis (2004) reminds us, is derived from the Latin *convertio*, "living together" and is an emergent form that cannot be predetermined, prespecified, but requires that we listen, attend to and be present to the other (p. 177). My responsibility as an educator is to engage in this complicated conversation with openness, to embrace the indeterminacy of meaning, and to keep knowledge alive through acknowledging the polyphonic, generative, divergent lines of becoming.

Embracing indeterminacy, living with contradiction, irony, and ambiguity has been a struggle for me. Perhaps, that is why in the past I always found comfort in ideologies (feminism, critical theory) that had a vision/plan/direction/goal for a utopian society. Having faith in the processes of becoming/emergence/indeterminacy requires improvisation, play, and embeddedness in the relationality/vitality of life. In other words, there is no truth or meaning that can be uncovered/discovered, instead we are continuously constituted in the flow of life/breath/spirit. We are entangled in the web of life and cannot step outside of it. Ethics, according to Levinas (1985), "does not supplement a preceding existential base," instead our subjectivity "is knotted in ethics understood as responsibility" (p. 95). Ethics or relationality is not about "right" response to the "other," but about the responsibility "for the lively relationalities of becoming of which we are a part" (Barad, 2007, p. 93). This relational responsibility focuses not on understanding the other (there is no such subject) or on meaning (since this is always in flux), but on practicing/doing/performing/being in the dance of connectivity and intra-action. It is this dance, repeated over and over again, like the Easter Vigil, that is a process of "embodied sensibility" or relational ethics through which we engage in and are present to the wonder and awe of the web of relationships that constitute our being. It has been an honor to engage in this dance with William Doll.

References

Barad, K. (2007). *Meeting the universe halfway: Quantum physics and the entanglement of matter and meaning.* Durham, NC: Duke University Press.

Davis, B. (2004). *Inventions of teaching.* New York, NY: Routledge.

Doll, W. (1987). Foundations for a post-modern curriculum. *Journal of Curriculum Studies, 21*(3), 245–253.

Doll, W. (1993). *A post-modern perspective on curriculum.* New York, NY: Teachers College.

Doll, W. (2012). Struggles with spirituality. In D. Trueit (Ed.), *Pragmatism, postmodernism, and complexity theory: The "fascinating imaginative realm" of William E. Doll, Jr.* (pp. 33–44). New York, NY: Routledge.

Hendry, P. (2011). *Engendering curriculum history.* New York, NY: Routedge.

Huebner, D. (1993). Education and spirituality. *JCT: An Interdisciplinary Journal of Curriculum Studies, 11*(2), 13.

Huebner, D. (1999). *The lure of the transcendent* (V. Hillis, Ed.). Mahweh, NJ: Erlbaum.

Levinas, E. (1985). *Ethics & infinity: Conversations with Philippe Nemo* (R. Cohen, Trans.). Pittsburgh: Duquesne University Press.

Ong, W. (1982). *Orality and literacy.* London: Methuen.

Quinn, M. (2010). "No room at the inn"? The question of hospitality in the post(partum)-labors of curriculum studies. In E. Malewski (Ed.), *Curriculum studies handbook* (pp. 101–117). New York, NY: Routledge.

Rorty, R. (1989). *Contingency, irony and solidarity.* Cambridge, UK: Cambridge University Press.

24 Afterword

William F. Pinar

> Bill sought to see with an owl's eyes.[1]
>
> Carl Leggo

After words comes silence. The voice of William E. Doll, Jr. has now fallen silent. There will be no more captivating courses, no more groundbreaking books, no more provocative presentations at academic conferences. Now there are our words about his words, words enacted in pedagogical practices worldwide. These words and practices are embodied in Doll's students and colleagues: particular people in particular places, expressive of, responsive to, particular times. Doll—and his wife and intellectual compatriot Donna Trueit—always emphasized relationality; now the term feels like a lifeline to a great teacher, original scholar, congenial colleague, and invaluable friend. Bill Doll was all these and much more. While he is among us no longer, he remains in relation to us through the words published here.

These words—the ones you're reading now—may comprise an afterword, but here there is no silence, as words continue to be composed and spoken, words inspired by the still reverberating presence of William E. Doll, Jr. This ongoing echo—his words, his voice incorporated into ours, the raising of voices Doll supported throughout his long and astonishing career—is audible throughout this collection that Molly Quinn has so ably assembled, a collection that is, in her inspiriting words:

> a kind of polyphonic harmony or symphony of voices that are themselves each echoes of a sort of Doll's divine laughter—as it also seeks to express something of/at the heart of his thought, teaching, work, influence, legacy, life, and person: certainly, an art born of spirit, and its expression of playfulness and delight in being in the world and creatively participating in its becoming.

---

1. Unless otherwise indicated, all quoted passages can be found in this text.

Afterword

This collection, then, is a complex echo[2]—utterly earnest in its playfulness, an academic juxtaposition of Mardi Gras and Lent (as Hendry implies)—that sends shock waves through those of us touched by his thought, presence, and practice. We mourn his loss, but we can still hear that still reverberating laughter, that constant questioning, threaded through his sustaining study that has brought us insight, understanding, even joy. Let us celebrate this man.

What gift you were—are—Bill Doll, a judgment exclaimed in each of these distinctive chapters. Those who did not know in person this man can nonetheless hear him in our words, often his words that have now become ours. Maybe you can almost sense that expansive subjective presence it has been my personal privilege to know for forty-one years.[3] All of us gathered in this text remember too. You who come afterward—after these words—can re-experience him through your study of his work, relocating his words into yours. Allow this collection to serve as a cordial invitation to enter the "fascinating imaginative realm" of William E. Doll, Jr.[4] It is a realm he inhabited in time and place and expressed through teaching.

Time

> Doll's art too embraces complexity, paradox, tensionality, and temporality—complexifying curriculum studies, it challenges much of accepted, endorsed educational and curricular ideology and certitude.
>
> Molly Quinn

Especially in the U.S.—William E. Doll, Jr. was an American from head to toe—the nightmare that is the present continues.[5] Like the owl Carl Leggo

---

2. Referencing Greek mythology, Quinn points out that "Echo's is a playful spirit, born of and inhabiting and cavorting about in the high and exalted places, in conversational art and companionship with the divine. . . . Doll is apt to appreciate Echo's mischievous adventures, as well, overturning the established order of things and revelling in that which it would define as diverting or excessive."
3. We met in an airport after an academic conference in 1976, discovering that we lived an hour apart in upstate New York. I acknowledge our friendship in my 2006 collection (see Pinar, 2006). My introduction to his 2012 collection—edited by Donna Trueit—focuses upon his intellectual accomplishment; my introduction to the 2016 book by Hongyu Wang is focused on Doll's teaching. I dedicated the second edition of *What Is Curriculum Theory?* to both Bill and Donna. This present statement chronicles the consequences of Doll's teaching and scholarship for others, consequences that exceed what you read here, consequences that continue to reverberate among those who study him.
4. One place to begin is Trueit (2012).
5. School reform has now been hijacked by profiteers who see public education not as a sacred public trust but as a financial market to be plundered. "Many of the country's largest tech companies," Kang (2017, September 27, B6) reports, "including Amazon, Facebook, Google, Microsoft, and Salesforce, have pledged "$300 million for computer science education, part of a partnership with the Trump administration meant to prepare

invokes in his essay, Doll could see through the darkness that shrouds us, could hear what was moving underneath the surface of the soil, could glide effortlessly through the jagged terrain of the present moment. Even within the nightmare of standardized tests, teacher scapegoating, and moving curriculum online, Doll kept education alive, made it seem easy, even fun. Morally committed to children and to those who teach them, Doll courageously continued his effort to enliven curriculum despite others' determination to reduce it to a computer program.[6]

The darkness within which educators work is worldly; it references the centuries-old tendency to stifle the spirit[7] of students and teachers and the knowledge they study. In that darkness ghosts haunt us, imperiling our commitment to keep knowledge alive. For Doll, the ghost of control was the key culprit. For Eero Ropo and Veli-Matti Värri, the ghost that haunts education is control, but it is control that fails, burdening us with by-products of technological progress (they name pollution as one) that haunt the future we bequeath to children. They liken that ghost to a "hyperobject," a term denoting the scale of what haunts us. For Doll, "control" itself was on such a scale; like pollution and the climate change pollution produces, the ghost of (now technological) control disables us from breathing freely, seeing clearly, gliding through the air like an owl.

---

students for careers in technology." Not only do these mega-companies intend to convert public schools into private-sector job-training centers, "these efforts coincide with a larger corporate initiative to sell computers and software to U.S. schools, a 'market' projected to reach $21 billion by 2020" (Singer, 2017, June 7, A14).

6. While "captains of American industry have long used their private wealth to remake public education," Singer (2017, June 7, A14) reminds, "with lasting and not always beneficial results," today the huge technology companies—Apple, Google, Microsoft—attempt to sell their products (curriculum has become one) directly to students, teachers, and parents, often using social media. These companies also cultivate (through free dinners and trips) administrators and teachers—sometimes violating public ethics laws—to accept that their products ensure students learning (despite study after study that contests such claims). These unethical and sometimes illegal strategies enable these mega-corporations to influence public schools far more quickly than in the past, creating unquestioning faith in technology that spreads like an oil slick to legislators and education officials. "Another difference," Singer reports, is that "some tech moguls are taking a hands-on role in nearly every step of the education supply chain by financing campaigns to alter policy, building learning apps to advance their aims and subsidizing teacher training" (A14). This massive intervention represents an "almost monopolistic approach to education reform," said Larry Cuban, an emeritus professor of education at Stanford University. "That is starkly different from earlier generations of philanthropists" (quoted in Singer, 2017, June 7, A14). While Doll was open to the use of technology in education, he was no unquestioning believer in its omnipotence in student learning. And he always affirmed the public character of public education, e.g. its formative role in the cultivation of citizens capable of critical and creative thinking.

7. "Spirit," Hendry points out, is for Doll the "breath of life" and it "gives force, passion, and commitment to an event."

When haunted by ghosts, words can sometimes seem inadequate. Nel Noddings examines "the four criteria at the center of Doll's vision," wondering "what remains of them," pointing to "current developments that might renew our hope." Because ideas persist despite present circumstances, I suggest that even without "current developments" everything remains of Doll's ideas. They stand at the ready for anyone who walks into his fascinating imaginative realm. Noddings adds moral commitment to Doll's four R's (richness, recursion, relations, and rigor), but moral commitment vivifies Doll's vision from beginning to end. He could not agree more with Noddings' assertion that "our aim is to produce better people, and what we mean by that is perpetually open for transformative exploration." Doll's pedagogy is morally committed to that progressive aim.

Control was the ghost Doll identified as haunting the curriculum, but maybe that same ghost can come to our rescue, or so Ropo and Värri seem to suggest. "We need a global curriculum," they argue, "something that responds to the very basic needs of the whole humankind, to develop global citizens, transform people towards universally positioning thinkers, and to help them grow into responsible agents, willing to serve the universal good, equity, equality, and democracy," adding, humorously, "maybe we also have to introduce a new PISA test promoting the common understanding of the world and ghosts we have with us." They conclude: "This is the legacy from Bill Doll. Thank you Bill! Is it time to start the work, together?" That apparent paradox—control for the sake of freeing us from control—haunts progressive thinkers from Dewey to Doll, haunts all of us who position education as a means to an end.[8]

After Progressivism in the U.S. came powerful propaganda[9] followed now by out-of-control profiteering. Education remains a means but the end is no longer democracy and the self-realization of citizenry but the enrichment of the few. Doll lived through this wrenching outraging sequence. Rather than becoming submerged in it, Doll, like the owl of Minerva, took flight. What this means, the great Canadian educator George Grant suggested, "is that human beings only pursue philosophy, a rigorous and consistent attempt to think the meaning of existence, when an old system of meaning is coming to the end of its day."[10] Doll

---

8. Not that I oppose paradox. Control of climate change *is* urgent; intolerance of intolerance is as well. In Germany, anti-Semitism among new residents of the country may be addressed—or so a recent proposal suggests—by requiring new immigrants to visit Nazi concentration camp memorials. Of course, there remain too many instances of anti-Semitism among native-born Germans, despite student trips to Nazi concentration campus being "regular elements of German school curriculums" (Gladstone, 2018, January 11, A4). Still, democracy requires a strong—even anti-democratic—response to those who would end it.
9. For an early analysis see Berliner and Biddle (1995).
10. Grant (1966[1959], p. 5).

studied pragmatism just as it disappeared from U.S. public schools and university-based schools of education; he critiqued modernity just as it dissolved into post-modernity; he theorized the curricular implications of complexity theory just as the standardization of assessment rendered education simplistic. Like the owl of Minerva, Doll glides through this deepening darkness, his eyes alert to enemies and to progressive possibilities, his wings gently enfolding friends, protecting authentic knowledge (in contrast to empty information), keeping knowledge alive. Quinn knows:

> Of "sunny elegance" is an apt description for Bill as well, and his playful laughter and thought have been a healing balm time again, bringing me happiness and hope amid melancholy, as I am sure it has been for many others also (to which some here attest)—and the curriculum field itself amid dark times. Occasions with him, too, are ever festive, and often toasted with spirits as well—of which colleagues in this collection also speak.

One such close colleague is Petra Munro Hendry, who remembers the "tension" between Doll's emphasis upon "indeterminacy" and her own demands for "a more just, humane society," a tension that had "animated" many conversations ... [that] taught me much about embracing the temporality and spirit of education."

The darkness in which we move is not only worldly; it is also spiritual. Doll's "struggles with spirituality"—as Petra Munro Hendry testifies—"remind us that, not only are we intertwined and connected to a larger ecology and cosmos, but also that in the end, our individual lives have little meaning except as part of a much larger whole." She continues:

> Embracing this dynamic tension, or spirit, between chaos and order, what Bill calls perturbation/dissonance/vitality is central not only to understanding our temporality, but illuminates an understanding of education as a breathing, living, spirit that surpasses all understanding.

So the concept of relationality—so central to Doll's *oeuvre*—is surely spiritual as it is intellectual, ecological, and social, interlacing domains of experience interpersonally engaged in classroom conversation.

For Doll, however, spirituality suffered an ambivalent relation to the institutions pledged to protect it, a relation not unlike that of education to schools. That is evident in Doll's "struggles with spirituality," housed as these were within Catholicism. Like Petra Munro Hendry, Steve Triche points out that Doll's Catholicism was "heretical"—playful even: "For instance, when he goes to mass, he goes on Monday rather than Sunday." Hendry too acknowledges this fact, but she points out that for Doll Lent was a different matter, a season he observed, she notes, "with a great deal of reverence."[11]

Ugena Whitlock wonders whether Doll's theology is queer, by which she means odd or eccentric, not Queer. Whitlock recounts several episodes, the first of which she names (as does M. Jayne Fleener) the Mysterium Tremendum, a phrase Doll employs "to represent the ever-contriving complexity and creativity in the cosmos," adding that "he furthers the concept of tremendous mystery to also hold feelings of repulsion that works together with awe and fascination. Herein is the nature of struggle with our participation in divine life." Between the "intense fear and trembling concurrent with ecstatic attraction," Whitlock writes, "Doll finds the cosmologic, ecological awakening to an awe-some power of the universe." Queer here means awe, the "awe-some" complexity of the universe. Relationality is, then, not only social and intellectual and historical, it also denotes our embeddedness in what we might not understand.

Whitlock remembers her days as a graduate student, living among fellow graduate students: "we traveled as a pack, seven or eight sharing a hotel room—room, not suite—at conferences, dashing to each other's presentations, clustering in star-struck awe at networking receptions." Suddenly it was ending, and Whitlock recounts: "Toward the end of my studies the last Bergamo I attended as a doc student was weighing heavily on me in my nostalgic way of missing a place in time rather than being joyfully mindful of it." It was at a conference where another episode unfolded, paired she was with Doll at a keynote session.

> Although his theorizing is brilliant and provocative—and inspirited, probably the one word I remembered from senior seminar—his topic is usually superfluous to me. It's worth the price of a ticket just to see him present, because he walks the audience through his thought processes, itself a journey into chaos and complexity that ends in illumination.

Whitlock's subject was queer theory, and the question/answer session was "rich and spirited," perhaps because she depicted "engagement with the divine as orgasmic."

Stymied by a question on method, Whitlock was waiting for an answer when Doll "walked over to me.... He paused, breathed, smiled, and said,

11. Doll, Hendry continues, "observed all the Lenten rituals: giving alms, sacrifice (no meat on Fridays), repentance and confession. The three traditional practices to be taken up with renewed vigor during Lent are prayer (justice towards God), fasting (justice towards self), and almsgiving (justice towards neighbors). I don't believe he did this in the 'spirit' of following the 'law' of the church." He also observed Mardi Gras, as Hendry—and everyone in this collection—can recall.

Try prayer." That advice answered *her* question: "Yes, I am talking about transcending intellectual limitations—but not by turning to God in a fundamental, Judeo-Christian way; I am suggesting a *currere* in which there is a bending backward and forward, apart and together, across space and time, in our search—whatever the ground of being, the ultimate concern may be. All that from two words."[12]

Recall that M. Jayne Fleener also points to the *mysterium tremendum*, the phrase Doll invoked to reference the mystery of religious experience. This sense of "spirituality," Fleener notes, Doll placed alongside science and story. This triumvirate incorporated, she continues, complexity theory, including conceptions of "process, perturbation, emergence, transformation, and recursive dynamics in an ongoing and unfolding hermeneutic." These concepts accent the "unfolding" of Doll's *oeuvre* over the course of his career, itself, Fleener suggests, "a complex adaptive system with recursion, emergence, and increasing layers of complexity defining the evolving story and pathways of understanding." The "largeness" of the work and the man was embodied as well as conceptualized: Fleener recalls Doll's booming voice and his "enormous laugh" filling the classrooms of LSU's Peabody Hall. Quinn too recalls Doll's "laugh . . . so unique, robust, jovial, infectious, and surely unforgettable."

This symmetry of subjective and physical presence was also audible, as one heard it, Fleener points out, in his "booming voice" and "enormous laugh." The scale of Doll's achievement seems almost somatized too, in what for Whitlock was a seemingly seven-foot-tall Doll, "mostly limbs, [a] silken shock of white hair neatly combed, thick eyeglasses, signature bow tie. And the laugh." Doll laughed, Whitlock notes, "with his whole being . . . a joyful, howling roar." She emphasizes *joy*. So does Noel Gough: "Bill's great gift to all who know him is his seemingly limitless capacity to find wonder and joy in almost everything he experiences, no matter how trivial or insignificant they might seem to those of us who are more suspicious or cynical. Long may we cherish the echo of Bill's laughter." The words that echo through us now are not only serious, then, they make us smile, chuckle, even laugh.

That resounding echo—joyful, playful, pedagogical—filled through the ears of those occupying the institutions where Doll taught, as he challenged established hierarchies of knowledge and sequences of learning. "The fragile edifice of disciplinary superiority crumbled," Douglas McKnight remembers, "when in walked this tall, thin, gangly, bespectacled man with wispy white hair and a bow tie, a Dickensian character come to life in the halls of LSU." What he offered, McKnight continues, was "something . . . strange yet seductive, a concept of curriculum that challenged years of

---

12. Recall that James B. Macdonald also invoked curriculum theory as a prayerful act: see 1995.

schooling . . . a gift, a curriculum of hermeneutic play, of playfulness, of keeping knowledge in play." Kathleen R. Kesson also invokes the metaphoricity of Doll's subjective and specifically physical presence:

> So thank you Bill . . . for offering your—very tall—shoulders for us to stand on, to gaze into the stellar distance and feed our imaginations with educational possibilities as yet undreamed, and visualize the space/time bridges that might connect the Now and the New, and to approach the infinitute and the vast unknown with the awe, and wonder, and humility which it deserves.

Reminiscent of a religious icon, Bill brought/took our attention from here to eternity. Not only a movie title, the phrase postulates the space between materiality and spirituality, implying that the two can be traversed, can even become entwined.

Hua Zhang implies as much when he notes the unity of the heavenly and the human that informs "the ancient state and wisdom of curriculum." Both "charming and enchanting," Hua Zhang characterizes that ancient curriculum as "enchanted." After the Renaissance, Hua Zhang reminds, science and technology replaced enchantment with industrialization and social efficiency, both of which restructured school curriculum and curriculum theory, now, in late modernity, "disenchanted." It is within these circumstances, Zhang reminds, that Doll makes his "great contributions to the field." First, he notes, Doll criticizes the disenchantment of curriculum, and second, he proposes a reenchantment of curriculum, his post-modern curriculum theory. These contributions, Hua Zhang knows, hold "great significance to our time and world."

Place

> It's not surprising, either, that laughter is physically tied to play—a notable characteristic of Doll's theoretical and pedagogical gifts (signature elements in his approach to theory and pedagogy) to us.
>
> Molly Quinn

Just a month before Doll's death on December 27, 2017, Louisiana State University established a fellowship in his name, the third honor that institution has conferred, having already named a conference room after him, and having established the William E. Doll, Jr. Archive at the LSU Library. Appreciation for his academic accomplishment is hardly limited to Louisiana, as Hua Zhang would testify. Tero Autio focuses on the "Finnish receptivity to the style of curriculum research Bill Doll's insightful and imaginative scholarship embodies." In contrast to "the self-sufficient and arrogant grasp of the Anglophone mainstream instrumental rationality and system closure," Finnish basic education policies acknowledge complexity, chaos, and contingency as "natural," in sync, Autio points out, with "the spirit, theoretical and moral sensitivities exemplified in Bill Doll's scholarship." Autio characterizes Doll's scholarship "as an intellectual struggle for an education worthy of its name," opposing the instrumental rationality that Adorno and Horkheimer criticized as "half-education." For Autio, Doll's oeuvre demonstrates that "there *are* alternatives for that global, anti-intellectual and antidemocratic waste of human talent, imagination and creativity in the name of education." Talent, imagination, and creativity were all at work in Doll's pedagogy, amply explicated in Hongyu Wang's astute study.[13]

Noel Gough remembers the year—1987—his travels with Bill Doll began, "a journey that began in the academic landscape of American curriculum studies but took us in directions that neither of us anticipated." In the absence of email, it was not likely "that an Australian and an American curriculum scholar—neither of whom had any previous knowledge of one another's work—would initiate and sustain a productive personal and professional working relationship that would grow and strengthen across three decades." Meeting at conferences and finally at LSU, Gough saw "how special Bill was to his graduate students, and of the reasons that so many of them remain lifelong friends." In honor of his "stature and leadership" in the field, Doll was, Gough acknowledges (as do others in this collection), crowned the King of Chaos.

Jie Yu tells the backstory of that appellation, one in which "a monkey born from a rock in a big storm at the far end of the East China Sea" became a "monkey king . . . famous for his untiring battles against rigid social structure. He is also called the King of Chaos because of both his birth from chaos and his adventures against all dead orders such as the caste system." Jie Yu remembers that during Doll's lecture tour of China that one of his hosts, a middle school principal, pronounced him the "King of Chaos" after hearing him speak. When the principal explained, Doll was "fascinated" and quickly accepted his new title, a title that traveled across the Pacific Ocean back to Baton Rouge.

Recently returned from China, Nicholas Ng-A-Fook writes directly to Doll, reporting that the curriculum of the Wuhan Yucai Second Primary School "draws on your initial conceptions of a 3S's curriculum," replacing science with STEM and story with "social practice," emphasizing moral and aesthetic education as "spirit." Still addressing Bill directly, Ng-A-Fook reports that "What I witnessed in Wuhan, at that school, and in our conversations, is that your intellectual work continues to provide a reflective window for us to rethink our approaches to [quoting Doll] 'life and our activities in life, including teaching and curriculum design,

---

13. See Wang (2016).

in a way that allows the spirit or soul of these activities and of ourselves to come forth.'" Ng-A-Fook concludes: "To be a small part of the community that studied and lives your teachings, I thank you."

Teaching

> Doll's enlivening presence, pedagogy and thought are so unforgettably influential and surely inspiring.
>
> Molly Quinn

"Creating his own space in the midst of difference," Hongyu Wang appreciates, "had cultivated in him the capacity to stand on his own while at the same time initiating conversations across differences." Wang focuses on "play" and "difference," noting that the former is "usually associated with early childhood and elementary education," and the latter with "social and cultural differences." While acknowledging there is "no inherent relationship between the two," in Doll's curriculum and pedagogical theory and practice, "play and difference take on quite different meanings," concluding that "his playful engagement with difference as a teacher and as a scholar has opened up a new landscape in education." For Doll, Wang emphasizes, play enjoys "an essential role in students' and teachers' intellectual growth," and, she continues, "the key to opening students and teachers to growth is 'playful engagement' with intellectual difference." In other words, "openness to something different is the precondition for transformative learning and teaching."

For Doll, Wang continues, "playing with different ideas and playing with patterns of subject matter, which bring newness and surprise, are important for 'keeping knowledge alive.'" She explains: "As students play with ideas and craft an experience, richer and deeper understandings as well as creativity can come forth." Moreover, "playing with ideas is also related to the spirit of questioning," encouraging students to examine issues from multiple points of view. And in multiple venues, one might add: "The blending of sharing food, walks, and talks in his intellectual relationships with students and colleagues infuses social dimensions into intellectual life, which is usually marked by independence and seriousness," in service to creating "a communal space for everybody's intellectual exploration and personal growth." Refusing to reduce a person to a single dimension, Doll declined identity politics, emphasizing "the necessity of playing with tensionality in the relational in order to negotiate more room for educative possibilities." Wang reminds:

> In his curriculum visions, whether the four R's, five C's, or three S's, playful engagement with relations is an important component, as reflected in Relation in the four R's (Richness, Recursion, Relation, and Rigor), Community in the five C's (*Currere*, Complexity,

Cosmology, Conversation, and Community), and the relational quality of Story in the three S's (Science, Story, and Spirit).

For Doll, then, play and difference are "not only social and human, but also ecological and cosmological, which leads to the next dimension of play: spiritual play with difference." Wang concludes that "Doll's play is simultaneously intellectual, social, and spiritual."

Knowing his life history, she knows that Bill Doll was a "playful child." As Doll's student, she knows he was a "playful educator." And as students of his work we can all appreciate, as Wang does, that William Doll was "a playful scholar." His legacy, Wang concludes (quoting Doll quoting Kundera), "lies in '*the fascinating imaginative realm where no one owns the truth and everyone has the right to be understood*,'" a legacy, she asks us to remember and carry on: "May we all be inspired to play with difference to reach deeper and fly higher, embracing the complexity of life and of education."

Embracing the complexity of life and education was evident in Doll's capacity to embrace intellectual difference. After my diatribe against identity politics at LSU's Curriculum Camp one year, it was Bill Doll who broke the stunned silence, asking me a definitional question that defused the moment. I am hardly alone to have experienced Doll's determination to keep the conversation going, a Rortyian phrase Doll practiced at every turn. Respecting—playing with—difference is also evident in Petra Munro Hendry's acknowledgment that:

> While our politics were radically different—I was a feminist, critical, post-structuralist seeking social change, and Bill was a postmodernist, complexity theorist who sought to embrace chaos; it seemed that Bill never saw our differences as opposition, but as pedagogical spaces to explore multiple sites of meaning, to generate more questions as a way to keep knowledge alive.

Keeping knowledge alive: this moral-pedagogical commitment was enacted through Bill Doll being subjectively present in the educational lives of students and the concepts they studied.

"Bill Doll's thoughtfulness," Jung-Hoon Jung testifies, "combined with his wholehearted presence, makes personal growth possible. His thoughtfulness sustains his interpretive and reflective intelligence, intuitiveness, sensitivity, and openness to students' subjectivity." What Whitlock remembers is precisely "his *presence*, as always. Contemplative, gentle, deliberate." She recalls the "silence in the room as he towered over the podium with spectacles, bow tie, and shock of hair in tact." Whitlock was inspired by Doll's capacity for "contemplation," inspiriting study "with a sacred spirit of wisdom," and "the mindfulness . . . with which he is present in the briefest of encounters in such a way that they stay with you more than a decade later—if these are all I know of Bill Doll, I know him in abundance."

That fine phrase of David W. Jardine's[14] seems especially apt when invoking the subjective presence—that "enlivening presence," in Quinn's phrase—of William E. Doll, Jr. That presence was profoundly expressive of his own distinctive, original theory: at once progressive, post-modern, and complex. It was expressive too of his practice: assiduously communicative, earnestly playful and irreverently reverent. Doll exemplified the very concept of educator he depicted in his scholarship, true to the uniqueness of his life history while encouraging those in his midst to be faithful to theirs.

"Understanding education spiritually requires our subjective presence within the complex relationships within which we are embedded," Petra Munro Hendry sagely observes, "and such presence enables us [now quoting Doll] 'to be alive to the awe, wonder, and process of being.'" Such subjective presence structured as it animated his classroom conversation, as Jardine himself remembers: his "unwavering joy in conversation, commiseration, his whiling over a question, a spark, bespeaks a lightness that produces joy while it seeks it." Jardine emphasizes Doll's capacity to listen—to be "all ears"—and the glow that his listening amplified, adding that: "the joy he takes in being 'all ears' *creates* joy."

Nicholas Ng-A-Fook remembers the places where such listening, glowing, and joy occurred. He recalls specifically the Friday seminars, time spent—still speaking to Doll directly—"together in complicated conversations about ghosts in the curriculum . . . whether that was in Peabody Hall, or later over lunch at Arzi's, was us, with you, becoming community." He continues: "For you, of all the five C(s) –*Currere*, Complexity, Cosmology, and Conversation—Community was the most important. . . . I was fortunate enough to experience as a graduate student, a friend, and a colleague, a familial community during my studies at Louisiana State University."

That community occurred among those physically present at LSU but also among those absent, as Doll emphasized historical figures and out-of-fashion ideas, figures and ideas he kept alive as enlivening memories. Ng-A-Fook affirms that dimension of disciplinary conversation, remembering Doll's own work as a graduate student, providing "glimpses of your past political activism," among them Doll's protesting of the closure of the Johns Hopkins University Department of Education (where Doll had studied for the PhD degree). There, and later at the State University of New York, the University of Redlands, at Louisiana State University, and at the Universities of Victoria and British Columbia, Nicholas notes, "you

---

14. See Jardine et al. (2006). Also I am reminded of Paula Salvio's depiction of Anne Sexton as a teacher of "weird abundance (see Salvio (2007))."

continued to trouble the false dichotomy between theory and practice in relation to the coming of a post-industrial society," adding that that phrase (now out of fashion) denoted "social organization . . . as influenced by changing economic and technological forces." Characterized variously as an "automated society, a knowledge society, a leisure society, a technological society, a change society, and a service society," in a post-industrial society "the prime commodity will be knowledge, but not just knowledge, for the axial principle of post-industrialism is the 'centrality of theoretical knowledge.'" Nicholas wonders what has stayed the same and what has changed since the suggestion that theoretical knowledge would be central.

Denise Egéa wrestles with Doll's work—like Ng-A-Fook, in historical terms—noting that Doll wrestled with others, among them Morin, Mandelbrot, and Poincaré, on whose work Egéa pins key concepts, including complexity and chaos. Over one hundred years ago Poincaré knew that precise prediction of important human affairs was impossible (breaking news to the U.S. Department of Education). Still, "the many irregular shapes that make up our natural world at any scale (clouds, smoke, surf, etc.) are not random, but follow some organizing principles," a fact Egéa associates with Doll's fascination with fractalness and self-organization, the very "nature" of complexity. The latter Egéa links with *cheminement* . . . "a journey on the continuous path of learning, of change." In such a conception, the curriculum would "engage our students [not only] in a quest for knowledge which should take them way beyond the boundaries of their immediate socio-politico-cultural context in space and time . . . but which would encourage them to become constructors and generators of meaningful knowledge, meaning makers."

Fused with the screens in front of us—I am staring at one now—reactivating the past (as Egéa and Ng-A-Fook have done) might afford us some separation, even if just one degree of separation, from the present. Immersion in the moment followed by detachment from it—not always in sequential fashion of course, perhaps in dialectical tension—is evident in Doll's pedagogical practice, summarized in a phrase Bernard P. Ricca recalls: "Be engaged. Pull back." That phrase means—"sometimes to engage we must pull back and regroup"—but Ricca suspected "a deeper meaning," one with "multiple levels." One meaning has to do with the problem with "explanations of emergence that rely on emergence across levels." A second has to do with hierarchies, as creating patterns does not, evidently, proceed only in one direction, but are "inherently geometric in nature." Ricca prefers "topology," similar to "the study of networks," concluding that "topology is a better branch of mathematics on which to base investigations into complex systems in general, and for the particular exploration here." Translated into "best practice," this means that "openness" not "control" is prerequisite for "emergence to occur," indeed "a very radical openness." Ricca returns to Doll's suggestion—"Be Engaged. Pull Back"—again, summarizing:

Full engagement, then, implies a rather radical openness: We do not know what will come out, and we cannot control it; in fact, control is the opposite of engagement. And pulling back is an essential part of this engagement: We must remove ourselves from that with which we engage—while still maintaining engagement—so that we may allow the system to become itself.

Acknowledging that "no two sentences can sum up Bill Doll (or anyone else, for that matter), but I believe that it is this ability to be engaged while pulled back that are a hallmark of Bill Doll"; Ricca reminds readers of Bill's "expansive personality" that—in contrast to control—connects with others so all can "grow." Put differently, Doll's curriculum theory is less wedded to the ideas than it is to student growth, the promotion of "emergence."

Emergence, it seems, is developmental, intellectual, and spiritual. Is it also historical? Is post-modernity another phase of (late) modernity? Doll implied as much, insisting on hyphening the term post-modern. Peter Appelbaum admits his misreading of Doll's four R's as "modernist," missing that how this conception traversed the "slow and confusing transformation underway in culture, social institutions, and knowledge/curriculum." No new set of objectives, he concludes, "these concepts also exist in a transformative, process-based world of flux and becoming, a post-modern plasma of complexity and uncertainty." Doll understood, Appelbaum appreciates, that "we are still in a transition period between paradigms, still entering that new world." That sense of drama is communicated too in McKnight's remembrance of the man who embodied the transitional period Appelbaum identifies.

Unfurling the flag of curriculum, McKnight writes, remembering his time with him at LSU, Doll "uttered four words that changed everything— 'This is your curriculum.'" McKnight's "brow furrowed in concern" was "soon transformed into utter joy." For McKnight, too, play was the most significant element of Doll's multidimensional curriculum theory, playing with ideas and with each other, changing curriculum into an "active rather than passive notion that encouraged the child's inherent capacity to interact with the world through basic playful curiosity." Such playfulness occurs through language, emphasizing interpretation. A curriculum of complexity would be hermeneutical, no longer a game of "determining an author's meaning, but as an act in which I participate in a spirit that animates human life."

Through this complex hermeneutical curriculum theory McKnight "came to believe Dr. Doll had been joyfully dancing with Hermes from the beginning. Hermes is the ultimate player, the creator of language and messenger of the Gods." Etymologically, McKnight notices, knowledge means "the state of being or of having to become," an archaic conception very much in play for William E. Doll, Jr. Now McKnight appreciates that "knowledge is a form of play, a gift, a state of being and becoming." That state McKnight likens to a dance: "And every time William Doll appeared in our classroom, Hermes appeared alongside him, each dancing with the other and inviting us to join in the play by creating our own new ways of knowing." Among these new ways, as McKnight emphasizes, were old ways, including spiritual ones.

Not entirely different from religious associations of reverence with revelation, Fleener associates the concept of emergence with spirituality. "Opening up the curriculum to create spaces for emergent learning," she suggests, and such opening "reveals the importance of the *Mysterium Tremendum*, the mysterious energies that drive an intellect. These mysterious energies emerge when one focuses less on the science and embraces personal story and spirit." Doll, Sarah Pratt reminds, knew "the significance of stories." Alongside science and spirit, she notes, story conveys "complexity" as it fosters "emergent thinking." Indeed, "stories invite complexity into the classroom and the curriculum." Pratt quotes Doll: "a good story, a great story, induces, encourages, challenges," and it includes just enough "*indeterminacy*" to allow for an "open form of narrative." Thus, Pratt concludes, "indeterminacy is integral to story."

And vice versa it would seem, as story can be crucial to indeterminacy: "Just like in story," Pratt writes, "an emergence is just on the horizon, not to be controlled or predicted. In nonlinear dynamics, a chaotic system is one in which patterns can be understood in retrospect." Moreover, story is "also about recursively reflecting." Pratt emphasizes that "recursion is not the same as repetition; it is the act of doing again but looking for a difference based on initial conditions." She continues:

> Additionally, story is a reciprocal relation of interactions. Story is a dance of mutual reciprocity in which the context, the conversants, and the topics help shape and influence the story. This is significant, for the networks of relations and playfulness all impact the dance when teachers and students engage in the act of learning.

That engagement is a series of "complex conversations," a concept that depicts "learning and teaching that moves away from the mode of 'teaching-as-telling' toward an embodiment of thinking this world together." Here is an instance of Doll's moral commitment to an enlivening conversational pedagogy resounding in the words of those whom he taught.

That fact is also evident in Triche's reflection on Bill Doll's "pedagogic creed." Students are invited to join a close and democratic community wherein open discussion is the rule, including the disclosure of students' struggles with new ideas. Triche tells us he has included a version of Doll's "pedagogic creed" in his syllabi "during his entire university teaching career," working "hard to live up to it, sometime succeeding, but often failing." The creed includes patience, inspiring Triche to be "empathetic to the needs of my students," as Doll, he notes, was with him. Play was part of Doll's pedagogical creed—the "most serious aspect" Triche tells us—that Doll's "sense of play has certainly influenced my scholarship as well," as the man was always playing with ideas. "For Bill Doll," Triche continues, "play is the ground out of which knowing emerges." The creed, he concludes, "requires the teacher to have a different type of presence in the classroom," one that promotes "learning that refreshes the soul."

Lixin Luo experienced such learning as well, depicting it as "seeing the whole in parts," interweaving her personal stories with Doll's teachings, showing the space that was opened for her personal, professional, and academic development. "The change Bill occasioned in my thinking was nothing but subtle, yet it would take me a much longer time to enact this level of change. As the intense summer study [at the University of Victoria] with Bill subsided, I entered a recursive journey of re-encountering complexity and its accompanying chaos and hopeful transformation." She references the change in her teaching as grappled with complexity theory, on which she focused during her doctoral study. Her "renewed understanding of complexity" enabled Luo to shift from "reflection" to "recursion." noting that "the question in recursion, then, is not just how to reflect, but also how to loop back." She adds:

> Undoubtedly, recursion lies at the heart of Bill's post-modern curriculum: It is through the process of recursion that one can see relations among isolated topics and understand richer and deeper, hence recursion brings forth the other three R's in Bill's transformative curriculum.[15]

Through study of Doll's scholarship, Luo "learned to listen better to my personal experiences and stories," cultivating a "willingness to be led by one's personal experience and to answer its call," enabling her to "make sense of one's experience and make personal experience educational."

For Lixin Luo, Doll has been a teacher who "embodied" what he taught: "a mentor, inspiring, and full of life." He taught big ideas, leading her to a "land of creativity and imagination." Working with her "patiently" and "with care," teaching her "patience and faith." Did Doll's exemplary teaching derive, in part, from his exemplary study? Lixin Luo seems to suggest so, characterizing him "a fellow student," enacting "complexity thinking" that "can lead oneself and others to a space of infinite possibilities. Bill has kept the knowledge alive!"

15. Petra Munro Hendry concurs: "It is this sense of recursion that I now also understand not only as central to Bill's teaching, but his very vision of education. We return again and again, this iteration is not repetition but a recognition that the dynamic process of education cannot be reduced to a linear story, an objective or method."

"An extraordinary teacher of our time," Jung-Hoon Jung characterizes William Doll as a pedagogue of "unfailing excitement, generosity, hospitality, and thoughtfulness." He is, Jung summarizes, a *susung*, "a Korean concept that can be translated in English as *teacher, mentor*, or *advisor*." The concept, he continues, is historically associated with "Confucianism, whose ideas have sustained the ideals of education in Korea." Those ideals emphasize virtue, ethics, and morality, elements of being human. "Thus," Jung continues, "a *susung* is a person who provides teaching (or learning opportunities) for reaching or achieving" these ideals. They can be achieved in many ways; the concept of *susung* is not limited to official educators but can be extended to anyone who affirms one's "agency." Jung explains that "the concept of *susung* should not be understood as undermining the centrality of the teacher in education: instead, it expresses the significance of pedagogical relationships between teachers and students."

Jung recalls Doll's "way of being in the conversation," a form of "pedagogical thoughtfulness" that is "neither a science nor a behavioral code . . . [which] cannot be taught formally . . . [but is, rather] an intuitive sense of doing and being in concrete personal embodiment." Jung too recalls that while officially the instructor, Doll acted also as "a student in the course," wherein "participants were all asked to write reflections on the weekly readings, and Bill unfailingly wrote his reflections and shared them with us." "The power of Bill Doll's being overcame the institutional and geographical limitations. The relationships developed through his efforts made the class a familial learning community." Jung testifies to his membership in this community by sharing with readers that, despite living "thousands of miles" away from Doll, "my sense of connectedness with him never decreases; it gets stronger as my desire to be with him grows. . . . I am together with him. The fact that he was there and he prayed for my well-being reminds me of the caring relationship between a *susung* and a student."

That caring relationship is implied in David W. Jardine's insight that "someone had to simply say, 'Stop!' in a voice loud enough to break the spell, loud enough to remind everyone that we are surrounded by ancestors who can help us, quite literally, *out*," Doll prominent among them. "Once we summoned them, they broken our fixed gaze and cultivated our readiness. We studied our circumstance instead of falling for it. They provided us with a field rich enough to work *out* what was happening, here. They helped us be all ears." Remembering "the past thirty years of friendship and camaraderie with Bill Doll," Jardine emphasizes "Study. Light air that bears a sword. Terrifying but not petrifying. Readiness. And, too, somehow fragile and perishable." These poignant phrases convey the character of William E. Doll, Jr. as they challenge us to preserve the gifts he gave to us by keeping that knowledge alive.

Legacy

> Come, then, let us attend what strange, marvellous, fascinating and sweet delights/insights await us, and in curriculum studies, as we venture forward thus with Bill Doll in these echoes of/on his divine laughter.
>
> Molly Quinn

Kathleen R. Kesson likens Doll to "Planet Nine, circling the known world of educational theory in his own orbit, his revolutionary ideas slowly manifesting as adventurous seekers begin to infer the presence of something of enormous import just outside our range of perception." Kesson points out that "postmodern theories of curriculum, embodying as they do notions of uncertainty, relationship, complexity, indeterminacy, self-organization, chaos, and transformation circle far beyond the known orbits of modernist curriculum, teaching, and learning practices." Continuing with the metaphor, Kesson notes that "Professor Doll, with telescopic vision, has helped to bring the unknown closer into the orbit of the known, enriching our lives and our thinking in multiple ways." Opening new universes for us to explore, perhaps? "In that vast distance, he saw the emerging sciences of chaos and complexity as having the power to push our understandings of teaching, learning, and curriculum into entirely new spaces," including "fresh understandings of the connections between spirituality and science." Doll provided "a bridge between the innovative educational thinkers of the recent past and the experimentalists of the time."

Moving well beyond the "fixed . . . orbits of the behaviorists and the constructivists," Kesson continues, Doll entered that outer space "opened up by the new sciences—ideas such as synchronicity, self-organization, non-local causality, intuition, connectedness." While espousing no "particular form of spirituality," Doll was "wonderfully open to the multiplicity of ways that people expressed their own soulful commitments. In this, he was a model for how we might embrace difference in a post-modern world, in which truth can no longer be spelled with a capital T." Kesson concludes:

> Perhaps my most fiercely held educational belief is that everyone possesses within their being a psychic compass that steers them into the development of their potential, and that this manifests differently in all of us as curiosities, interests, and passions. We can call it soul, we can call it spirit, or we can call it an organism's capacity to self-organize, but I believe, with the Romantics, that these inclinations need to be honored and that education really should be a "drawing, or leading out" (*ēdūcere*) and development of these emergent intentions.

Doll shared that Truth, however buried it can be in truths and even falsehoods.

Carl Leggo remembers the 7th Biennial Provoking Curriculum Studies Conference (that he and Erika Hasebe-Hudt organized), in particular the celebration he and Erika engineered on the evening of February 20, 2015, a circle of curriculum scholars located in Canada, among them William E. Doll, Jr. "A highlight of the evening," he remembers, "was Antoinette Oberg's tribute to William E. Doll," an Argentinian tango Antoinette danced with her partner Daniel. It was, in Leggo's words, "sensual, fluid, lyrical, delightful!" The dance, Leggo continues, "represented a kind of love story," a love that Doll has enjoyed "in Canada among students and colleagues," an abiding love for a teacher who "lives with a poet's delight in language and dialogue and questioning." Carl Leggo—a poet, our poet—would know. He also articulates a quality of colleagues' response to Bill. We can treasure the responses students have expressed, but Carl Leggo captures colleagues' response, one of:

> bemused reverence. Bill Doll was loved! When I finally met him, I understood immediately that he is a man of singular charm. Bow ties always breathe with an air of stylish exuberance! Bill lives poetically in the spaces between his primary two names. On the one hand, he is William E. Doll, Jr.—a name with enough gravitas to gain entrance to a prestigious golf club! On the other hand, he is Bill Doll—like a Dr. Seuss play on words, the name reverberates like a bell, a spondee with two stressed syllables, singing out a psalm of delight.

There may well be no "after" to append to those words. But in-between them maybe we can allow Leggo to slip a few more, among them Leggo's recognition of Bill as "living the conviction of the slow professor long before the concept was invented," there by teaching "us how to live in the academy . . . with compassion, care, and conscience."[16] A "teacher of the heart," Leggo affirms Doll's "commitment to integrity and interrogation and interconnection. Bill is constantly curious, motivated by awe and wonder."

"Comfortable in his own presence, and therefore comfortable in the presence of others," Doll seems "always the host . . . never arrogant, loud, extroverted, self-centred . . . always gracious and generous. He lives with his feet in the earth, the *humus*. He lives with humility. And he lives with his heart, the source of all courage for living well." These qualities Doll and Donna Trueit thread through their teaching, as Leggo recounts: "I often heard from students how Bill and Donna created caring and loving communities where everybody took creative risks with language and ideas and possibilities." His teaching and writing, Leggo continues, "full of voice—the unique voice that he has honed and sustained in a lifetime

---

16. For the slow professor see Berg and Seeber (2016). There is also slow art: see Reed (2017).

of devotion to scholarship and education. One of his lasting gifts is his invitation for us to learn to hear our own voices, especially as we learn to hear the voices of others." Through yours, Carl Leggo—and those of the others in this collection—we have once again heard the voice of Bill Doll. May it resound through all those who hear it.

References

Berg, M., & Seeber, B. K. (2016). *The slow professor: Challenging the culture of speed in the academy*. Toronto: University of Toronto Press.

Berliner, D. C., & Biddle, B. J. (1995). *The manufactured crisis: Myths, fraud, and the attack on America's public schools*. Cambridge, MA: Perseus.

Gladstone, R. (2018, January 11). Germans' idea To fight bias gains support. *The New York Times* CLXVII, 57(839), A4.

Grant, G. (1966). *Philosophy in the mass age*. Toronto: Copp Clark Publishing. (Original work published in 1959)

Jardine, D., Clifford, P., & Friesen, S. (Eds.). (2006). *Curriculum in abundance*. Mahwah, NJ: Lawrence Erlbaum Associates Publishers.

Kang, C. (2017, September 27). Tech titans to pour money into push to teach coding. *New York Times* CLXVII, 57(733), B6.

Macdonald, J. B. (1995). *Theory as a prayerful act*. New York, NY: Peter Lang.

Pinar, W. (2006). *The synoptic text today and other essays: Curriculum development after the reconceptualization*. New York, NY: Peter Lang.

Reed, A. (2017). *Slow art: The experience of looking, sacred images to James Turrell*. Berkeley, CA: University of California Press.

Salvio, P. M. (2007). *Anne Sexton: Teacher of weird abundance*. Albany, NY: State University of New York Press.

Singer, N. (2017, June 7). Tech billionaires reinvent schools, with students as beta testers. *The New York Times* CLXVI, 57(621), A1, A14.

Trueit, D. (Ed.). (2012). *Pragmatism, postmodernism, complexity theory: The "fascinating imaginative realm" of William E. Doll, Jr*. New York, NY: Routledge.

Wang, H. (2016). *From the parade child to the king of chaos: The complex journey of William Doll, teacher educator*. New York, NY: Peter Lang.

Contributors

Peter Appelbaum
Arcadia University

Peter Appelbaum is a musician, sound artist, juggler, and professor of education at Arcadia University in Philadelphia, USA. He is a past president of the American Association for the Advancement of Curriculum Studies, past chair of the Critical Issues in Curriculum and Cultural Studies special interest group of the American Educational Research Association, and vice president of the International Commission for the Study and Improvement of Mathematics Education. Appelbaum's *Children's Books for Grown-Up Teachers: Reading and Writing Curriculum Theory* was awarded the Outstanding Book Award for Curriculum Studies by the American Educational Research Association in 2009.

Tero Autio
University of Tampere, Finland

Professor Tero Autio's scholarly interests are related to curriculum theory and history, education theories, theories and practices of politics, and education policies and their effects on teacher's work and teacher education. Except his country of origin, Finland, he has worked as invited international professor of curriculum theory at Tallinn University, Estonia, funded by the European Union. He has done and is doing research and consultancy on curriculum issues in North and South America, Europe, South Korea, Mainland China, Hong Kong, and Saudi Arabia. He is vice president of the European Association of Curriculum Studies.

Denise Egéa
Nazarbayev University and Louisiana State University

Denise Egéa is Distinguished Professor, W. H. "Bill" LeBlanc Professor Emeritus at Louisiana State University, USA, and Professor in the Graduate School of Education at Nazarbayev University, Astana, Kazakhstan. She is a Fellow of the American Philosophy of Education Society, a Phi Kappa Phi scholar, and an Officier dans l'Ordre des Palmes Académiques. Recent publications include "Derrida's Archive and Legacy to Education: Between Past and Future" in *The International Handbook of Philosophy of Education*, edited by Paul Smeyers (Springer, 2018); and "Education as/is Ethics" in *The Wiley Handbook of Educational Ethics*, edited by Richard Smith (2018, Wiley-Blackwell).

M. Jayne Fleener
North Carolina State University

Dr. Fleener has served as dean of the colleges of education at NC State and Louisiana State Universities and associate dean at the University of Oklahoma. She is currently a professor in the College of Education at NC State. She utilizes philosophical inquiry and chaos and complexity theories to explore complex problems in social and educational systems. Her current projects include books on Heidegger and education, and transformational learning for communities of the future. Dr. Fleener has her bachelor's and master's degrees in philosophy from Indiana University and the University of North Carolina at Chapel Hill, respectively, and a second master's degree and PhD in mathematics education and curriculum studies, also from UNC-CH.

Noel Gough
La Trobe University, Melbourne, Australia

Noel Gough is professor emeritus in the School of Education at La Trobe University, Melbourne, Australia, where he was Foundation Professor of Outdoor and Environmental Education (2006–2014). His teaching, research, and publications focus on research methodologies and curriculum inquiry, with particular reference to environmental education, science education, internationalization, and globalization. With Bill Doll, he co-edited (and contributed to) *Curriculum Visions* (Peter Lang, 2002), and contributed to the formation of the Chaos and Complexity Theories Special Interest Group of AERA. He is founding editor of *Transnational Curriculum Inquiry* (the journal of IAACS), and is a past president (2008) and honorary life member of the Australian Association for Research in Education.

Petra Munro Hendry
Louisiana State University

Petra Munro Hendry is the St. Bernard Chapter of the LSU Alumni Association Endowed Professor in the School of Education at Louisiana State University where her research focuses on post-structural, feminist analysis of the discourses of curriculum history, narrative research and oral history research. She served as co-director of the LSU Curriculum Theory Project from 2006 to 2017. She is the author of five books, including *Engendering Curriculum History*, as well as numerous scholarly publications in journals including *Journal of Curriculum*

Theorizing, History of Education, International Journal of Qualitative Studies in Education, and *Qualitative Inquiry*. In 2016 she received the Lifetime Achievement Award from Division B, American Educational Research Association.

Hua Zhang
Nanjing Normal University

Hua Zhang is a professor and the dean of Graduate School of Education Studies at Hangzhou Normal University; former president of International Association for the Advancement of Curriculum Studies (IAACS); the main expert for National Curriculum Reform in China. His research interests include curriculum studies, curriculum history, wisdom traditions (Confucianism, Taoism, Buddhism), curriculum reform, pedagogy, and teacher education. He has published 9 books and more than 160 papers in academic journals. He is the author of *The Theory of Curriculum and Instruction* (2000), *The Theory of Experience Curriculum* (2001), and *On Research-based Pedagogy* (2010).

David W. Jardine

David W. Jardine is a retired professor of education. His recent books include *In Praise of Radiant Beings: A Retrospective Path Through Education, Buddhism and Ecology* and, with Jackie Seidel, *The Ecological Heart of Teaching: Radical Tales of Refuge and Renewal for Classrooms and Communities*.

Jung-Hoon Jung
Chinju National University of Education

Jung-Hoon Jung teaches at the Department of Education of Chinju National University of Education, South Korea. He was a student of Bill Doll at the University of British Columbia, Canada. Jung-Hoon also worked as Bill's teaching assistant for three years, which was a blessing for him. His research interests include curriculum theorizing, teacher education, inter-cultural studies, and autobiographical inquiry. He is the author of *The Concept of Care in Curriculum Studies: Juxtaposing Currere and Hakbeolism* (Jung, 2016) among other works. He co-authored *Ugly Duckling: First Year Elementary School Teachers' Lives* (Mooneumsa, 2006) and co-translated Sleeter and Grant's *Making Choices for Multicultural Education* (2009). His works attempt to resist theoretically and practically the instrumental rationality in education.

Kathleen R. Kesson
LIU-Brooklyn

Kathleen R. Kesson is Professor of Teaching and Learning and Chair of the Department of Teaching, Learning, and Leadership at LIU-Brooklyn, where she teaches courses in the social and philosophical foundations of education, arts in education, and teacher research. She has authored and co-authored over forty books, journal articles, and book chapters on topics including education and democracy, aesthetics, and education, teacher inquiry and reflective practice, ecological education, and curriculum decision-making. She is currently researching the implementation of personalized learning legislation in Vermont.

Carl Leggo
University of British Columbia

Carl Leggo is a poet and professor at the University of British Columbia, Vancouver, Canada. His research interests include creativity, arts-based research, poetic inquiry, contemplative practices, and well-being. His books include: *View From My Mother's House; Come-By-Chance; Lifewriting as Literary Métissage and an Ethos for Our Times* (co-authored with Erika Hasebe-Ludt and Cynthia Chambers); *Creative Expression, Creative Education* (co-edited with Robert Kelly); *Sailing in a Concrete Boat: A Teacher's Journey; Arresting Hope: Prisons That Heal* (co-edited with Ruth Martin, Mo Korchinski, and Lynn Fels); *Arts-Based and Contemplative Practices in Research and Teaching: Honoring Presence* (co-edited with Susan Walsh and Barbara Bickel); *Hearing Echoes* (co-authored with Renee Norman); and *Poetic Inquiry: Enchantment of Place* (co-edited with Pauline Sameshima, Alexandra Fidyk, and Kedrick James).

Lixin Luo
University of Alberta

A former high school mathematics teacher, Lixin Luo is currently a PhD candidate at the University of Alberta, focusing on secondary mathematics education. Since her first encounter with Dr. William E. Doll, Jr., and his works during her masters' program at the University of Victoria in 2003, Lixin has embarked on a recursive journey to study education and life through the lens of complexity thinking and enact what she has learned in both education and daily life. Lixin's dissertation *Towards a Recursive Mathematics Curriculum* is rooted in Doll's works and complexity thinking. It aims to complexify Doll's concept of recursion theoretically and practically.

Douglas McKnight
The University of Alabama

Douglas McKnight is a professor of curriculum studies at The University of Alabama. He is the author of *Place, Race, and Identity Formation: Autobiographical Intersections in a Curriculum Theorist's Daily Life* (New York: Routledge, 2017); and *Schooling, the Puritan Moral Imperative and the Molding of an American Identity: Education's "Errand into the Wilderness"* (Lawrence Erlbaum Associates, Inc., 2003).

Nicholas Ng-A-Fook
University of Ottawa

Dr. Ng-A-Fook, a Professor of Curriculum Studies, is Director of the Teacher Education Program at the University of Ottawa. He is the President of the Canadian Society for the Study of Education, the largest professional educational research association in Canada. In these administrative, educational, and research capacities, he is committed toward addressing the 94 Calls to Action put forth by the Truth and Reconciliation Commission in partnership with the local Indigenous and school board communities. He is collaborating with colleagues to create a state-of-the-art teacher education program that promises to prepare teacher candidates for the social, economic, and cultural demands of the 21st century.

Nel Noddings
Stanford University

Nel Noddings is Lee Jacks Professor of Education Emerita at Stanford University. She is the author of twenty-one books and more than three hundred articles/chapters. Her latest book (with Laurie Brooks) is *Teaching Controversial Issues*. She is a past president of the John Dewey Society, Philosophy of Education Society, and the National Academy of Education.

William F. Pinar
University of British Columbia

William F. Pinar worked with William Doll for forty-one years, first in upstate New York, then in Louisiana, and finally in western Canada. Along with close colleagues and friends Mary Aswell Doll and Donna Trueit, Pinar and Doll worked closely together to advance our common cause: a curriculum studies field at once pedagogically progressive and intellectual sophisticated. Pinar organized a conference—"In Praise of the Post-modern"—and a banquet in honor of Doll's 70th birthday, spoke of their close work together at the celebration of the 15th year of the LSU Curriculum Theory Project and, later, at the establishment of the Doll-Pinar Conference Room at the LSU School of Education. Pinar was invited by Dr. Trueit to give the eulogy at Doll's funeral, and he spoke of Doll's professional and personal significance to him to faculty and students assembled at a celebration of his life held at the University of British Columbia.

Sarah Smitherman Pratt
University of North Texas

Sarah Smitherman Pratt is an assistant professor in curriculum studies and mathematics education at the University of North Texas in Denton, Texas. Her research and teaching focus at the intersections of mathematics education and curriculum theory, with a special interest in complex conversations in education. She is the former program chair and chair of the AERA SIG: Chaos and Complexity Theories, and she currently serves as the section editor of book reviews for *Complicity: An International Journal of Complexity and Education*. She engages in mathematics teacher education and professional development, and recently joined the new AERA SIG: Lesson Study to join with other researchers to discuss how to empower teachers as professionals to work collaboratively in a supportive environment.

Molly Quinn
Augusta University

Molly Quinn is honored to have been a student of William Doll, whose life and work has influenced her immeasurably. Professor of curriculum studies at Augusta University and president of the American Association for the Advancement of Curriculum Studies, she is author of *Going Out, Not Knowing Whither: Education, the Upward Journey and the Faith of Reason* (2001; Peter Lang); *Peace and Pedagogy* (2014; Peter Lang); and *Theorizing Justice, Justly Theorizing, in Education* (forthcoming; Routledge); as well as numerous book chapters and articles. Much of her scholarship engages "spiritual" and philosophical criticism toward embracing a vision of education, and curriculum, that cultivates wholeness, beauty, awareness, compassion, creativity, and community.

Bernard P. Ricca
St. John Fisher College

Bernard (Barney) P. Ricca is Director of Statistics and Data Sciences at St. John Fisher College, which, coincidentally, is not far from where Bill Doll started his teaching career. He has been involved in STEM education for more than a quarter century, and counts Bill as one of the influences that moved him from his training in classical physics toward a more post-modern approach to education. Barney likes to work on interesting problems in almost any field, and considers himself lucky to have found employment doing just that. Additionally, he enjoys biking and eating (not necessarily in that order) and being with his family and their dog.

Eero Ropo
University of Tampere, Finland

Eero Ropo is a professor of education (particularly, teacher education and learning research) since 1996 at the Faculty of Education, University of Tampere. He has made his doctoral degree in 1984 at the University of Tampere, Finland. Since then he has acted as a researcher, lecturer, associate professor and professor in general education, primary teacher education, and secondary teacher education. He has been a visiting scholar and professor at the LRDC, University of Pittsburgh, USA (1984–1985), Texas Tech University (1992–1993) and Vanderbilt University (1996, 1997). Currently, Ropo is head of the international MA program in teacher education and has also a part-time position at the Nord University, Norway. Ropo pursues international research interests specializing in teacher education, narrative research on learning and identity, curriculum theory, and ICT in education.

Stephen S. Triche
Nicholls State University

Stephen S. Triche, PhD, is a Professor of Education at Nicholls State University. He has served on the faculty in the Department of Teacher Education since the summer of 2000. During this time, Dr. Triche has taught graduate and undergraduate education foundation courses in philosophy and history of education, as well as curriculum studies, multicultural education and instructional issues for teaching diverse learners, and social studies. He is the coordinator for the masters' program in elementary and secondary education. Dr. Triche regularly presents and publishes on the history and philosophy of curriculum as well as curriculum studies.

Veli-Matti Värri
University of Tampere, School of Education, Finland

Docent (senior lecturer) in ethical education at National Defence University, Veli-Matti Värri is a philosopher whose expertise consists of the central issues of educational philosophy and theory, teacher education, ethics of education, and philosophy of dialogue. The most of Värri's publications deals with the basic questions of educational ethics and the critique on instrumental rationality in education. His monograph *Hyvä kasvatus—kasvatus hyvään*, 1997 (*Good Education—Education for Good*) has reached its fifth edition in 2004. In his current project, Värri's main interest is to reconceptualize the ontological, socio-cultural, and ethical reference points for constituting moral identity in the ecological sphere of late-modern education.

Hongyu Wang
Oklahoma State University–Tulsa

Hongyu Wang is a professor in curriculum studies at Oklahoma State University–Tulsa. Her research and teaching areas include nonviolence education, curriculum theory, international curriculum dialogues, psychoanalysis and education, and college curriculum and teaching. She has authored books and articles in both English and Chinese, including *From the Parade Child to the King of Chaos: A Complex Journey of William Doll, Teacher Educator* (2016; Peter Lang), *Nonviolence and Education* (2014; Routledge), *Cross-Cultural Studies in Curriculum:*

Eastern Thought, Educational Insights (co-edited with Claudia Eppert) (2008; Lawrence Erlbaum), and *The Call From the Stranger on a Journey Home: Curriculum in a Third Space* (2004; Peter Lang).

Ugena Whitlock
Kennesaw State University

Ugena Whitlock is Professor of Curriculum and Instruction and Chair of the Department of Educational Leadership at Kennesaw State University. Her works include a book, *This Corner of Canaan: Curriculum Studies of Place and the Reconstruction of the South* (2007) and an edited collection, *Queer South Rising: Voices of a Contested Place* (2013). She considers her current work to be queer theological curriculum theory, particularly exploring the possibilities queer Christian sexual ethics might hold to inform a broader ethics for humankind.

Jie Yu
Rollins College

Jie Yu is Associate Professor of Education at Rollins College in Winter Park, Florida. She received her PhD in Curriculum and Instruction from Louisiana State University. Her major research interests include curriculum studies, narrative inquiry, classroom teaching and learning, and multicultural education.

Index

Adorno, T. 40, 226
adventure 17
Alhadeff-Jones, M. 197
American Educational Research Association (AERA): annual meeting, 1987 59–61; "Chaos and Curriculum Inquiry" symposium 63–64; Complexity SIG 19, 51, 64, 165; excursions post- (1989–1993) 61–63
Analects of Confucius 124
Andrighetto, G. 82
Anglophone curriculum theory 38–40, 225
Aoki, T. T. 87, 122, 132, 155, 202
Appelbaum, P. 52
Aristotle 118
Arrien, A. 202
Art of the Novel, The 9
Astro, R. 65
authentic action 5
Autio, T. 19, 225, 226

Back to the Basics of Teaching and Learning 55
Bacon, F. 42
Barad, K. 215
Barthes, R. 183
Bateson, G. 91, 130, 131
behaviorism 140–141, 144, 157–158
Bell, D. 157
Bell-Robinson, V. 154
Berg, M. 202
Berman, M. 143
Berry, W. 77, 203
big data 31–32
Bittner, J. 45
Bobbitt, F. 140
Bohm, D. 143

Bohr, N. 158
Bolyard, C. 154
"Bonds of Laughter, The" 8
Bonhoeffer, D. 147
Book of Rites, The 121–122, 123
bounded infinity 154
Brueggemann, W. 207
Bruner, J. 34, 61, 118, 142; constructivist theory and 140; on distancing oneself from one's thoughts 178; emphasis on structure of subject matter 92; on modes of thought 129
Bush, G. W. 39

Calvin, J. 115, 116
Calvino, I. 75–78
Cannery Row 58–59
caring relationships, pedagogy of 125–126, 234
Carson, T. 201
Cervantes, M. de 66
Chambers, C. 77, 201
chaos 94–95, 103, 107–108, 137, 173–174; chaotic order 192; curriculum and 140–142; Doll as King of 22, 63–64, 103, 135, 137, 163, 165–166, 226; dynamic 193; Morin on 196
Chaos, Complexity, Curriculum and Culture 165
"Chaos and Curriculum Inquiry" symposium 63–64
Charters, W. W. 140
Chicago Lab School 159
China 226–227; complexity theory in 165–166; curriculum reforms in 35–36, 137, 159; Doll and 163–168; "third way" in 166–168

Christianity 41–42
Cleese, J. 8
Cobb, P. 84
Coleman Report 44
Combs, A. 157
community 187–188
complex conversations 132–133, 182–189, 232
complexifying reflections 2–3
complexity: chaos and 94–95, 103, 107–108; Doll's "dancing curriculum" and 191–199; Edgar Morin and the paradigm of 195–198; in the five C's 5, 53–54, 185–186; of story, pedagogical 128–133
complexity theory 21–22, 107–108, 165–166
Complicity 19, 64
Complicity: An International Journal of Complexity and Education 166
Confucius 32, 33, 121–123, 125–126
constructivism 140–141, 144
Contingency, Irony, and Solidarity 65
conversation 34–35, 186–187; complex 132–133, 182–189, 232
cosmology in the five C's 5, 53–54, 186
Crary, R. W. 155
creativity, relational 33
Crowther, B. 49
C's (currere, complexity, cosmology, conversation, and community) 34–35, 55–56, 155, 173; complex conversations in 132–133, 182–189; with the four R's and three S's 53–54; from perspective of emerging narratives of the world 184–188; playful engagement with 89
culture of complaint 74–75; lightness in 75–76
Culture of Method 45
currere (self-study) 5, 69, 139, 155, 185; making sense of one's experience in 99–100; and the sacred in complexity 53–54; spirituality and 34–35, 150–151
curriculum 3–4; addressed in an inspirited letter by Ng-A-Fook 153–160; Anglophone curriculum theory and 38–40; behaviorism and constructivism in 140–141, 157–158; changing technologies, mores, gender roles, and power relationships and their effects on 51–52; chaos and 140–142; as closed system 140; complex conversations on 132–133, 182–189; dancing 53–54, 191–199; disenchanted 29, 30–32; Doll's influence in 17–18; enchanted 29; expressed in the school and society 171–174; four R's, five C's, and three S's in 53–54; imagination and storytelling in 55; neoliberal 44–45; play in (*see* play and playful engagement); provoking 201; rationalization of 31–32; reconceptualized 29, 55–56, 136, 139; recursive 97–100; reenchanted 32–35; R's, C's, and S's in complex 53–54; three states of 29–30; Tyler Rationale in 4–6, 32, 34, 35; urgency to save complexity again in education and 43–44; vision for post-modern 176–181
curriculum theory 107–109, 117, 139–140; Doll as father of post-modern 164–165
Curriculum Theory Project (CTP) 148–149
Curriculum Visions 19, 56, 63, 64
Curriculum Windows: What Curriculum Theorists of the 1980s Can Teach Us About Schools and Society Today 154

dancing curriculum 53–54, 191–199
"dancing curriculum" 191–199
Davies, P. 143–144
Davis, B. 216
de-complexification in education 40–43
Democracy and Education 36
Dennison, G. 156
Descartes, R. 19, 41–44
Dewey, J. 4–5, 18, 32, 61, 118, 140, 157–158; Chicago Lab School 159; *Democracy and Education* by 36; influence on Doll of 24–25, 69, 128, 131; on knowledge 33–34, 141; *School and Society* by 171; on scientific concepts having starts and stops, ebbs and flows 130
dialogic community 89–90
difference: intellectual 87–89; social-relational 89–90; spiritual play with 91–93
Discourse on Method 41, 43

248 Index

disenchanted curriculum 29, 30–32
Diverse Perspectives on Curriculum and Pedagogy 205
Doll, W. E., Jr.: at AERA meeting with Gough 60–61; in China 25, 35–36, 163–168; complexity theory as lens to examine 21–22; critique of method by 116; echo in endowment of 4–7; echoing God's laughter 1–3, 9–11; ensemble logic and 118; on ghosts (*see* ghosts); influence of Dewey on 24–25, 69, 128, 131; inquiry web of work of 23, 23–26; as King of Chaos 22, 63–64, 94–95, 103, 107–108, 135, 137, 163, 165–166, 226; laughter of 7–9, 65–66, 218–219, 225, 235; legacy of 7–9, 235–237; living poetically 201–209; on methodization and the disenchantment of curriculum 30–32; *Mysterium Tremendum* of 21–27, 23, 148–149; on paradoxical dualism of modernism and postmodernism 128–129; pedagogical complexity of story and 128–133; pedagogic creed of 114, 115, 232; in place 225–227; on play (*see* play and playful engagement); on postmodern curriculum as reenchanted curriculum 32–35; post-modernism of 2, 24, 25, 35, 48–49, 116–117, 164–165, 176; praxis of 114–115; presentation style of 60–61; on pulling back 81, 84; readiness to be all ears of 69–70, 73–79; recursion and 97–100; on scientism and education 43; significance to our time and world of 35–36; on spirit 210–216; struggles with spirituality (*see* "Struggles With Spirituality"); as *susung* 121–126, 234; teaching by 227–234; in time 219–225; utopian aspirations of 2–3; at UVic 64–65; on world beyond technocratic mind-view 158
Dominique, N. 8

Easter Vigil 212–213, 215
echo: of Doll's endowment 4–7; of God's laughter 1–3, 9–11, 65
eduction as spirit 211–214
Egan, K. 55
Egéa, D. 173, 230
Einstein, A. 158

emergence 81–82, 231; engagement and 84–85; of narratives of the world, curricula and five C's from perspective of 184–188
Emile 43
enchanted curriculum 29
engagement 4, 18, 69; culture of complaint and 74–75; emergence and 84–85; playful, with difference 87–93; pulling back in 81–85, 230–231; readiness to be "all ears" in 73–79
Enlightenment, the 29, 192
ensemble logic 118
experimental method 42

Finland 19, 38–40, 226
Finney, S. 202
Finnish Lessons: What Can the World Learn From Educational Change in Finland? 39
First Street School 160
Fisher 182
Fleener, M. J. 18, 136, 165, 224, 232; work with Bill Doll 22–23
Force of Character and the Lasting Life, The 205
Foucault, M. 194
"Foundations for a Post-modern Curriculum" 60
fractal geometry 82–83, 107–108
Frankfurt School 40
Fruits of the Earth 205

Gadamer, H. G. 73, 76, 87, 109
Galilei, G. 42
GERM (Global Education Reform Model) 41
ghosts 182–183, 220–221; as narratives in education 183–184; wicked 186, 188
Ghosts of Control 44
Gide, A. 205
Gleick, J. 141
Glenn, L. N. 206
Gnosticism 42
God and the New Physics 143–144
Gordon, D. 171
Gough, A. 63, 64
Gough, N. 19, 224, 226; at the 1987 AERA annual meeting 59–61; "Chaos and Curriculum Inquiry" symposium 63–64; at UVic 64–65; work with Doll, 1989–1993 61–63

Grant, G. 221
Grapes of Wrath, The 58
Gravemeijer, K. 84
Green, E. 179
Greene, M. 77
Grimmett, P. 201
Grumet, M. 185, 202

Hakbeolism 121
half-education 40–41
Hanh, T. N. 77
Hasebe-Ludt, E. 201, 208, 236
Haynes, K. 192
Heidegger, M. 11, 18, 21, 25, 26
Heisenberg, W. 158
Hendry, P. M. 222, 174, 228, 229
Herbart, J. F. 44
hermeneutics 110–113
Hill, G. R. 49
Hillman, J. 205, 207
Hitchcock, A. 63
Holmes Elementary Program 25–26
Horkheimer, M. 40, 226
Hua Zhang 18, 165–166, 225
Huebner, D. 155, 202, 211, 215
humanism 157
Hunter model 177
hyperobjects 183–184, 220

IAACS 19
Illich, I. 76
imagination and storytelling 55
indeterminacy 222, 193; story and 193
In Dubious Battle 58
inductive reasoning 42, 116
industrialization movement 29
inertia and opacity of the world 75–76
inert ideas 118
inquiry and story 130
intellectual difference, playful engagement with 87–89
Intentional Monogamy 147
International Association for the Advancement of Curriculum Studies 147
Irwin, R. L. 201

Jackson, P. 212
Jansen 187–188
Jardine, D. W. 55, 69, 201, 202, 229, 234
Jewett, L. 155
Jie Yu 226
Johnson, M. 143
Johnston, I. 201

Journal of Curriculum and Supervision 192
Journal of Curriculum Studies 59–60, 61
Jung, J.-H. 104, 228, 234

"Keeping Knowledge Alive" 122
Kesson, K. R. 63, 136, 225, 235
Kincheloe, J. 64
King, J. 61
King, M. L., Jr. 63
Klein, F. 61
knowledge: Dewey on 33–34, 141; as form of play 111–113, 118; modes of thought and 129; as relational 33–34; secularized concept of 42; and spirit kept alive 214–216
Kofman, M. 195
Kreutzer, C. 21
Kundera, M. 1–3, 9–11, 33, 65–66, 103, 110, 214

Lakoff, G. 143
La Méthode 195, 197, 198
language, play of 110–113
Latour, B. 183
laughter and Doll's legacy 7–9, 65–66, 218–219, 225, 235
learning, pedagogy of 124
Lee, G. 125
Lee, K. 125
legacy, Doll's 7–9, 235–237
Légaré, S. 8
Leggo, C. 173, 203, 218–220, 236–237
Leibniz, G. W. 10
Lenten season 213–214
Les Sept savoirs nécessaires à l'éducation du futur 198
Lessons from Finland 39
Levinas, E. 216
Li Bai 160
Logic 24
Luo, L. 70, 233; on complexity thinking and recursion 98–100; continued interaction with Doll on mathematics instruction 96–98; entry into Doll's world 94–96

Marijuán, P. 8
Maturana, H. 131
McKnight, D. 104, 224, 231–232
meditative thinking 21
Medusa, legend of 76–77
metaphors and metamorphosis 143–145

Index

method-beyond-method 11, 150, 173
Methodization Movement 29, 30–32
Meyer, K. 201
Miller, J. 90
ministerium 135
misterium 135
Möbius strips 80–81, 83, 84
modes of thought 129
Monod, J. 196
Montuori, A. 195
moral and aesthetic education 159
Morin, E. 173, 191, 195–199
Morton, T. 183–184
Munby, H. 60
mysterium tremendum 21, 137, 159; driving forces for Doll's 26–27; inquiry web of Doll's work to reveal 23, 23–26; struggles with spirituality and 148–149

National Steinbeck Center 58
natural dialectic 118
Navarro, J. 8
neoliberalism 44–46
network topology 83–84
Newton, I. 19, 43, 44, 61
New York Times 45, 49
Ng-A-Fook, N. 137, 226–230; curriculum addressed in inspirited letter by 153–160
Nietzsche, F. 3
No Child Left Behind 25, 45, 84
Noddings, N. 125, 172, 221
Nuova Scienzia 42

Oberg, A. 64, 173, 201, 202, 236
Of Mice and Men 58, 66
O'Leary, K. 74
Oliver, M. 203, 206
Ong, W. 213
Orderism 45–46
"Origins of Laughter, The" 8
Orr, G. 204
Oswald, L. H. 62
Otto, R. 148

paradigm of simplification 197
paradox 194
paradoxical dualism of modernism and post-modernism 128–129
pedagogical complexity of story 128–133
pedagogy: of being a learner 124; of caring relationships 125–126, 234; creed of Doll 114, 115, 232; of thoughtfulness 122–123

personalized learning (PL) 145
Piaget, J. 34, 54, 61, 87, 118, 140; on self-regulation 194
Pinar, W. 32, 60, 77, 154, 197, 201, 202; AERA meetings and 64; on *currere* 185; Curriculum Theory Project (CTP) 148; on genius of Doll 18, 151, 218–219; on historical succession of U.S. mainstream education policy 45; on impoverishment of theory in curriculum and pedagogy 203; as leader of Reconceptualization movement 29
PISA rankings 19, 39
place 225–227
play and playful engagement 3, 194, 227–228; with intellectual difference 87–89; knowledge as form of 111–113, 118; of language 110–113; as praxis 118–119; with social-relational difference 89–90; spiritual, with difference 91–93
poeisis 130–131
Poetter, T. S. 154
Poincaré, J. H. 193
Popham, J. 157
post-industrial society 156–157
post-modernism 24, 25, 35, 44, 48–49, 116–117, 164–165; disenchanted curriculum in 29; four R's in curriculum of 176–181; paradoxical dualism of modernism and 128–129; reenchanted curriculum in 32–35; worldliness and 35
Post-modern Perspective on Curriculum, A 2, 25, 35–36, 50, 54, 60, 94, 176, 191; Chinese translation of 164, 168
Pragmatism, Post-Modernism, and Complexity Theory: The "Fascinating Imaginative Realm" of William E. Doll 165
Pratt, S. S. 105, 132, 232
praxis: of Doll 114–115; play as natural 118–119
Prigogine, I. 34, 54, 61, 87, 118, 158–159
Prigonine: A New Sense of Order, A New Curriculum 60, 158–159
Principia Philosophiae 41
Progressivism 221
Provoking Curriculum Studies Conference 201–202, 208–209, 236
pulling back in engagement 81–85, 230–231
Puritan-Protestant ethics 29, 32

queer theology 147–148, 150, 223
Quest for Certainty, The 45
questioning in play 88
Quinn, M. 63, 105, 125, 216; on Doll's divine laughter 218–219, 225, 235; on Doll's enlivening presence, pedagogy and thought 227; on sunny elegance of Doll 222

Rabelais, F. 66
racism 62
Ramism 34
Ramus, P. 41, 44, 114–116
Rationalism 41
rationalization, curriculum 31–32
Reconceptualization movement 29, 55–56, 136, 139; 3S's in 159–160; birth of 140–142
recursion 21, 35, 50, 54, 97–100, 105, 117; AERA on 52; basics of 55; in China 164; differentiated from repetition 131; in mathematics 70; playful engagement and 89; in post-modern curriculum 172, 177–178
recursive reflection 55, 131
reenchanted curriculum 29; post-modern curriculum as 32–35
Reenchantment of the World, The 143
reflection and story 131
reflexivity 154
Rcid, B. 60
relational creativity 33
relations/relationships 8, 35, 50–51, 53–55, 97–98; in China 164; complex conversations and 132; double-bind 26–27; between facts 33; logic of 24; pedagogy of caring 125–126, 234; playful engagement and 89–90; in post-modern curriculum 178–180; reality of 33; space for emergence in 129; spiritual 91–92; three S's and 34
Relier les connaissances—The challenge of the 21st century 198
repetition differentiated from recursion 131
resonating ideas 3
"Restricted Complexity, General Complexity" 196
Reverence: Renewing a Forgotten Virtue 203
Ricca, B. 70, 166, 230–231
richness 19, 34, 35, 50, 54, 97, 117; AERA on 52; basics of 55; in China 164; play engagement and 89; in post-modern curriculum 172, 176–177
Ricketts, E. 58–59
rigor 5, 19, 25, 35, 50, 54–55, 97, 105, 117; AERA on 52; in China 159, 164; in complex conversations 132–133; playful engagement and 89; in post-modern curriculum 172–173, 180–181; in science 159
Rittel, H. 188
Ropo, E. 173, 220, 221
Rorty, R. 65, 101
Rousseau, J. J. 43
R's (rich, recursive, and rigourous) 50–53, 70, 117, 172–173, 194–195, 221; with the 5 C's and the three S's 53–54; in China 165; as modernist categories 53; playful engagement with 89; in post-modern curriculum 176–181
Ryan, A. J. 82

sacredness of being 11–12
Sagal, J. T. 202
Sahlberg, P. 38–39, 41
Santa Fe Institute 24
Santanya, G. 212
Sawada, D. 61
School and Society, The 171
schools and society, curriculum expressed in 171–174
Schools Are Killing . . . Vital Learning Force Natural to Every Child 156
Schools in a Post-Industrial Society 157
Schubert, B. 60, 63
Schwab, J. 61
science and spirituality 143–145
Sea of Cortez 59
secularization 42
Seeber, B. K. 202
Seeing Off Meng Haoran for Guangling at Yellow Crane Tower 160
Seeking a Method-Beyond-Method 150
"seeking a method-beyond-method" 11
self-organization 193–194
self-regulation 193–194
Serres, M. 118
shared flourishing 90
Simola, H. 39, 40
Slow Professor: Challenging the Culture of Speed in the Academy, The 202
Smith, D. G. 77, 209
Smitherman, S. 154
Snow, C. P. 59

social efficiency movement 29
social practice 160
social-relational difference, playful engagement with 89–90
spirit: education as 211–214; and knowledge kept alive 214–216
spirit courses 159
spirituality: *currere* and 150–151; Ng-A-Fook on curriculum and 153–160; science and 143–145; and spiritual play with difference 91–93; temporality of life and 210–216
spiritual methodology 18
S's (science, story, spirit) 6, 34, 129, 173; complex conversations and 132–133; with the four R's and the five C's 53–54; playful engagement with 89, 90; reconceptualizations and 159–160
Stanley, T. 153–154
Steinbeck, J. 58–59, 62, 65–66
Steinberg, S. 64
STEM courses 159, 226
St. Julien, J. 24
story: indeterminacy and 130–131; of inquiry, indeterminacy, and reflection, example of 131–132; inquiry and 130; pedagogical complexity of 128–133; reflection and 131
Structural View of Curriculum, A 157
"Struggles With Spirituality" 147, 148, 151, 210, 211
studying and the arts of writing 77–78
susung 234; concept of 121–122; pedagogy of being a learner of 124; pedagogy of caring relationships of 125–126; pedagogy of thoughtfulness of 123–124
Synoptic Text Today and Other Essays: Curriculum Development After the Reconceptualization, The 151

Taylor, F. 158
Teachers College Record 154
teaching, Doll's 227–234
temporality of life 210–216
"Thinking Complexly" 131–132
Thoroughly Modern Millie 19, 48–51
thoughtfulness, pedagogical 122–123
three states of curriculum 29–30

time 219–225
topology 83–84
transactional play 88
Travels with Charley in Search of America 58–59, 66
Triche, S. S. 222, 24–25, 104, 232–233
Trueit, D. 1, 22, 24, 65, 125, 130, 132, 163, 165, 203, 205, 212, 218
Truth and Method 109
Tsong-Kha-Pa 76
Tyler, R. 41, 44, 140, 195
Tyler Rationale 4–6, 32–35, 121, 164, 177, 191–192; cause-effect epistemology and 193

Varela, F. 131
Värri, V.-M. 173, 220, 221
von Bingen, H. 66
Vygotsky, L. 140, 141

Waldrop, K. 154
Wallace, G. 63
Wang, H. 6, 64, 70, 103
Wang, Hongyu 227
Warhol, A. 62
ways of knowing 206–207
Webber, M. 188
Weber, M. 29–32
Wen Jiexia 65–66
West, C. 54
Westbury, I. 60, 61
What Knowledge Is of Most Worth? 44, 109
Whitehead, A. N. 25, 33–34, 54, 61, 118, 122, 129
Whitlock, U. 136, 223–224; conversations with Doll 148–150
Wholeness and the Implicate Order 143
wicked ghosts 186, 188
wicked problems 183
Wilson 177
Wittgenstein, L. 26, 114, 118, 129
Wolf, F. 144
Wood, G. 180
Woodruff, P. 203
worldliness 35

Yan Hui 125–126
Yan Yui 125
Yrjänäinen, S. 187